India as an Asia Pacific Power

The emergence of India as a regional and potentially global power is forcing us to rethink our mental map of the Asia Pacific. We are only just beginning to discern how India may alter the global economic landscape. How will the rise of India change the strategic landscape of Asia and beyond?

This book provides a comprehensive assessment of India's strategic relations in the Asia Pacific, a region which has not traditionally been understood to include India. It examines India's strategic thinking about the Asia Pacific, its relationships with China and the United States, and India's increasingly close security ties with other major countries in the region. It considers the consequences of India's rise on the Asia Pacific strategic order and asks whether India is likely to join the ranks of the major powers of the Asia Pacific in coming years.

David Brewster is a Visiting Fellow with the Strategic and Defence Studies Centre at the Australian National University. He has written widely about India's strategic relationships in the Asia Pacific and Indian Ocean.

Routledge Security in Asia Pacific Series
Series editors
Leszek Buszynski, International University of Japan and William Tow, Australian National University

Security issues have become more prominent in the Asia Pacific region because of the presence of global players, rising great powers and confident middle powers, which intersect in complicated ways. This series puts forward important new work on key security issues in the region. It embraces the roles of the major actors, their defense policies and postures and their security interaction over the key issues of the region. It includes coverage of the United States, China, Japan, Russia, the Koreas as well as the middle powers of ASEAN and South Asia. It also covers issues relating to environmental and economic security as well as transnational actors and regional groupings.

1 Bush and Asia
America's evolving relations with East Asia
Edited by Mark Beeson

2 Japan, Australia and Asia-Pacific Security
Edited by Brad Williams and Andrew Newman

3 Regional Cooperation and Its Enemies in Northeast Asia
The impact of domestic forces
Edited by Edward Friedman and Sung Chull Kim

4 Energy Security in Asia
Edited by Michael Wesley

5 Australia as an Asia Pacific Regional Power
Friendships in flux
Edited by Brendan Taylor

6 Securing Southeast Asia
The politics of security sector reform
Mark Beeson and Alex J. Bellamy

7 Pakistan's Nuclear Weapons
Bhumitra Chakma

8 **Human Security in East Asia**
Challenges for collaborative action
Edited by Sorpong Peou

9 **Security and International Politics in the South China Sea**
Towards a co-operative management regime
Edited by Sam Bateman and Ralf Emmers

10 **Japan's Peace Building Diplomacy in Asia**
Seeking a more active political role
Lam Peng Er

11 **Geopolitics and Maritime Territorial Disputes in East Asia**
Ralf Emmers

12 **North Korea's Military-Diplomatic Campaigns, 1966–2008**
Narushige Michishita

13 **Political Change, Democratic Transitions and Security in Southeast Asia**
Mely Caballero-Anthony

14 **American Sanctions in the Asia-Pacific**
Brendan Taylor

15 **Southeast Asia and the Rise of Chinese and Indian Naval Power**
Between rising naval powers
Edited by Sam Bateman and Joshua Ho

16 **Human Security in Southeast Asia**
Yukiko Nishikawa

17 **ASEAN and the Institutionalization of East Asia**
Ralf Emmers

18 **India as an Asia Pacific Power**
David Brewster

India as an Asia Pacific Power

David Brewster

LONDON AND NEW YORK

First published 2012
by Routledge
711 Third Avenue, New York, NY 10017

Simultaneously published in the UK
by Routledge
2 Park Square, Milton Park, Abingdon, Oxon OX14 4RN

Routledge is an imprint of the Taylor & Francis Group, an informa business

First issued in paperback 2013

© 2012 David Brewster

The right of the David Brewster to be identified as author of this work has been asserted by him in accordance with sections 77 and 78 of the Copyright, Designs and Patents Act 1988.

All rights reserved. No part of this book may be reprinted or reproduced or utilised in any form or by any electronic, mechanical, or other means, now known or hereafter invented, including photocopying and recording, or in any information storage or retrieval system, without permission in writing from the publishers.

Trademark notice: Product or corporate names may be trademarks or registered trademarks, and are used only for identification and explanation without intent to infringe.

British Library Cataloguing in Publication Data
A catalogue record for this book is available from the British Library

Library of Congress Cataloging-in-Publication Data
Brewster, David.
India as an Asia Pacific power / David Brewster.
p. cm. – (Routledge security in Asia Pacific series; 18)
Includes bibliographical references and index.
ISBN 978-0-415-61761-1 (cloth : alk. paper) – ISBN 978-0-203-63768-5 (ebook : alk. paper) 1. India–Foreign relations–Asia. 2. Asia–Foreign relations–India. 3. India–Foreign relations–Pacific Area. 4. Pacific Area–Foreign relations–India. I. Title. II. Series: Routledge security in Asia Pacific series ; 18.
DS33.4.I4B74 2012
355'.033054–dc22
2011016300

ISBN: 978-0-415-61761-1 (hbk)
ISBN: 978-0-415-72572-9 (pbk)
ISBN: 978-0-203-63768-5 (ebk)

Typeset in Times New Roman
by Taylor & Francis Books

Contents

Acknowledgements		viii
Introduction		ix
1	India as a great power	1
2	Developments in Indian strategic thinking about the Asia Pacific	18
3	Sino-Indian strategic competition and the Asia Pacific	34
4	The United States and India's strategic role in the Asia Pacific	49
5	Northeast Asia: India's peer relationship with Japan	64
6	Indochina: India's political partnership with Vietnam	90
7	Archipelagic Southeast Asia: India's strategic relationships with Singapore, Malaysia and Indonesia	102
8	India's uncertain partnership with Australia	119
9	India's maritime security ambitions in Southeast Asia and the western Pacific	134
10	Understanding India's engagement with the Asia Pacific	144
11	India as an Asia Pacific power	156
Notes		165
Bibliography		193
Index		214

Acknowledgements

Thanks to Christine, Jack, Juliette, Bronte and Essie for their love, patience, support and understanding. Many thanks also to my dedicated editorial team.

18 April 2011

Introduction

The emergence of India as a major regional and potentially a global power is forcing us to rethink our mental map of the Asia Pacific. We are only just beginning to discern how India may alter the economic landscape. India's impact on the strategic picture of Asia is even less clear. Although India is not traditionally understood to be part of the Asia Pacific, it is now claiming an important strategic role in that region. This book will examine the consequences of India's rise on the Asia Pacific strategic order and ask whether India is likely to join the ranks of the major powers of the Asia Pacific in coming years.

The consequences of India extending its power into the Asia Pacific are significant for itself, the region and the world. The Asia Pacific is the most economically vibrant region in the world and since the end of the Cold War has become the primary locus of interaction and competition between most of the world's major economic and military powers. The Asia Pacific is also becoming increasingly unstable, with numerous unresolved territorial disputes and shifting alignments in the face of China's growing power. India has the potential to profoundly alter the dynamics of the region. Some see the Asia Pacific's strategic landscape in coming decades as essentially involving competition and even conflict between the United States and China in East Asia. The rise of India has the potential to swing the regional balance for or against China, or even lead to a multipolar contest played across a wider space of the Pacific and Indian Oceans. India could bring greater stability to the region or it could make the Asia Pacific strategic order increasingly complex and unpredictable.

India has long been recognised as the leading power of South Asia. However, its potential as a major power must now be understood in several dimensions. India is in the process of extending its strategic reach beyond South Asia into the entire India Ocean region, westwards into West Asia and, perhaps most significantly, east towards the Asia Pacific. Its emergence as a power of regional and global significance has been largely driven by its remarkable economic growth over the last 20 years. If its growth continues as many predict, India will become one of the largest economies in the world. This will expand its political and economic influence and give India the capability, if it so chooses, to project military power far beyond its borders. Will the rise of India as an economic giant cause it to expand its strategic reach into the Pacific Ocean, or will it remain relatively cautious and inward looking within its traditional area of influence?

Along with the development of its material capabilities there has also been a revolution in India's strategic thinking. In the years following independence, India worked within a strategic paradigm of nonalignment in which it generally avoided security alignments, while also seeking an important 'moral' role in the world system. For much of the Cold War, India effectively acted as the 'shop steward' of the Third World. In practice this paradigm also inhibited the extension of India's power beyond South Asia. The end of the Cold War has allowed India to refashion traditional ideas about strategic autonomy, the balance of power and space in a way that is now helping India extend its strategic reach. This has particular impact on India's role in the Asia Pacific.

Two major factors drawing India into the Asia Pacific are China and the United States. India identifies China as its principal long-term strategic competitor. With the economic rise of China and now India, competition between them has become multidimensional and more geographically spread, extending through much of the Indian Ocean region and the western Pacific. A need to balance against China's rising power and economic influence has become a driving force in India's engagement with the Asia Pacific. Over the last decade or so, India has also developed a much more cooperative strategic relationship with the United States, which sees benefit in building India as a counterweight to China in the Indian Ocean and the Asia Pacific. Although few in New Delhi will care to admit it, the United States is shaping India's role in the Asia Pacific.

There are, however, important constraints on India's ability to project power into the Asia Pacific. India is not physically part of the Pacific Ocean and despite its remarkable economic growth in recent years, its military and economic capabilities are limited. There is also a deep-seated understanding within much of East Asia that India occupies a separate cultural and strategic sphere. These factors limit India's ability to project power into the Asia Pacific and give particular importance to India's strategic partnerships in the region. For many years to come, India will to a significant extent need to cooperate with local partners to project power into the region – much more so than major powers situated on the Pacific Ocean, such as the United States, China, Japan and Russia. An examination of India's key relationships in the region and the willingness of India's partners to facilitate the projection of India's power is therefore necessary to understand India's future role.

The evolving 'peer' relationship between Japan and India will be important in defining India's strategic role in the Asia Pacific. Until recently Japan and India have shown an extraordinary degree of indifference towards each other. Each has seen the other as being largely beyond its sphere of strategic interest and each has seen little common cause in their relationships with China, the giant that lies between them. However, in recent years, shared concerns about China's growing power have led to an informal partnership. This may help legitimise India's claims to be recognised as a great power of Asia.

India's relationships with the middle powers in Indochina, archipelagic Southeast Asia and the South Pacific are also important to India's future strategic role. India has long recognised Vietnam's important geostrategic position dominating Indochina and the South China Sea and has long supported Vietnam against attempts by other major powers to dominate Indochina. However India has had only limited success in recent years in transforming its political partnership with Vietnam into a closer security relationship. India has had greater success in building a role in archipelagic Southeast Asia where Singapore has been a major focus of India's strategic ambitions. Singapore has positioned itself as India's strategic gateway to Southeast Asia and is increasingly seen by India as an eastern anchor to its strategic space that extends into Southeast Asia. Indonesia is also likely to play an increasingly important role in India's strategic ambitions in Southeast Asia. As Southeast Asia's largest power and a gatekeeper between the Indian and Pacific Oceans, Indonesia is likely to have a key role in India's ability to project power into the Pacific. India has also been improving its relationship with Australia, an active middle power in the Asia Pacific. India and Australia share many common interests in promoting maritime security and regional stability and there is significant scope for them to build a relationship that could facilitate the extension of India's influence into Southeast Asia and even the South Pacific.

In developing a role in the Asia Pacific India has not articulated any 'grand strategy' and seems unlikely to do so in the near future. However, one can identify several imperatives for India to play a greater role in the region. India is becoming increasingly wary of Chinese influence in South Asia and the Indian Ocean. India also sees the possibility of Chinese hegemony in East Asia as inimical to its aspirations to play a major role in a multipolar regional order. Together these create an imperative for India to balance against China in the Asia Pacific. But India's strategic motivations in the Asia Pacific go well beyond balancing against China. The extension of India's influence into Southeast Asia and beyond might be seen as a natural consequence of India's rise as a major power and the expansion of its strategic space. India has aspirations to become the leading power of the Indian Ocean region and some see India as having a natural sphere of influence extending into archipelagic Southeast Asia and Indochina.

In short, several factors are pushing India to adopt a major strategic role in the Asia Pacific. But many questions remain. It is not clear whether India will have the material capabilities or political willingness to project power into the western Pacific beyond Singapore. Although Asia Pacific states see India as a potentially important strategic partner, few see it as naturally 'belonging' to the region and legitimately exercising a direct security role. But should we see India as occupying a separate strategic sphere to the Asia Pacific, or should we begin to think about the Asia Pacific and the Indian Ocean region as a strategic whole? This book examines these questions and considers whether India will become a major power of the Asia Pacific.

1 India as a great power

India has always believed it would shape the future of the world. In recent years India's dream of claiming its rightful place has come ever closer. On the back of its remarkable economic transformation, India is projecting its power and influence out of South Asia into West Asia and the Indian Ocean and, most significantly, into the Asia Pacific. But does India have what it takes to become a great power?

India's 'destiny' as a great power

Indians have long believed that India is destined to become a great state of global significance. Jawaharlal Nehru saw India's role in bringing morality and stability to the world as not a policy but as implicit in India itself. He spoke of India's 'manifest destiny' to become the third or fourth greatest power in the world.[1] In recent years it has become commonplace for Indian leaders to talk of India's 'destiny' as a 'great power'.[2] A widespread belief among India's elite of its destiny – and even of its obligation – to play a major role on the world stage distinguishes India from other important regional powers such as Indonesia or Brazil. However, India failed to achieve this destiny in the 50 years after its independence. The reasons are many, including relative economic failure, the constraints of the Cold War and India's security preoccupations in South Asia. But India's past failures have done little to diminish this underlying belief. As Stephen Cohen, a leading analyst of Indian strategic affairs, puts it: 'Despite foreign policy failures and much debate over tactics, the Indian elite holds fast to a vision of national greatness.'[3]

India's purported destiny has been received much more hesitantly outside India. During much of the Cold War, India was treated by many in the West and Asia as more of a problem or international irritation than a serious power to be reckoned with. Even in the mid-1990s, Henry Kissinger would only cautiously concede that India 'has yet to assume a role commensurate with its size on the international political stage'.[4] Nonetheless, since the beginning of the twenty-first century a great many political leaders and analysts throughout the world have increasingly accepted that India will in coming years be recognised as a great power in the region and even the world.[5] The United States, in particular, made its view plain when a White House spokesman announced in 2005 that the US would 'help India become a major world power in the 21st century'.[6] This change in expectations has been largely driven by the remarkable transformation in India's economy since the early 1990s and predictions of sustained high growth in future decades. It has also been driven by major transformations in Indian strategic behaviour, such as its 1998 declaration as a nuclear weapons state, and the development of new strategic relationships with the United States and other key states. These have all opened the way for India to project its power and influence beyond the traditional confines of South Asia.

While there are growing expectations of India's emergence as a great power, there is still much debate within India about the nature of its destined 'greatness'. There has long been a strong element of exceptionalism among the Indian elite who see India as a spiritual or moral leader of the world, and this perspective continues to be a significant factor in the way in which it exerts its influence.[7] Many Indians believe that as one of the world's largest and most enduring civilisational entities, India is not only destined but also has a moral *obligation* to fulfil an international leadership role. Some see this combination of destiny and obligation as a legacy of India's nationalist independence movement as articulated by Nehru.[8] Others link it with Hindutva beliefs about the superiority of Hindu civilisation over others.[9] A perceived obligation to demonstrate moral and spiritual leadership in the international arena was one of the key ideological foundations of India's nonaligned posture during the Cold War. This was contrasted with what was often disparagingly referred to as the 'power politics' practised by the United States and other powerful states in the international system. Although during the post-Cold War period there has been less emphasis on spiritual or moral leadership and more emphasis on conventional capabilities backed by economic power, perceptions of Indian exceptionalism remain strong, if perhaps not always clearly articulated. As Indian Foreign Minister Yashwant Sinha commented in 2004:

> It is important therefore that India distances itself from the conventional idea of power, as the ability of a nation to bend other nations to its will through coercive use of force. It is also essential to make clear at the very outset that India approaches the notion of power with an alternate vision and a deep consciousness of responsibilities. There can be no other way for India.[10]

However, India's exceptionalism seems to have little following outside India, at least in the post-Cold War world. On the contrary, the self-proclaimed moral dimension in India's strategic rhetoric and the particularly didactic approach of some Indian officials to international issues can sometimes be a source of puzzlement and irritation to many of India's interlocutors.

Despite widespread expectations that India's economic and political power will increase considerably in the coming decades, there remains more than a little scepticism about India's ability to achieve its 'destiny' to become a great power, even in conventional terms. While India clearly has many attributes that could make it a major Asian power – and these will be discussed below – many believe that it will continue to be constrained by such factors as its difficult regional circumstances, incomplete economic reforms, flawed governance institutions and a lack of strategic thinking.[11] Some see India as having just enough power to resist the influence of others, but consider that it must make great strides before it can attain significant power over other states.[12] Cohen, who long argued the case for India's emergence as a great power, now concludes that India is less likely to emerge as a military great power than an economic great power – with an influence in the region perhaps equivalent to that of Japan. Cohen argues that the Indian political community is too domestically focused and the Indian security community is 'hopelessly unstrategic'.[13] Many Chinese analysts in particular have long been publicly sceptical about India's great power aspirations, seeing India as weak and divided with unrealistic and unachievable 'big power dreams' (*daguomeng*).[14]

A significant gap also exists between what might be called India's strategic self-perceptions and its actual role in the international order. India has been described as a 'status inconsistent' power – that is, there is a discrepancy between its perceptions of its own achievements and its ascribed status at an international level.[15] Among the international community, India is often regarded as *currently* possessing only some great power capabilities (e.g. nuclear weapons, a large population and military), and having the *potential* to possess others (e.g. economic strength and military power projection capabilities). However, many in New Delhi believe that India is unfairly denied recognition of its global importance through being denied such things as permanent membership of the UN Security Council, formal recognition as a nuclear weapons state and membership of Asia Pacific regional entities such as APEC. In other words, many in India perceive an entitlement to international status based on India's *potential* rather than *actual* capabilities. This impatience for an enhanced international status contrasts with what Paul Kennedy, author of *The Rise and Fall of Great Powers*, sees as a 'normal' time lag between the trajectory of a state's relative economic strength and the trajectory of its military/territorial influence.[16] As Selig Harrison, a US expert on South Asia, put it, 'Many Indians have what might be called a "post-dated self image." They are confident that India is on the way to great power status and want others to treat them as if they had, in fact, already arrived.'[17] The gap between India's ambitions and its capabilities is an oft-noted feature of Indian strategic behaviour.[18]

As will be seen later, a perception of status inconsistency is an important factor shaping India's strategic ambitions in the Asia Pacific. Although Asia Pacific states are to some extent willing to deal with India on the basis of its great power *potential*, the gap between its current capabilities and its ambitions will nevertheless cause its recognised strategic role to fall short of its ambitions. How might we judge whether India has the capability to become a great power in the Asia Pacific?

India's capability to become a great power

There is no settled understanding in international relations theory as to what constitutes a great power. While various criteria have been put forward, many theorists have ended up concluding that while great powers are difficult to define in the abstract, they nevertheless 'know one when they see one'. There is certainly a degree of consensus as to which states should be regarded as great powers during different historical periods.[19] Realists argue that at the heart of a great power is its ability to project military power.[20] However, most international relations theorists suggest that there needs to be an examination of a state's material and non-material resources as well as social or cultural factors in determining whether it should be regarded as a great power. Kenneth Waltz, the founder of the neorealist theory, argues that the key material factors determining whether a state should be regarded as great power include: population and territory; resource endowment; economic capability; political stability and competence; and military strength.[21] In recent decades there has been particular focus on economic power as a key source of power in other dimensions. In *The Rise and Fall of Great Powers*, Kennedy documented the close long-run connection between the economic and military power and influence of rising states, arguing that not only are economic resources necessary to support a large scale military establishment, but also that the international system essentially operates on the basis of *relative* wealth and power. While Kennedy claims that economics plays a key role in the rise and fall of great powers he also avoids what he calls 'crude economic determinism', stressing that other factors such as geography, military organisation, national morale and alliances can, along with economics, be key to the success or failure of nations.[22] Geopolitical theorists emphasise the fundamental role of space and geography in a state's capacity to be a great power.[23] This can be a function of size and location and especially the impact of geographic features on a state's ability to defend itself and to project power. Easy access to markets through maritime trading routes and other geographic factors can also play a major role in a state's economic development and therefore its potential military power.

Many international relations theorists also emphasise the importance of non-material factors in understanding whether a state should be regarded as a great power. These include such things as national 'will' and political stability which can directly affect a state's willingness and practical ability to project military power. Hedley Bull, the noted Australian strategic theorist, also emphasised that great power status was a socially constructed role in the international system. Bull argued that in addition to material factors, great powers must be:

> recognised by others to have, and conceived by their leaders and peoples to have, certain rights and duties. Great powers, for example, assert the

right, and are accorded the right, to play a part in determining issues that affect the peace and security of the international system as a whole. They accept the duty, and are thought by others to have the duty, of modifying the policies in light of the managerial responsibility they bear.[24]

Bull's definition in effect would require that a state recognise itself as a great power and be recognised by other states in the international system. The recognition of great power status by other states can be important at least in some circumstances. As will be seen later, the recognition of the legitimacy of India's role by key Asia Pacific states is a significant factor in its ability to act as a great power in that region.

Putting aside these debates over the definition of a 'great power', this book will consider whether India is likely to have the capacity and willingness to project power in the Asia Pacific that places it broadly within a category occupied by what are currently recognised to be the great or major powers of the region: the United States, China, Japan and, perhaps, Russia. Just as importantly, will these and other important states of the Asia Pacific treat India as an Asia Pacific power?

India is endowed with many of the attributes of a great power, arising from its huge population and geographic position. It is the second most populous state in the world with an estimated population of around 1.17 billion in 2009 and is expected to become the world's most populous state in the next two decades. It is one of the world's largest countries in area (with around 3.3 million square kilometres) and possesses large areas of arable land as well as significant reserves of coal, iron ore and other minerals. Its location, essentially dividing the northwest and northeast Indian Ocean, gives it the capacity to militarily dominate the Indian Ocean region, while the Himalayas provide a major defensive barrier to invasion from the north. Its position and long coastline (approximately 5,700 km) also provides easy access to the main trading routes between East Asia, the Middle East and Europe. India's democratic system provides it with political stability and resilience, although perhaps impedes long-term strategic planning and execution. Some believe that India also has significant 'soft power' attributes – that is, the ability of a state to get what it wants through attraction rather than coercion or payments – at least in the cultural dimension.[25]

India also has significant military capabilities. Its military expenditure was the ninth largest in the world at US$36.3 billion in 2009 (less than Saudi Arabia but more than Italy).[26] India is a declared nuclear weapons state with approximately 50–60 nuclear devices as of 2007.[27] Its military establishment is also very large in size: with the world's second largest army (around 1.1 million active regular personnel); the world's fourth largest air force (around 850 combat aircraft); and one of the world's largest navies. However, India's ability to project power beyond South Asia is somewhat constrained. Although it has a huge standing army, much of it is deployed to deal with domestic insurgencies or in defensive roles along its western and northern borders. The Indian Navy is well trained and efficient, but is deficient in many areas, including in maritime reconnaissance, extended logistical support and expeditionary forces. Much of its equipment requires modernisation. There are also significant limitations in India's long-range nuclear weapon delivery capabilities, meaning that while India can deploy nuclear devices against all of Pakistan, it cannot deploy nuclear devices against China's eastern cities. India's nuclear doctrine calls for the development of a triad of air, land and sea-based delivery capabilities, however the development of some, such as a submarine launched ballistic missile delivery system, are reportedly a long way off.[28]

Rapid economic growth in recent years is being translated into expanded military capabilities, particularly India's ability to project power. Military expenditure has increased significantly from Rs 196 billion (US$13.8 billion) in 1991 to Rs 1,851 billion (US$36.6 billion) in 2009, although as a percentage of GDP, military spending declined from around 3 per cent to 2.6 per cent over the same period.[29] Given the projected growth in the Indian economy, Indian military spending is likely to increase significantly in future years and there is also claimed to be broad political support for an increase in military spending as a percentage of GDP.[30] Much of the increase in India's defence expenditure in recent years has been devoted to modernising army and air force capabilities and transforming the Indian Navy into a blue water navy. The navy's share of defence expenditure (and particularly of capital expenditure) has increased very significantly in recent years. Nevertheless, it will be more than a decade before the Indian naval modernisation and expansion programme has a significant impact on India's ability to project maritime power.

Despite having many attributes of a great power, throughout much of its modern history India has had material deficiencies in several areas. These include economic underdevelopment, a strategic preoccupation with South Asia and policies that have inhibited the projection of power and influence beyond South Asia. Only in the last two decades has it taken significant steps to overcome these deficiencies, allowing India to claim to be a major power beyond its immediate neighbourhood.

From the biggest loser of the Cold War to an Asian juggernaut?

At independence, India was one of the poorest nations in the world. This was compounded in the following decades by policies that promoted economic autarky and a high level of government control of the economy, which in practice led to economic isolation and stagnation. The so-called 'Hindu rate of growth' averaging around 3 per cent per annum that India experienced from the 1950s to the 1980s,[31] made India a by-word for failed economic policies and contrasted sharply with the 'economic miracles' being experienced in East Asia during that period. India's strategic doctrine also led it up a dead end. India sought to maintain its strategic autonomy during the Cold

War by avoiding taking sides between competing US and Soviet blocs and positioning itself as a leader and spokesman for the Third World. In practice, though, India became increasingly reliant on the Soviet Union as a strategic guarantor, arms supplier and trading partner. India's never-ending conflict with Pakistan kept it strategically preoccupied with South Asia and it failed to exert any real political or strategic influence elsewhere in Asia.

The collapse of the Soviet Union and the end of the Cold War exposed many of these deficiencies, leading some to call India one of the biggest losers of the Cold War.[32] In 1990 and 1991 India experienced an unprecedented series of crises that would ultimately overturn the Nehruvian political, economic and strategic systems that had underpinned the country since independence. The electoral defeat of the Congress Party in 1989 and the assassination of its leader, Rajiv Gandhi, in 1991 appeared to mark the end of the Nehruvian political dynasty. At the same time, India suffered its greatest economic crisis since independence. It was hit by a series of external economic shocks triggered by the disintegration of its export markets in the Soviet bloc and a doubling of oil prices following Iraq's invasion of Kuwait. A severe balance of payments crisis virtually exhausted India's foreign exchange reserves and by May 1991, the Indian Finance Minister believed that, 'the country was on the verge of bankruptcy'.[33]

The political and economic crises were mirrored by a strategic crisis. The collapse of the Soviet Union left India strategically isolated. Not only had India's superpower guarantor disappeared, but the end of the Cold War seemed to destroy the *raison d'être* of the Nonaligned Movement that had provided India with a degree of international stature. When the bipolar world disappeared, its cherished policy of nonalignment had little meaning. The collapse of the Soviet Union also meant the loss of a major source of economic aid and India's primary supplier of military equipment. By late 1991 India's strategic outlook seemed bleak. According to one commentator: 'India's reach for great power status is in shambles. The keystone of Indian power and pretence in the 1980s, the Indo-Soviet link, is history. ... India has no "useful friends".'[34]

From the low point of the early 1990s, India has taken major steps to address its strategic and economic deficiencies. From being the subject of condescension through the second half of the twentieth century, India is now widely regarded as one of the rising economic powers of Asia, if the not the world. Under Prime Minister P.V. Narasimha Rao, in 1991 India began a process of transforming India's economy which can be compared with the transformation of the Chinese economy from the late 1970s under Deng Xiaoping. This involved the progressive removal of many barriers to international trade and investment that had been in place for decades and the dismantling of the so-called 'Licensing Raj', under which the manufacture of many products was licensed to a handful of monopoly suppliers. These reforms led to a dramatic acceleration in India's economic growth, from 0.8 per cent per annum in 1991/92 to an estimated 8.3 per cent per annum in

2010. India's GDP has grown from US$267 billion in 1991 to an estimated US$1,430 billion in 2010.[35] India's current rate of growth appears to be sustainable for some time to come. PricewaterhouseCoopers has projected India's growth to average around 7.5 per cent per annum in coming decades, predicting that in 2050, India's GDP will be around 58 per cent of US GDP in US dollar terms and equivalent to the United States in purchasing power parity terms.[36] Goldman Sachs has predicted that India's GDP (in US dollar terms) will exceed the United States by 2050.[37]

The world's bookstores are now awash with accounts and predictions of India as a major economic power.[38] The current reality is somewhat different. India is, in the aggregate, the twelfth largest economy in the world in current exchange rate terms and fifth largest in purchasing power parity terms (estimated at US$4,046 billion in 2010).[39] India nonetheless remains a poor country with per capita GDP in purchasing power parity terms of US$3,100 per annum on 2009 estimates, placing India far below any other country claiming to be a regional power. By comparison, annual per capita GDP for the United States was US$46,400; Japan was US$32,600; Russia was US$15,200; China was US$6,500; and Indonesia was approximately US$4,000.[40] Similarly, India ranks 115 out of 162 countries on the UN Human Development Index (a composition of variables of life expectancy, literacy, school enrolment and GDP per capita).[41] Although the aggregate size of India's economy is relatively large due to its huge population, the low per capita GDP is a major constraint on India's ability to mobilise an economic surplus for the purposes of projecting power (e.g. its ability to purchase sophisticated foreign weaponry). In short, while there are remarkable projections for India's future economic growth, its economic resources are far less than states recognised to be major powers in the Asia Pacific.

Over the last two decades, while reforming its economic system India has also made major changes to its strategic posture. Although the end of the Cold War left India isolated, it also expanded its strategic options. The removal of many Cold War tensions and ideological certainties has allowed India to engage with Asia in a way previously not possible. As will be discussed in detail in Chapter 2, in the post-Cold War years, India has shown a willingness to discard many of the old imperatives of nonalignment and there has been an overall ideological reorientation of the Indian elite towards the West. India's post-Cold War foreign policy has been characterised by an omni-directional expansion of its political, economic and strategic links with key stakeholders in Asia and beyond.

The dimensions of India as a major power

As India overcomes many of the deficiencies which long inhibited its strategic reach, it can now be viewed as a power in several dimensions. Among other things, India can be perceived as a major regional power in South Asia, West and Central Asia, the Indian Ocean region and the Asia Pacific. These should not necessarily be seen as alternatives, although India may find it easier and more profitable to extend influence in one direction rather than another. Some of these characterisations are also complementary. For example, the assumption by India of a role as a leading maritime power in the Indian Ocean region would likely underpin its potential role in the Asia Pacific.

India as a South Asian power

For a long time India has been recognised as the predominant power of South Asia, a region which is generally recognised to include the states of India, Pakistan, Nepal, Bhutan, Bangladesh, Sri Lanka, Maldives and, sometimes, Afghanistan. This predominance is a result of many factors. India is by far the largest state in South Asia in demographic terms (its population comprises approximately 75 per cent of the region),[42] in economic terms (Indian GDP comprises approximately 79 per cent of the region)[43] and in geographic terms (India's land area represents 75 per cent of South Asia). It has also by far the largest military establishment in the region. Its central position means that it borders each other state in South Asia, while none of its South Asian neighbours border another. India sees itself as a civilisational state that essentially defines South Asia.

Since independence, India has sought to exercise its strategic predominance through imposing its own version of a Monroe Doctrine in South Asia, in which it claimed a right to intervene in the internal affairs of other South Asian states – something that has occurred on several occasions.[44] However, India's regional predominance has never been accepted by Pakistan, which has challenged it since independence and will probably continue to do so even as its own credibility wanes. India's other South Asian neighbours have also sought to partially hedge against India's overwhelming size and power through developing relationships with extra-regional powers. India's Monroe Doctrine has also not been accepted by some outside powers, notably China and the United States, although what might be called its 'leading role' in South Asia is generally accepted by the international community.

Over the last two decades, India has demonstrated a determination to transcend its traditional strategic preoccupations in South Asia. It has had some success in 'de-hyphenating' itself from Pakistan in its international relationships. The asymmetry in economic and military power between India and Pakistan has grown over the last decades, reducing any conventional threat from Pakistan (while India has also reduced its conventional threats against Pakistan), and the declaration by both India and Pakistan of nuclear weapons capabilities in 1998 also arguably helped stabilise the relationship. Pakistan, however, continues to be a significant source of terrorist violence against Indians. The so-called 'Gujral doctrine', as enunciated by Indian Foreign Minister I.K. Gujral in 1996 and more or less followed by Indian governments since that time, has led India to be generally less demanding and more generous in its relations with its neighbours in South Asia. This has led to some improvements in its relationships with the region. These factors have, to some extent, allowed India to pay greater attention to projecting economic, political and military power beyond the confines of South Asia.

India as a West and Central Asian power

Since the end of the Cold War, India has also considerably enhanced its regional role in West and Central Asia. While India has had deep and long-standing cultural, economic and political connections with West Asia, its post-independence relationships in the region were for a long time constrained by Cold War alignments and its conflict with Pakistan. As with the Asia Pacific, the end of the Cold War (and then the 1991 Gulf War) forced India to review its relationships in the Middle East, leading it to seek closer economic and political links with several important regional states. Of particular significance is Israel, with which India has developed a close relationship in defence technology and intelligence.[45] Simultaneously, India is seeking to renew colonial-era economic and security relationships with smaller states in the Persian Gulf, where British India played a dominant strategic role prior to 1947. India has also cautiously renewed its political relationship with Iran, which is both a major energy supplier to India and an important regional counterweight to Pakistan.[46] In 2005, India sought to give greater coherence to its relationships in West Asia by launching a 'Look West' policy, intended to act as a counterpoint to its 'Look East' policy in East Asia. India has sought a major strategic role in post-Taliban Afghanistan and has been hesitantly developing relationships with the newly independent Central Asian states. Since 2003, the Indian Air Force has had an active role in developing the Farkhor Air Base in Tajikistan, which was intended to support India's interests in Afghanistan.

There are, however, some important limitations on India's ability to expand its influence in West Asia. These include the Islamic factor arising out of India's continuing conflict with Pakistan and the overwhelming military dominance of the United States in the Persian Gulf. This has sometimes left little room for major initiatives by India.[47] India's relationship with Iran in particular is currently severely constrained by Iran's hostile relationship with the United States. India's relations in Central Asia are also limited by physical access to the region, which makes trade, particularly trade in energy, difficult.[48] In short, while it seems likely that India will play a much greater strategic role in West and Central Asia in forthcoming years than it did during the latter half of the twentieth century, its role is likely to be constrained for the foreseeable future.

India as an Indian Ocean power

India is increasingly claiming to be the leading maritime power of the Indian Ocean. This geographic area includes Indian Ocean littoral states stretching from Southern and East Africa, to the Middle East, Southeast Asia and

Australia. There is some question as to whether the 'Indian Ocean' constitutes a meaningful region in strategic terms or is in reality merely a collection of subregions. The Indian Ocean has little economic, political or security coherence comparable to the regional identity that now exists in the Asia Pacific. Nevertheless, the Indian Ocean plays an obvious central geographical role in linking its littoral states, as well as forming the transport routes linking East Asia to the Middle East and Europe.

The Indian Ocean region has been one of the key spheres of the expansion of India's strategic influence over the last two decades. India arguably has a 'natural' role as a great power in the region, particularly in the maritime security dimension. The Indian peninsular dominates the northern Indian Ocean, and India is by far the largest and most powerful littoral state in the region. India began to assert a leading role in the Indian Ocean in the 1970s, when it sought to exclude or limit any military presence by extra-regional powers (principally the United States) in the region through international treaty, while also beginning to build its own capacity to project maritime power throughout the Indian Ocean. India currently acts as a security provider to, and even a security guarantor of, several smaller island states in the region. India's ambition to be recognised as the leading Indian Ocean power is helped by the limitations of other littoral states. Many Indian Ocean states are very small, poor and/or have negligible military capabilities (such as most African and Indian Ocean island states), or have largely a continental rather than a maritime strategic focus (such as most states in the Middle East). Others traditionally have a geostrategic perspective primarily facing the Asia Pacific, not the Indian Ocean (such as most Southeast Asian states and Australia). Although in recent years India has shown a willingness to accept a continuing US security presence in the Indian Ocean (at least around the Persian Gulf) it is very sensitive to a security presence of other extra-regional powers, particularly China.

India's strategic ambitions in the Indian Ocean are intimately tied to its naval capabilities and the development of a greater maritime perspective (which is discussed in detail in Chapter 2). During the Cold War, India's ability to pursue its maritime ambitions was severely constrained through a combination of superpower rivalry in the Indian Ocean and a lack of economic resources. For decades following independence the Indian Navy was the 'Cinderella' of the Indian armed forces, while India focused on immediate security threats on its western and northern land borders. However, since the mid-1990s, India has embarked on a major programme to develop a blue water navy involving significant increases in naval expenditure.[49] The proportion of the navy's budget allocated to capital expenditure significantly exceeds the proportions allocated by the army or air force. At the same time, the Indian Navy's force structure has been undergoing significant change with an emphasis on sea control capabilities. Plans announced in 2008 call for a fleet of over 160 ships by 2022, including three aircraft carriers and 60 major combatant ships, as well as almost 400 naval aircraft. According to Admiral

Arun Prakash, the former Indian Chief of Naval Staff, India aims to exercise selective sea control of the Indian Ocean through task forces built around three aircraft carriers that will form the core of separate fleets in the Bay of Bengal, the Indian Ocean and the Arabian Sea.[50]

In conjunction with an increase in its naval capabilities over the last two decades, India has been quietly expanding its sphere of influence throughout the Indian Ocean. The Indian Navy has actively developed security relationships with states throughout the Indian Ocean region intended to enhance India's ability to project power and restrict China's ability to develop similar relationships. India's strategic ambitions are primarily focused on the northern Indian Ocean. In the northeast Indian Ocean, India has developed a strong security relationship with Singapore and is in the process of developing a security relationship with Indonesia – relationships that will be discussed in detail in Chapter 7. India has also developed a close security relationship with the Maldives (where the Indian Navy/Air Force has been granted use of the old British airbase on Gan island and India is building a system of electronic monitoring facilities) and in the Persian Gulf, where the Indian Navy has security relationships with Oman and Qatar. India has also made significant progress in developing maritime security partnerships with island states in the southwestern Indian Ocean including Mauritius, Seychelles, Mozambique (where the Indian Navy assists in providing maritime security) and Madagascar (where India operates signals intelligence facilities). Arguably these relationships form the basis for a sphere of naval influence covering much of the Indian Ocean.[51] The Indian Navy has also sought to institutionalise a position for itself as the leading Indian Ocean power through such initiatives as sponsoring the Indian Ocean Naval Symposium, modelled on the US-led Western Pacific Naval Symposium.[52]

The strategic role which India envisages for itself in the Indian Ocean region remains a work in progress. To a significant extent this will be determined by the extent to which India's naval expansion plans come to fruition. Drawing on the experience of the United States in the Western Hemisphere in the nineteenth and twentieth centuries, Holmes, Winner and Yoshihara, strategic analysts at the US Naval War College, have identified three basic roles which the Indian Navy could play. These are, first, a 'free-rider' navy, in which the Indian Navy could play a growing role in maritime policing and humanitarian assistance and disaster relief (HADR) while the United States continued to play a dominant strategic role; second, a 'constable' navy, in which the Indian Navy would, sparingly and with tact, intervene in littoral states, and third, a 'strong-man' navy where it would seek to establish hegemony in the Indian Ocean and had the capability of mounting forward defence beyond the Indian Ocean.[53] They conclude that the Indian Navy's expansion programme in the coming decades would give it the capability to act somewhere between a 'free-rider' navy and a 'constable' navy.

Apart from the constraints of India's naval capabilities, there seem few insurmountable obstacles to India taking the role of a 'great power' of the

Indian Ocean, at least in cooperation with the United States. The United States currently exercises naval predominance in the Indian Ocean, but, as will be discussed in Chapter 4, is actively facilitating the expansion of India's naval ambitions and power projection capabilities. Although China has significant interests in the sea lines of communication (SLOCs) that cross the Indian Ocean and may perhaps establish a naval presence there, it is questionable whether it could seriously challenge the Indian Navy throughout much of the Indian Ocean. In claiming a role as a 'great power' of the Indian Ocean region, India will, however, need to be mindful of the perceptions of important regional states such as Indonesia and Australia.

India's strategic role in the Indian Ocean has a significant impact on its role in the Asia Pacific. First, India's strategic ambitions in relation to the Indian Ocean chokepoints into the Pacific Ocean (principally the Malacca Strait) create imperatives for it to develop security relationships in Southeast Asia and potentially play a direct security role there. Second, perceived 'intrusions' by other powers (principally China) into the Indian Ocean may create an imperative for India to respond by projecting its own power into the South China Sea and further into the western Pacific basin. Third, India may seek to rely on an increased awareness of the interconnectedness of security of the Asia Pacific and Indian Ocean regions by leveraging a leading role in the Indian Ocean into that of a major 'Indo-Pacific' power.

India as an Asia Pacific power?

The most potentially significant strategic role for India, and the subject of this book, is India's role as an Asia Pacific power. India is not now part of the Asia Pacific, as that term is currently understood, but wants to be recognised as a major power in the region.

Although the phrase 'Asia Pacific' is ubiquitous today, it is easy to forget that it only came into common usage in the 1980s. The term was coined as part of an effort sponsored by Japan and Australia to promote a regional policy in which the developed Pacific states (primarily the United States, Japan and Australia) would engage with the less developed Asian states. The origin of the phrase was therefore as much to achieve a political end as it was a geographic description.[54] The formation of the Asia-Pacific Economic Cooperation (APEC) gave impetus to the development of a number of 'Asia Pacific' regional institutions under the auspices of APEC and ASEAN. These institutions and multilateral networks have been instrumental in developing a degree of regional identity for the 'Asia Pacific' in the economic, political and security dimensions. India was not a part of these developments. It was not invited to be a member of ASEAN on its formation in 1967 and nor of APEC on its establishment in 1989. APEC has since been expanded to 21 states, including Chile, Peru and Russia – but not India.

The scope of the 'Asia Pacific region' nevertheless remains a subject of debate, particularly between those who have sought to focus on a narrower

East Asian (or 'Pacific Asian') identity and a wider Pacific identity that includes the United States, Australia and New Zealand. It is, however, clear that the idea of the Asia Pacific, as currently understood, does not extend to India or the other countries of South Asia. This book will use the term 'Asia Pacific' essentially to describe the countries located in the western Pacific basin, including Northeast and Southeast Asia and the South Pacific, while also recognising the crucial economic, political and security role played by the United States in the region.

India's engagement with key states in the Asia Pacific is the most important part of its regional strategy and is arguably crucial to its broader global ambitions. The extent to which India is able to make itself part of the Asia Pacific will be of major significance to the economic and strategic future of both India and the Asia Pacific region. The integration of the (heretofore, largely closed) Indian economy with East Asia is already a major factor driving the development of the Indian economy and is likely to become a major economic factor for Southeast Asia, Japan, South Korea and Australia. The Asia Pacific is the most economically vibrant region in the world and the site of potential rivalry between most of the world's great economic and military powers: the United States, China, Japan and Russia. As a result, the assumption of a major political and security role in the Asia Pacific would provide a significant enhancement to India's international status, which is arguably not achievable if India simply focuses its energies on the Indian Ocean region.

However, the likelihood of India being recognised as an Asia Pacific power is far from certain. India is currently perceived as being outside the Asia Pacific region and as playing only a relatively peripheral role in the region, certainly in the political and security arenas. As will be discussed later, during the twentieth century and before, the regional security dynamics of South Asia operated largely independently of East Asia/Asia Pacific and most East Asian states found little reason to engage at a strategic level with India. Similarly, India showed little strategic interest in East Asia. During most of the Cold War it eschewed the development of regional security relationships and saw its interests as largely limited to rhetorical efforts to minimise the intrusion of other major powers into the region.

It is only in the last two decades that India has really begun to strategically engage with the Asia Pacific. India's regional initiatives in the immediate post-Cold War years were to a significant extent motivated by economic crisis and the need to expand trade and attract investment. As noted previously, in 1992, in the depths of India's post-Cold War crisis, the Rao government launched the 'Look East policy', designed to expand economic, political and security ties with East Asia. The policy initially had the expansion of economic links with Japan as a primary objective, reflecting Japan's position as a world economic power and as Asia's major source of capital. Japan was seen by many in New Delhi as the first economic success story of Asia and the epitome of non-Western modernity, something to be emulated by India.[55] Although Japan had played a crucial role in averting India's economic crisis in 1991,[56] attempts by India through the 1990s to encourage Japanese investment in India had little success. Japanese companies saw India as too difficult a place in which to do business. India had much greater success in developing links in Southeast Asia, which soon became the primary focus of the Look East policy. India saw its inclusion in the regional political, economic and security groupings based in Southeast Asia as an important way to avoid marginalisation in the post-Cold War international landscape. As will be seen later, India moved to improve bilateral security links with key Southeast Asian states and in the early 1990s identified Singapore as its key gateway into the region. India also sought to further develop links with its long-standing political ally Vietnam and more recently with Indonesia. These bilateral relationships have come to form the key points in India's Southeast Asian strategy. With the assistance of Singapore in particular, India's institutional links in Southeast Asia developed quickly, becoming a sectoral ASEAN dialogue partner in 1992 and a full ASEAN dialogue partner in December 1995. India also sought a security role in the region and joined the ASEAN Regional Forum (ARF) in 1996.

India also sought to create subregional organisations to help develop its relationships to its east. In 1997, India and Thailand sponsored the establishment of the BIMSTEC grouping[57] to promote technical and economic cooperation among states in the northeast Indian Ocean region (including Malaysia, Thailand and Burma). In 2000, India, again with Thailand, founded the Mekong Ganga Cooperation group, among other things, to promote greater east–west transport connectivity between South Asia and Indochina (through Thailand). Both organisations are symbolically significant in joining several Southeast Asian states with India – without the participation of China or Pakistan. However, neither have yet played a significant role in promoting intraregional trade or in extending India's strategic influence.

In the late 1990s, India signalled a broadening of its Look East policy to the entire western Pacific basin. As Indian Foreign Minister Jaswant Singh described it, 'our Look East policy will be integrated into a larger regionalization strategy which encompasses ... the Asia Pacific.'[58] The so-called 'Phase 2' of the Look East policy involved a deepening of India's relationships in Southeast Asia, including the entry into bilateral and multilateral free trade arrangements, expanding India's focus to a broader region extending from Australia and the South Pacific to Northeast Asia with ASEAN as its core, and pursuing a broader agenda involving security cooperation.[59] As E. Ahamed, the junior Indian Foreign Minister, commented: 'the Look East policy is not merely an external economic policy, but a "strategic shift in India's vision".'[60] India's institutional relationships in the region continued to develop in the early years of this century. It participated in a separate 'ASEAN plus One' summit with ASEAN leaders in 2002, in the first East Asian Summit in December 2005 and in the first meeting in 2010 of the Defence Ministers of ASEAN plus Australia, China, India, Japan, New Zealand, Russia, South Korea and the United States (known as ADMM + 8).

Despite the broader focus given to India's relationships in the region, economic integration with the Asia Pacific remains the most important driver of India's engagement with the region. In August 2009, India signed a multilateral ASEAN–India Free Trade Agreement which will substantially reduce tariffs on most manufactured items, with the exception of important sectors such as textiles, chemicals, automobiles and steel. The deal will be largely confined to manufactured goods, allowing India to continue to protect agriculture, while ASEAN states will continue to protect their services sectors. In recent years India has also pushed for a non-exclusive 'Asian Economic Community' which would bring together Japan, ASEAN, China, India and South Korea. However, Indian proposals have been in competition with other proposals supported by China for an East Asian economic community that exclude India.[61] These competing proposals were the subject of controversy at the East Asian Summit in December 2005. The prospects for any Asia Pacific economic grouping of any substance seem unlikely for some years to come.

While India has made significant progress in developing multilateral links in the Asia Pacific, in many ways it is still an outsider to regional groupings. India is not a member of ASEAN + 3 or APEC and it remains uncertain whether it will be allowed to join APEC when its membership is next considered. Some perceive that it has only second-ranking status in the East Asian Summit. Indian Prime Minister Vajpayee argued that: 'India's belonging to the Asia-Pacific community is a geographical fact and a political reality. It does not require formal membership of any regional organisation for its recognition and sustenance.'[62] Nevertheless, it is clear that India, as a late starter in the process of economic and political engagement with the region, is nowhere near approaching the depth of the economic and security relationships that the United States has across most of the region nor the economic relationships that China has in the region.

Although some ASEAN states (in particular, Singapore) have welcomed an increased regional security role for India, others (e.g. Indonesia) have been more cautious, though not necessarily unwelcoming. India is generally seen as a benign security presence. However, there are concerns about the potential for strategic rivalry between India and China. There is also a sense (although this may be gradually fading) that India's credibility as a regional security provider may be undermined by an inability to create a stable security environment in South Asia. As one commentator put it at the turn of this century:

> More than any power projection capabilities, ASEAN's main expectation vis-à-vis India in terms of security would be its capacity to ensure the stability of the subcontinent itself ... India's aspirations to a political role in Southeast Asia would certainly be more credible if it was able to settle its dispute with Pakistan.[63]

India has also radically recast its relations with the key major powers of the Asia Pacific – the United States, China, Japan and Russia. The end of the

Cold War forced India to partially recast its relationship with China that had been largely frozen since the early 1960s. This led to important improvements in the relationship, opening the way for major increases in bilateral trade. However, relations with China remain uneven at best and new areas of strategic rivalry have developed over energy, the Indian Ocean and Southeast Asia. The development of India's strategic partnership with the United States since the turn of the twenty-first century has transformed is position in the Asia Pacific, allowing it to develop strategic partnerships with US allies and friends and potentially legitimising a direct security role in the region. India's relationship with Japan, which could be viewed as a relationship between two major power peers, is of particular significance. India has also sought to partially renew its relationship with Russia, a country which continues to have significant emotional resonance in parts of India's security community. Russia remains India's largest supplier of defence technology, a role which is likely to continue for some time. While Russia is an important international partner for India, it is not currently a major factor in India's strategic role in the Asia Pacific.

Although India's economic power and strategic influence in the Asia Pacific have grown considerably over the last two decades, its role is subject to significant constraints. For many East Asians in particular, India is beyond the bounds of what they conceive as 'Asia' in either a cultural or geographical sense and therefore India is not seen as having a 'natural' role in the region (although, of course, similar objections could be made in relation to the United States, Australia, New Zealand and Russia, each of which is now recognised to be part of the broader Asia Pacific region). In addition, India is not located on the Pacific Ocean and faces considerable geographic hurdles in projecting naval power into the Pacific basin. These factors limit India's ability to unilaterally assert or project power in the Asia Pacific and make India highly reliant on its relationships with key Asia Pacific states in order to play a major strategic role in the region. These relationships will be discussed in subsequent chapters.

2 Developments in Indian strategic thinking about the Asia Pacific

Since the end of the Cold War, India's economy has been transformed. India's strategic thinking has also undergone a revolution, as the country that prided itself on nonalignment moved closer to the West. But India's culture, history and geography still fundamentally shape its worldview. In engaging with the Asia Pacific, India is guided by a mosaic of strategic objectives about extending its sphere of influence, developing a multipolar regional system and balancing against China. The interplay of these objectives will frame India's role in the Asia Pacific.

Nehruvian strategic doctrine and the post-Cold War revolution in Indian strategic thinking

India's engagement with the Asia Pacific since the end of the Cold War has been accompanied by a revolution in Indian strategic thinking. Through much of the Cold War, Nehruvian strategic doctrine formed the intellectual foundation of Indian strategic analysis. At its core was the concept of nonalignment, which brought together several long-running strands of Indian strategic thought.[1] The key principles of nonalignment were non-violence, international cooperation and the preservation of India's international freedom of action through refusing to align India with any Cold War bloc. Nonalignment represented an insistence that even relatively weak powers could choose to stay aloof from great power rivalries. Although Indian strategic practice was progressively modified towards a more realist, and even militant, stance following India's defeat at the hands of China in 1962 and India's strategic alignment with the Soviet Union in 1971, India's leadership insisted that the Nehruvian 'consensus' remained in place. As a result, Nehruvian strategic principles remained an intellectual anchor to Indian strategic thinking and dominated Indian strategic rhetoric up until the end of the Cold War.

Nehruvian strategic doctrine inhibited India from playing a significant role in the Asia Pacific until the early 1990s. Throughout much of the Cold War India saw its interests in the Asia Pacific as largely limited to rhetorical efforts to minimise the influence of other major powers. As a result, India abdicated any leadership role that it could have had in Southeast Asia and only really sought to exert its influence in negative terms, such as its emphatic rejection of regional security relationships with the United States.[2] Although this position was progressively moderated under Indira Gandhi and successive Indian leaders, the basic temper of India's relationship with Southeast Asia continued until the early 1990s. Nehruvian strategic doctrine also contributed to distant relations with many other Asia Pacific states. Throughout most of the Cold War, Indian leaders viewed Japan, South Korea, Taiwan and Australia as little more than protectorates of the United States and therefore of little interest to India except, in the case of Japan, as a potential source of capital and technology.

The end of the Cold War forced India to re-examine the viability of the Nehruvian principles in guiding India's strategic stance. With the collapse of the Soviet Union the idea of nonalignment seemed to lose its *raison d'être*. India's leaders were forced to fashion a new set of strategic goals based on a more pragmatic view of the world. India's strategic options included attempting to continue with the logic of nonalignment, joining the US alliance system or attempting to balance against the United States through joining with other second-tier powers. Alternatively, it could pursue a multipolar world in which it would establish itself as one of the major powers in the international system without recourse to any alliance. While the notion of a triangular security relationship among India, Russia and China was debated within the Indian strategic community during the 1990s, it was realised that there was little to gain from trying to create a countervailing bloc against the United States. By the end of the 1990s, the dominant emphasis in Indian strategic thinking had settled on building a new partnership with the United States as part of a multidirectional engagement of the major powers.

Many believe that India's Pokhran II nuclear tests in 1998 became the fulcrum around which India's post-Cold War strategic thinking turned. Before the tests, India's ambiguous nuclear status created significant obstacles to improving relations with the United States and its allies. Although the nuclear tests caused a storm of protest internationally, it led to a transformation of India's relationship with the United States and provided India with a new status in Asia. According to C. Raja Mohan, a leading 'modernist' in Indian strategic thinking, after Pokhran II, India's self-perception as an emerging great power armed with nuclear weapons allowed it to negotiate with other powers without the sense of defensiveness that permeated earlier relationships. India's successful transition to a nuclear power also moved India's intellectual balance in favour of realists and pragmatists and effectively ended the longstanding dominance of Nehruvians and left-of-centre internationalists over the foreign policy discourse.[3]

Nevertheless, Nehruvian ideas and other important cultural factors continue to have an important place in Indian strategic thought. In particular is the significance placed on strategic autonomy, which will be discussed later. Further, in considering India's likely future moves in the Asia Pacific, one must also take into account the longstanding gap between rhetoric and strategic action which is evident in India's strategic history. Stephen Cohen calls this a culture of 'strategic restraint', which is deeply rooted in the Indian strategic psyche and is derived from a political culture that stresses disengagement, avoidance of confrontation and a defensive mindset. Cohen believes that this has been a major factor in Indian strategic behaviour throughout its modern history and will continue to be an important limiting factor in Indian strategic behaviour even as India gains the material resources to play a more active strategic role outside South Asia.[4] Cohen's observations are an important reminder that, despite much of the rhetoric from Indian leaders and strategic commentators, at least outside South Asia, India is highly defensive and cautious in its strategic behaviour.

There have been several attempts to characterise and define the various ideological schools in Indian strategic thinking as they have developed since the end of the Cold War. Rahul Sagar proposes a categorisation between moralists (who uphold the Nehruvian tradition), Hindu nationalists (who advocate protecting national values through building strength), strategists (secularists who advocate developing strategic capabilities) and liberals (who emphasise attaining security through trade and interdependence).[5] Kanti Bajpai identifies three paradigms of Indian strategic thinking: Nehruvianism, neoliberalism and hyper-realism, each characterised by differing attitudes towards internal security, regional security and relations with great powers and each of which is broadly associated with differing political ideologies.[6] Although it is very much an oversimplification, in practice, over the last decade or so, Nehruvian traditionalists have been increasingly associated with leftist ideologies and realists and Hindu nationalists more with the Bharatiya Janata Party (BJP) and other rightist groups, sometimes leaving the Congress Party to follow a more liberal or pragmatic course.

These ideological categorisations can be useful in understanding the main streams of Indian strategic thinking and the political debates over India's strategic role and relationships. However, they can quickly become sterile in considering India's strategic engagement with the Asia Pacific where it can be difficult to discern any dominant or cohesive stream of strategic thought. This is partly a function of the immediate post-Cold War years, when Indian leadership allowed strategic policy to develop in a pragmatic way, generally avoiding a clear rejection of the past. As a result, India is unlikely to articulate a grand theory of strategic relations. Having flirted disastrously with grand concepts in the past, India's emphasis is on cautious *realpolitik*.[7] Ashley Tellis, a US expert on Indian strategic affairs, suggests that in the current strategic environment, India does not have the luxury of pursuing policies that are 'utterly transparent or completely straightforward' and instead must develop the institutional and psychological capacity to move deftly.[8] However, ambiguity or a lack of transparency over India's security objectives in the Asia Pacific has not prevented it from making significant steps towards engagement in the region.

A more useful way to comprehend India's strategic ambitions in the Asia Pacific is to understand the various long-running themes in Indian strategic thinking. One might see Indian strategic thinking in terms of a 'mosaic' of many different threads and contrasting themes and influences which often cross ideological boundaries, although these may sometimes be expressed in different ways and with different emphases. There are important differences, for example, between those who prioritise the economic over security dimensions of relationships in the Asia Pacific and particularly over India's relationship with the United States. However, despite New Delhi's rambunctious political culture there is a high degree of consensus within India's strategic elite about the importance of developing closer strategic relationships with most Asia Pacific states, because it is consistent with several themes or objectives. These include attaining strategic autonomy and a multipolar order; the development of a new Asian balance of power; the promotion of democracy; the growth of a maritime strategic outlook; and ideas about an Indian sphere of influence. Each of these will be discussed in detail below.

India's quest for strategic autonomy and a multipolar order

Throughout its modern history India has sought what has been called the 'Holy Grail' of Indian security policy: strategic autonomy.[9] Since independence and before, many of its leaders saw India's destiny as a great power, beholden to no-one, even if it lacked the resources to assert itself in traditional ways. The combination of a destined greatness and material weakness was a key reason for India pursuing its nonaligned policy, allowing it to claim strategic space and assert itself as an international leader. As has been discussed in Chapter 1, India's destiny as a great power is now almost universally accepted among Indian strategic thinkers and is virtually ubiquitous in strategic discussions; the only question is when the world will recognise India's emergence. Current thinking about strategic autonomy has been described as 'a realist mutation of the traditional non-aligned posture' and shares many of the underlying elements of Indian ideas on nonalignment.[10]

For many Indian strategists, strategic autonomy is the *sine qua non* of great power status. For some, particularly those influenced by Nehruvian traditions, it is an absolute imperative: any compromise of India's strategic autonomy will compromise India's destiny. According to Nehruvians this not only forbids significant security cooperation with the United States and its regional allies, but also casts doubt on any security alignments with states outside the US alliance system. Others see the goal of strategic autonomy in less absolute or immediate terms, conceding that India's interests may be served by entering into security relationships with the United States and others, provided that India retains significant freedom of action. Mohan believes that India should rethink its attachment to strategic autonomy, arguing that autonomy is for weak powers who are trying to insulate themselves from great powers and that Delhi's task in coming years will be to contribute to the management of the international order, not to seek autonomy from it.[11] Nevertheless, the idea of strategic autonomy is strongly ingrained in the Indian strategic psyche and is likely to be a guiding principle for many years to come. The concept may, however, evolve in coming years, just as Indian ideas about nonalignment evolved through the Cold War.

Closely related to India's 'destiny' as a great power and its quest for strategic autonomy is a desire for the development of a multipolar security order in the region and worldwide which, it is believed, is necessary to elevate India's status and maximise its freedom of action. To some extent, calls for a multipolar world have replaced nonalignment as a core concept of Indian foreign policy. India's twin goals of strategic autonomy and multipolarity have a profound impact on India's strategic engagement with the Asia Pacific. As will be seen below, in order to achieve a goal of regional multipolarity, India not only must cooperate with other major powers to balance against potential Chinese hegemony in East Asia, but arguably is also driven to establish its own maritime predominance in the Indian Ocean region. In pursuing these aims there are significant unresolved tensions between a desire for strategic autonomy and a perceived need to cooperate with the United States and its allies.

Indian ideas on an Asian balance of power

India's potential role in an Asia Pacific balance of power is an important theme in Indian strategic thinking. This might be expressed either in neorealist terms of creating a balancing coalition against China, or in more classical realist terms of seeking to create a multipolar regional balance. Mohan claims that balancing China is in 'the very DNA of India's geopolitics' and has been since the early 1950s.[12]

However, Indian thinking about an Asian balance of power is complicated by several factors. As discussed, Indian strategic thinking is still in the process of evolving from Nehruvian traditions in which talk of a 'balance of power' were frowned upon. Ideas of nonalignment still have resonance in Indian strategic debate, often with strong overtones of Indian exceptionalism. Varun Sahni, for example, sees India as playing a new nonaligned role in the developing Asian strategic order. He believes that India is destined to be a fence-sitter in Asia, relatively equidistant and nonaligned between the two poles of China and a US-led coalition, although making significant efforts to cultivate friendships with powers such as Russia and Japan.[13] In other words, India will *again* be able to transcend considerations of the balance of power, as Nehruvians claimed to have done during the Cold War.

Others such as Mohan believe that while it has not entirely discarded a commitment to liberal internationalist notions over the last two decades, Indian political discourse has had to come to terms with realist concepts of the balance of power.[14] Certainly there is much more open discussion about a balance of power in Asia than was the case during the Cold War.[15] Although there is some official acknowledgement from Indian leaders of what Defence Minister Mukherjee called India's 'crucial' role in maintaining a 'stable balance of power'[16] or an 'equitable strategic balance'[17] in Southeast Asia, at the same time there is considerable reluctance to acknowledge that any balancing might be aimed at China. New Delhi is acutely conscious of its limitations in the Asia Pacific and any implication that its relationships in the Asia Pacific are driven by a desire to balance against China.[18] India wishes to expand its strategic weight in the region while avoiding creating open rivalry with China.[19]

In addition to concerns about reactions to an overt balancing strategy, there is considerable sensitivity within India as to how such as strategy would affect India's 'Holy Grail' of strategic autonomy. In particular, to what extent would India need to ally itself with the United States and its regional allies in order to create an Asian balance against China? Many in India see a significant risk that the United States will build India as a junior alliance partner to contain China and that India will be caught in a web of bilateral arrangements that meshes with the so-called US 'hub and spoke' alliance system.[20] Thus there was considerable caution in portions of the Indian security community towards the 2007 'Quadrilateral' proposal for a security dialogue involving the United States, Japan, Australia and India not only on the grounds of unnecessarily provoking China, but also about the implications of being perceived to be part of a US-led security grouping. According to Tellis, even if an anti-China coalition led by the United States were to eventuate in the future, New Delhi's intuitive preference would be to assert its strategic autonomy even more forcefully. Short of the most extreme threats, India would prefer to deal with Beijing independently.[21] India has thus emphasised the development of strategic relationships in the Asia Pacific on a bilateral basis, which is regarded as being less provocative to China, and maximising India's freedom of action.

There is also a tendency among Indian strategic analysts of all stripes to see India as of significantly greater consequence to an Asian balance of power than might be perceived in Asia – where the focus is overwhelmingly on the United States, China and, to a lesser extent, Japan. Thus, a report from a US Central Intelligence Agency think tank calling India the most important 'swing state' in the international system is quoted widely and approvingly among Indian leaders and commentators.[22] Similarly, Kaplan suggests that India could emerge as the 'global pivot state supreme, tilting on some issues toward the United States and on others toward China'.[23] Comments such as these are taken as recognising an apparently powerful international role for India which, it is argued, could swing the international balance of power through choosing to side either with the United States, China or perhaps even another bloc.[24] In a similar vein, Mohan argues that India's objective is to become an *indispensable element* in the Asian balance of power.[25] To the extent that this claim assumes that India is likely to become an important element in an Asian balance of power, it is unexceptional. However, to the extent that claims about India's 'indispensability' imply that it has the option not to oppose Chinese hegemony over East Asia, they considerably overstate India's freedom of action. While there may certainly be some issues in the international arena on which India will choose to side with China against the United States, as will be seen, it is difficult to realistically conceive of India not seeking to balance against China in Asia. India is in fact compelled by its own great power aspirations to seek to form (limited) balancing relationships with the United States and its allies against China.

Spurred by dreams of strategic autonomy and a multipolar region, some Indian analysts have gone so far as to propose that India should develop an Indian-centred 'constellation' of Asian states linked by strategic cooperation and sharing common interests, including in counterbalancing China. Brahma Chellaney, a noted 'realist' commentator, sees the India–Japan relationship as forming the potential foundation of overlapping security relationships in Asia. India's security relationship with Vietnam is also widely viewed with approval in the Indian security community, partly at least, because Vietnam lies outside the US security sphere. Despite these dreams, there is a widespread understanding in the Indian security community that a relationship of some type with the United States is a necessary or desirable feature of Indian security, if only as a step towards other strategic objectives. Some believe that India's challenge will be to form part of an informal balancing coalition against China with the United States and its allies, while avoiding becoming part of a US-led web of relationships. Bajpai, for example, characterises Indian policy since the end of the Cold War as essentially bandwagoning with the United States, while also hedging in the sense of developing coalitions with first, second and third tier states that would assist it in standing up to the United States.[26] Others see the possibility of India occupying a middle ground of partial attachment to the United States while retaining significant strategic autonomy. Mohan endorses the idea that India can navigate between the 'two extremes' of an uncritical US alliance and what he calls the 'slogans' of a multipolar world. A somewhat more ambiguous outcome of this nature is likely both to be more realistic and to fit better with India's strategic tradition and domestic political imperatives. This ambiguity can be used to India's advantage, for example, in allowing India to be cast within the Asia Pacific as a potential benign balancer not only against a potentially threatening China, but also (if perhaps only symbolically) against potentially overwhelming US power.

The ideological dimension: flirting with values-based alliances

To what extent does India's strategic behaviour in the Asia Pacific involve an ideological dimension? A notable feature of Nehruvian strategic doctrine was that India rarely allowed the domestic political affairs of other states to be a significant factor in its foreign policy decision-making.[27] To the extent that India's foreign policy had an ideological dimension it often involved an alliance with communist or authoritarian states in opposing the supposed imperialism of the West. However, in recent years Indian leaders have begun to make considerable use of the rhetoric of 'shared democratic values' as justification for cooperation with Japan and other US allies in the region, to the exclusion of China. Prime Minister Manmohan Singh has called liberal democracy 'the natural order of social and political organisation',[28] describing India and Japan, the largest and most developed democracies in Asia, as 'natural partners'.[29] Such statements are consistent with efforts by the United States and Japan to use shared democratic values as an ideological foundation for strategic relationships with India.

Some Indian commentators have suggested that shared political values represent a 'secret weapon' against China in that it has much more to fear from ideological subversion than military threats,[30] while others have invoked the theory of 'Democratic Peace' to justify India forming alliances with other regional democracies.[31] The significance of alliances among democratic states is a matter of some theoretical debate. The so-called theory of 'Democratic Peace' proposes that democratic states never, or very rarely, go to war with each other. However, the theory does not in any way purport to support the idea that democracies will or should become alliance partners against non-democracies. Some theorists nevertheless suggest that members of ideological-based alliances may have similarities in threat perceptions,[32] and that alliances between democracies are both deeper and longer lasting than alliances with non-democracies.[33] It has also been argued that as a great power matures, it will increasingly seek to shape its region and the international order in ways that reflect its values and identity.[34] According to this argument, as a great power, India might eventually seek to impose its own values on Asia despite its avowed policy of not exporting ideology.

However, for the moment, ideology plays only a relatively minor part in India's strategic engagement in the Asia Pacific, either as a motivation or as a tool of 'soft power'. Democratic values form part of a rhetorical package of shared interests between India and the United States and others such as Japan, South Korea and Australia. India also finds it useful in differentiating itself from its two principal strategic adversaries, Pakistan and China.[35] India's democratic system probably also contributes to its relatively benign image in East Asia. In comparing international views of China and India, Lee Kuan Yew commented:

> What if India were [economically] well ahead of China? Would Americans and Europeans be rooting for China? I doubt it. They still have a phobia of the 'yellow peril.' One reinforced by the memories of the outrages of the Cultural Revolution and the massacres of Tiananmen Square, not to mention their strong feelings against Chinese government censorship.[36]

However, on the other hand, there is little history of democratic values playing a major role in East Asian strategic relationships. Democratic values (or the lack of them) seem to have been little impediment to the development of India's relationships with Vietnam, or for that matter, with Singapore. India has also demonstrated a willingness to abandon democracy as a guiding principle where it believes that its interests are otherwise threatened (e.g. when support for Burma's democratic opposition was reversed in the face of China's increased influence with the Burmese junta). As Indian Foreign Secretary, Shyam Saran, commented in February 2005, although 'democracy remains India's biding conviction, the importance of our neighbourhood requires that we remain engaged with whichever government is exercising authority in any country'.[37]

India as a maritime power

A new and potentially significant element in Indian strategic thinking is a partial reorientation in India's strategic outlook from purely continentalist towards a more maritimist perspective. This helps fuel India's ambition to become the predominant naval power in the Indian Ocean region, an ambition which has significant consequences for India's security role in Southeast Asia.

Indian security thinking has traditionally tended to take a 'continental' outlook. For thousands of years military threats to India have been perceived as coming primarily from India's northwest. This was reinforced by India's experience in the twentieth century, when any direct military threats to India were land-based: from the northeast (Japan, 1941–45), the northwest (Pakistan, 1947 and after) and the north (China, 1962 and after). The continuing threats on India's western and northern borders and from domestic insurgencies has led to the Indian Army holding an indisputably dominant position within the Indian military establishment, in comparison to which the Indian Navy and its supporters have had little strategic influence.

Despite this tradition there has been a developing view among some Indian strategists of India as primarily a maritime and not a continental power. According to some, New Delhi is making a conscious effort to expand the Indian 'mental map' in strategic affairs to include the seafaring dimension. This has been compared with the fundamental shifts in strategic culture previously experienced by Japan in the nineteenth century (as a result of US naval intrusion and the Sino-Japanese war) and the United States in the twentieth century (encouraged by its acquisition of Spanish colonial territories and the attack on Pearl Harbour).[38] Arguably, much greater Indian attention to naval affairs was prompted by Henry Kissinger's deployment of the nuclear aircraft carrier *USS Enterprise* to the Bay of Bengal in the closing days of the 1971 Bangladesh war, intended by Kissinger as a warning to India not to dismember West Pakistan. This was perceived in New Delhi as a seaborne nuclear threat to India at its moment of triumph over Pakistan and was remembered with bitterness for decades. Many Indian strategists now argue that India's peninsular character and central position in the Indian Ocean gives the sea a preponderant influence over its destiny. In 2000, Indian Chief of Naval Staff, Admiral Sushil Kumar, stated:

> in my view the continentalist era is over and the next millennium will witness the dawning of a new maritime period. I believe that during the

next century India will realise her potential as a full-fledged maritime nation and that India's maritime dimension will decisively shape our country's destiny in the years ahead.

Kumar further claimed that under the then government, 'India's national interest had been made coterminous with maritime security.'[39]

Some Indian leaders have drawn a close connection between India's maritime ambitions and its destiny as a great power. As Indian Foreign Minister Pranab Mukherjee commented in June 2007,

> Fortunately, after nearly a millennia [sic] of inward and landward focus, we are once again turning our gaze outwards and seawards, which is the natural direction of view for a nation seeking to re-establish itself, not simply as a continental power, but even more so as a maritime power, *and consequently as one that is of significance on the world stage* (emphasis added).[40]

Such thinking seems to echo other great power aspirants such as the former Soviet Union and now, China, that maritime power is at the very least a *sine qua non* of great power status. One could also argue that for geographic reasons any significant expansion of Indian influence can only take place in the maritime domain. The Himalayas provide a formidable barrier to India's ability to project power and influence northwards. As Rajiv Sikri, a former Secretary in India's Foreign Ministry commented: 'If India aspires to be a great power, then the only direction in which India's strategic influence can spread is across the seas. In every other direction there are formidable constraints.'[41]

India's standing as the most populous state in the Indian Ocean region and its central position in the northern Indian Ocean have long contributed to beliefs in New Delhi about India's destiny to control its eponymous ocean. Even before India's independence, K.M. Panikkar, India's most famous maritime strategist, argued that the Indian Ocean must remain 'truly Indian', advocating the creation of a 'steel ring' around India through the establishment of forward naval bases in Singapore, Mauritius, Yemen and Sri Lanka. According to some reports there is now a 'well established tradition' among the Indian strategic community that the Indian Ocean is, or should be, 'India's Ocean'.[42]

Not surprisingly, India's area of maritime interest is primarily focused on the northern Indian Ocean where it has developed strong security relationships with smaller states located near to, or at, choke points of entry into the ocean.[43] In 2000, Defence Minister George Fernandes spoke of an extended Indian *area of interest* from 'the north of the Arabian Sea to the South China Sea'.[44] In 2001, the Ministry of Defence Annual Report described what it called India's *security environment* as extending from the Persian Gulf in the west, to the Straits of Malacca in the east,[45] an area which the former BJP Foreign Minister Jaswant Singh called India's *sphere of influence*[46] and the current Prime Minister Manmohan Singh has perhaps more diplomatically called India's *strategic footprint*.[47] Many believe that the Indian Navy now sees itself as destined to be the predominant maritime security provider in a region stretching from the Red Sea to Singapore and having a significant security role in areas beyond, including the South China Sea.[48]

There is also a common view in New Delhi that control of the Indian Ocean (including the chokepoints into the Pacific Ocean) could give India the ability to dominate the whole of maritime Asia. Alfred Thayer Mahan, the nineteenth-century American naval strategist, is quoted widely and approvingly among Indian strategic thinkers, including a statement attributed to Mahan that: 'Whoever controls the Indian Ocean dominates Asia. ... In the 21st century, the destiny of the world will be decided on its waters.' Although the attribution of the statement has been shown to be fictitious, it has not inhibited the enthusiasm for the ideas that it carries.[49] Chapter 9 will examine how India's aspirations in the Indian Ocean underpin its security ambitions in maritime Southeast Asia.

An Indian sphere of influence?

Related to the increased prominence of maritime perspectives in Indian strategic thought is a revival in thinking about an Indian sphere of influence in the Indian Ocean region, potentially extending into Southeast Asia. While such ideas can, in part, be viewed as a reaction to perceived incursions by China into India's neighbourhood, they should primarily be seen as a natural consequence of India's ambitions as a great regional power.

Discussions of an Indian sphere of influence beyond South Asia find support from some Hindu nationalists, who emphasise an Indian 'cultural sphere' extending into maritime Southeast Asia (especially Indonesia) and Indochina. They claim that longstanding cultural, religious and linguistic associations make it natural for India to reassert its influence in these regions. Ideas of an Indian sphere of influence are also sometimes identified with Lord Curzon, the British Viceroy of India at the beginning of the twentieth century, who advocated that British India adopt a 'Forward Policy' to secure India. Curzon's so-called 'Forward School' argued that India's security demanded control of the maritime routes and key ports en route to India (including Aden and Singapore) and the creation of territorial buffers to insulate direct contact with other empires (including Afghanistan in the west, Tibet in the north and Siam in the east) and for British India to take an active role in managing the affairs of the buffer zones.

In many ways the policies of the British Raj represented a significant departure from Indian traditions, which had little history of territorial expansion or military or political adventure beyond the limits of the sub-continent. George Tanham's classic study of India's strategic culture in the early 1990s characterised Indian strategic thinking as being 'defensive' and having a 'lack of an expansionist military tradition'.[50] Certainly, any affirmation of an Indian security sphere beyond South Asia largely ceased following independence. After 1947, India effectively withdrew to the Indian subcontinent and asserted what has been called India's 'Monroe Doctrine', according to which India would not permit any intervention by any 'external' power in South Asia and related islands. The doctrine has been described as requiring that no country in South Asia should seek military aid from external powers; that no external power should intervene in disputes between South Asian states or in the domestic problems of those states; and that no South Asian state other than India should arbitrate the disputes and problems of South Asia.[51] However, India's assertions of a form of suzerainty over smaller neighbours encountered resistance from both regional and extra-regional powers.[52] Nevertheless, India's Monroe Doctrine was used to justify interventions in India's smaller neighbours such as Sri Lanka and Maldives in the late 1980s.[53] An important extension of India's perceived area of influence was in Indochina, where during the Cold War India developed a strong political relationship with Vietnam in an effort to limit the influence of China and other 'external' powers in that subregion. Through the Cold War and thereafter, Indian leaders and strategists claimed that Vietnam guarded the eastern flank of India's 'core sphere of influence' in South Asia.[54]

Since the end of the Cold War there has been a revival of discussion in India about a 'natural' sphere of influence extending well beyond the Indian subcontinent. This is related to attempts to move beyond India's strategic preoccupations in South Asia and re-engage with its extended neighbourhood, to rectify what Foreign Minister Jaswant Singh called India's unnecessary acceptance of 'the post-Partition limits geography imposed on policy'.[55] As noted above, over the last decade there have been repeated assertions at a political and military level in New Delhi that Southeast Asia forms part of India's 'sphere of influence' or its 'strategic footprint', at least in the maritime sphere. However, this vision extends beyond mere maritime predominance. Some have tried to re-articulate commonly understood geographical concepts through, for example, expanding the traditional concept of 'South Asia' (in which India is naturally predominant) towards a concept of 'Southern Asia', an area extending from the Persian Gulf to Singapore. K. Subrahmanyam, once called the 'doyen' of Indian strategists by Prime Minister Manmohan Singh, reportedly proclaimed that it is India's 'manifest destiny to control *Southern* Asia and the Indian Ocean sea-lanes around us' (emphasis added).[56] Subrahmanyam's words were no doubt intended to evoke claims by the United States to a special role in the Western Hemisphere.

Mohan has labelled India's reach into its extended neighbourhood over the last decade or more as a neo-Curzonian 'Forward Policy'. According to Mohan:

> The end of the cold war and the efforts to globalise the economy put India willy-nilly on the path of a new forward policy. India never consciously articulated its approach in terms of theory that demanded activism in the neighbouring regions to enhance its own security. Its regional initiatives were presented in terms of mutual economic benefit and the restoration of historic links, but their strategic significance was unmistakable.[57]

Mohan claims that this new Forward Policy includes the revival of commercial cooperation; the building of institutional and political links in the region; developing physical connectivity with neighbouring regions; initiation of defence contacts with key states; and strategic competition with China and Pakistan. Suggestions that India is pursuing (or should pursue) a new Forward Policy have been strongly criticised by some Indian strategists as an inappropriate, irrelevant or 'quixotic' attempt to return to imperial thinking. Despite such criticism, it is not difficult to view India's strategic engagement with the Asia Pacific, and particularly with Southeast Asia, as a part of a reassertion of British India's sphere of influence centred on the Indian Ocean and extending from Aden to Singapore. To the east, Indian is trying to develop Burma as a buffer state against China, while it gains maritime predominance in the Bay of Bengal/Andaman Sea and a major role in the Malacca Strait. Singapore would act as the eastern 'anchor' to this space. In the west, India exerts influence in Afghanistan while it renews its historical relationships with the Gulf States and Iran.

While there are indications of India's ambitions to build something that might be called a 'sphere of influence' there has been little guidance as to what it might look like, particularly in Southeast Asia. Certainly, India's approach to building a sphere of influence from Aden to Singapore differs significantly from Lord Curzon's. India has no choice but to accept that it must develop its influence in a non-confrontational way. As Foreign Minister Pranab Mukherjee commented (in relation to South Asia): 'India does not seek an exclusive sphere of influence, but a shared sphere of mutual development and cooperation.'[58] Similarly, Mohan argues that New Delhi is unlikely to attempt to regain the hegemonic role of British India in the Indian Ocean region.[59] India's cooperative approach to developing security relationships with smaller states has been particularly evident in Southeast Asia, where the Indian Navy has been successful in developing good relationships in the region and has displayed a degree of sensitivity towards local political concerns in relation to the Malacca Strait.

The failure of India to project military power beyond the limits of South Asia during the Cold War has placed India in good stead in the Asia Pacific. India has a noticeable lack of historical baggage in its dealings in much of the region, perhaps with the exception of the Islamic factor arising from India's conflict with Pakistan. India is commonly perceived in Southeast Asia as essentially a benign power and not a would-be hegemon, often in contrast with other external powers such as China, the United States and Japan. According to some, India's track record of non-aggression, its cultural and philosophical virtues, and its ethnic and religious ties to Southeast Asia lend credence to Indian soft power diplomacy.[60] While India is not in a position to exert significant power through military predominance or ideological means, it may be able to do so as a provider of public goods.[61] In the early 1990s, Tanham described India's regional ambitions in the following terms:

Strategically, India aspires to be a friendly international peacekeeper. It sees itself as a benevolent nation and a friendly policeman that seeks peace and stability for the entire Indian Ocean region. It denies any hegemonistic designs or territorial ambitions. It vehemently rejects and resents charges of being a regional bully. It wants not only to play the role of regional peace-keeper but also to be acknowledged and endorsed in that role by others, especially the great powers.[62]

India shows a strong desire to project power into the region as a benign maritime peacekeeper. There are indications that some in Southeast Asia (particularly Singapore) are now willing to cede India a role as a maritime security provider in the Malacca Strait, if only in the context of balancing other major powers. Mohan claims that as the Indian economy grows and it modernises its military capabilities it will become an attractive partner, generating strategic 'options that did not exist before in the Western Pacific'.[63] This may well become the case; however, as will be seen in subsequent chapters, few in the Asia Pacific currently see India as playing a major *direct* security role in the western Pacific.

As it expands its influence in Southeast Asia, India has had to accept that other major powers will continue to have significant interests in the region. The United States, particularly with its base at Diego Garcia and its naval facilities in Singapore and the Gulf, seems likely to remain the predominant naval power in the Indian Ocean region for some time to come. However, there are indications that the United States is willing to cede – and indeed encourage – a major regional naval role for India across the Indian Ocean and including in the Malacca Strait.[64] US thinking in this respect is considered further in Chapter 4. For its part, India's willingness to cooperate with the United States in achieving its ambitions is not as paradoxical as it may seem. As the former US Secretary of State, Dean Acheson, once conceded, the United States in developing its sphere of influence in the Western Hemisphere in the nineteenth century relied on the then superpower Britain (then in relative decline), to enforce the Monroe Doctrine until the United States was sufficiently strong to do so itself.[65]

Nevertheless, with the exception of the United States, which is unlikely soon to recognise India's predominance (except, perhaps, in specific areas), India will likely wish to cooperate with extra-regional navies in the Indian Ocean only as long as they recognise India's leading role.[66] Japan's apparent willingness to recognise India's role as the 'leading' maritime security provider west of the Malacca Strait forms a not insignificant element in the developing India–Japan security relationship. In contrast, others such as China and Australia seem unlikely to cede any such role to India.

Is the revival in Indian strategic thinking about a sphere of influence merely a defensive reaction to the rise of China and perceived intrusions of China into India's strategic space, or is it derived from India's ambitions as a great power? Neorealists argue that it is natural for especially powerful states to seek regional hegemony.[67] One study of India's regional plans concluded that:

> a rising India will try to establish regional hegemony in South Asia and the Indian Ocean Region ... just like all the other rising powers have since Napoleonic times, with the long term goal of achieving great power status on an Asian and perhaps even global scale.[68]

From a geopolitical perspective, spheres of influence are seen as a normal part of ordering the international system. According to Saul Bernard Cohen, a noted geopolitical theorist: 'spheres of influence are essential to the preservation of national and regional expression. ... the alternative is either a monolithic world system or utter chaos.'[69] From an Indian perspective the expression of a sphere of influence over the Indian Ocean region up to Singapore might be seen as India reasserting an historical or geographical role that was interrupted by India's post-independence self-limitations, limitations which India is now consciously seeking to overcome. Such a sphere of influence might also be seen as a 'natural' appurtenance of a great power.

However, China also provides good defensive reasons for the development of a sphere of influence. Many Indian strategists see China's actions in Southern Asia, including its consolidation of Tibet, its alliance with Pakistan and its relationships with Burma, Bangladesh and Nepal as part of a cohesive and successful policy of 'encirclement' or 'containment' of India. As will be discussed in Chapter 3, China's so-called String of Pearls strategy is widely viewed among the Indian security community as primarily motivated by a strategy of maritime encirclement of India. The development of a 'defensive' sphere of influence is thus justified by China's actions in South Asia and the Indian Ocean. As Admiral Arun Prakash, Indian Chief of Naval Staff (2004–6), commented: 'The appropriate counter to China's encirclement of India is to build our own relations, particularly in our neighbourhood, on the basis of our national interests and magnanimity towards smaller neighbours.'[70]

Many Indian security 'hawks' claim China's purported encirclement strategy justifies a more offensive approach by India, advocating a policy of 'counter-encirclement' of China, including the development of security relationships along China's periphery in Southeast and Northeast Asia and North and Central Asia.[71] The development by India of security-related facilities in Tajikistan and Mongolia is taken as evidence of India's counter-encirclement strategy in Central and North Asia and such a strategy is seen as driving India's relationships with Vietnam, Taiwan, South Korea and Japan on China's eastern periphery. A counter-encirclement strategy is also used to advocate the development of a direct Indian security presence on China's periphery, including Indian control of the Malacca Strait and ultimately an Indian naval presence in the South China Sea and even possibly in the Sea of Japan.[72] Many Indian strategists would strongly reject any proposition that India is involved in any counter-encirclement strategy against China.[73] Nevertheless, advocates of such a policy could gain greater influence in New Delhi in the event of a significant deterioration in the Sino-Indian relationship, particularly if China is perceived as being too assertive in the Indian Ocean region.

Proactive and reactive dynamics in Indian strategy

India has not articulated any 'grand strategy' about the Asia Pacific and seems unlikely to do so any time soon. While Indian strategic thinking about the Asia Pacific is best understood as a mosaic of perspectives and pragmatic goals, it is possible to identify two key factors that are driving Indian strategic thinking about the Asia Pacific: rivalry with China (which is essentially a reactive dynamic) and India's ambitions to achieve great power status (essentially a proactive dynamic).

Fears of possible Chinese hegemony in East Asia and of Chinese 'intrusions' into India's strategic space in South Asia and the Indian Ocean region have led to greater prominence in realist thinking about balancing China. From India's perspective this is a significant factor in its relationship with the United States and Japan and smaller powers such as Singapore and Vietnam (although, as will be seen, such motivations may not necessarily be reciprocated). However, India's ability to enter into any balancing coalition with the United States and its allies is limited by its objectives of maintaining strategic autonomy and avoiding overt rivalry with China.

Beliefs about India's destiny as a great power underlie a separate stream of strategic thinking, one more rooted in geopolitical perspectives. India's strategic outlook is increasingly maritime-orientated, driving its aspirations to become the predominant naval power in the Indian Ocean. Related to these ambitions are ideas about the development of an Indian sphere of influence which, among other things, would encompass the littoral states in the northeast Indian Ocean. As a result, India is increasingly projecting naval power into Southeast Asia, although it has been careful to do so in a cooperative manner.

3 Sino-Indian strategic competition and the Asia Pacific

China has never been far from India's mind. Many in New Delhi still remember India's humiliating defeat by China in 1962 and resent China's continuing support for Pakistan. As both India and China rise as economic powers, the rivalry between them has become more complex and wide-ranging. India now sees the Asia Pacific as a critical region in which it must compete with China and balance its rising power.

The evolution of the relationship

Despite sharing a long land border, the two great civilisations of India and China have had relatively little political interaction until modern times. The Himalayas have always served as a substantial geographical barrier and both civilisations were inward-looking for much of their history. Many Indians and Chinese have professed a particular incomprehension of the other, particularly in political and strategic affairs. It has been argued that each civilisation holds an idiosyncratic concept of its own centrality in the world, which contributes to a 'blindness' which each country has exhibited towards the other in modern times.[1] The relationship between India and China since the end of World War II has been characterised by periods of cooperation, conflict and competition, and a complex and relatively unstable relationship is evident today.[2]

From India's independence until 1962, one of the primary goals of Indian diplomacy in Asia was to preserve the goodwill and friendship of China. Nehru believed that notwithstanding ideological differences, there were strategic imperatives to develop a good relationship. According to Nehru, India's engagement with China would lead to China's engagement with the region as a whole, mitigating China's expansionist tendencies and drawing it away from its relationship with the Soviet Union. Nehru was aware of the underlying rivalry between India and China, commenting 'that some day or other these two Asian giants were bound to tread on each others' corns and come into conflict, and that would be a calamity for Asia'.[3] Throughout the first half of the 1950s India offered considerable diplomatic support to the People's Republic of China (PRC), which many then considered a pariah. India was one of the first non-communist states in the world to recognise the Communist Chinese government in 1949 and lobbied hard to give China's seat in the UN to the PRC. At the same time, both India and China moved to consolidate their positions in the Himalayas: India, through treaties with Bhutan, Nepal and Sikkim (which was later absorbed into Indian territory); and China, through its absorption of Tibet. In 1954, India formally recognised China's full sovereignty over Tibet in return for China's agreement on the Five Principles of Peaceful Coexistence (known as *Panchsheel*) – essentially principles of respect for sovereignty and mutual non-interference. The mid-1950s represented the honeymoon for the India–China strategic relationship, trumpeted by the Indians under the catchphrase '*Hindi-Chini bhai-bhai*' (in Hindi, 'India and China are brothers').

Nehru hoped that India's recognition of Chinese sovereignty over Tibet would address China's ambitions in the Himalayas. However, in 1962 disputes over the McMahon Line, the colonial-era border claimed by India, escalated into full-scale conflict. Chinese forces quickly defeated the Indian army and, after occupying significant areas of Indian-administered territory, declared a ceasefire and unilaterally withdrew to the current line of control. India's military defeat was a humiliating blow to the credibility of Nehru and his foreign policies and for many Indians established China as India's major long-term threat. The border dispute remains unresolved today and continues to be the most significant obstacle to improved relations between India and China. China's 'betrayal' of India in 1962 is still remembered with great bitterness in New Delhi. Despite talks over the issue since the 1980s, Beijing seems disinclined to reach a border settlement with India based on the existing line of actual control and periodically ratchets up bilateral tensions through claims over much of the populated area of the Indian state of Arunachal Pradesh, which China calls 'Southern Tibet'.

The second major historical issue in Sino-Indian relations is China's strategic relationship with Pakistan. China began pursuing this relationship following the 1962 war, establishing itself as a major supplier of arms to Pakistan and providing it with significant strategic support against India. The so-called 'all weather friendship' with Pakistan (alongside its relationship with North Korea) is the closest China has come to a long-term alliance. Since the 1960s, the China factor has played a significant role in limiting India's strategic options with Pakistan and keeping India strategically pre-occupied in South Asia. The perceived military threat from China and its alliance with Pakistan was a primary motivation for India's security relationship with the Soviet Union. During the 1980s and 1990s the Chinese 'threat' gained a new dimension when China played a key role in the proliferation of nuclear weapons and missiles to Pakistan. This will have a lasting impact on the balance of power in South Asia and is seen by some in New Delhi as China's second great strategic 'betrayal' of India.

The end of the Cold War and the dissolution of the Soviet Union allowed significant improvements in bilateral relations. While India no longer viewed

China as an immediate military threat, the relationship remained an uneasy one. The greatest shift in the relationship occurred as a result of India's 1998 nuclear tests, which formed a turning point in India's search for great power status. In seeking to justify this move, New Delhi pointed the finger squarely at China, calling it 'an overt nuclear weapons state on our borders, a state which committed armed aggression against India in 1962'.[4] Many see India's new status as a declared nuclear weapons state as redefining what Mohan calls the 'psychological framework' of India's relations with China.[5] Although the primary focus for strategic competition between India and China remains South Asia, in recent years, the scope of the relationship has extended to cover a much broader geographical area, including Central and West Asia, Southeast Asia and the Indian Ocean region. It has also involved important new dimensions, including a rapidly expanding economic relationship, growing competition in energy security and rivalry in maritime security. Each of these dimensions involve elements of competition and cooperation.

The economic dimension

In recent years, the Sino-Indian relationship has also developed a significant economic dimension. This has several aspects, including the impact of economic growth on overall national power and the potential impact of the bilateral economic relationship on strategic competition and cooperation.

China's head-start in implementing economic reforms and attracting foreign investment has led to a significant disparity between China's and India's GDP, a disparity that seems likely to grow in absolute terms in coming years. Goldman Sachs projected China's GDP in 2010 to be US$4,667 billion, compared with India's GDP of US$1,256 billion, and China's GDP in 2030 to be US$25,610 billion, compared with India's GDP of US$6,683 billion. Although India's rate of economic growth is expected to exceed China's from around 2015, China's GDP is still expected to be almost twice the size of India's in 2050.[6] It is apparent that China's political system has been much more successful than India's in driving economic development, although Indian optimists suggest that India's democratic system will deliver stronger economic benefits over the longer term. Nevertheless, for some, the growing disparity between Chinese and Indian economic power will make China an increasing threat to India in coming years.

The opening of the Chinese and Indian economies has led to some remarkable increases in Sino-Indian trade. Bilateral trade has grown from US$117 million in 1987 to US$51.7 billion in 2008 (up 34 per cent from 2007), making China India's largest trading partner. According to some forecasts, bilateral trade is expected to grow as high as US$100 billion by 2011. Some analysts suggest that rapidly increasing trade between India and China will lead to greater interdependence between them, perhaps moderating tensions and providing an environment for greater strategic cooperation.[7] However, there are major imbalances in the trade relationship. While China's exports are largely manufactures, Indian exports to China are largely low value-added commodities. There is also a massive numerical imbalance in China's favour. In the 12 months ending April 2009, exports from China (including Hong Kong) to India aggregated US$37.74 billion, while India's exports to China (including Hong Kong) were only US$15.93 billion, leaving a physical trade deficit for India of US$21.81 billion.[8] There are widely held concerns that India is being flooded with Chinese manufactured goods which will destroy local industries, increasing pressure on the Indian government to institute anti-dumping measures against China. A bilateral free trade agreement has been under negotiation since 2004, although there is reported to be considerable scepticism about it in light of these imbalances.[9] Bilateral investment between India and China is negligible, highlighting the relatively shallow nature of the economic relationship. Actual Chinese foreign direct investment in India between 2000 and 2009 was US$14 million[10] while approved Indian foreign direct investment in China between 1996 and 2004 was US$96 million.[11] The economic relationship between India and China may well mature and broaden in coming years, but the expansion of trade between China and India is currently as much a source of friction as a driver for strategic cooperation.

Energy security

Competition in the field of energy security is a significant and growing factor in the India–China relationship and has had a particular impact on India's strategic ambitions in the Indian Ocean and Southeast Asia.

In coming years, both India and China will have a growing dependence on energy imports, primarily from the Middle East, but also from Northeast Asia, Central Asia, Africa and Australia. In 2007, China imported approximately 55 per cent of its oil requirements (the great majority from the Middle East and Africa) and this is expected to rise significantly. In the same year, India imported approximately 69 per cent of its oil requirements (around two-thirds of which was from the Middle East), which is expected to rise to around 75–80 per cent by 2015. China has over the past decade or more taken what has been described as a 'diplomatic–mercantilist' approach to securing oil supplies. This has involved a centralised strategy of Chinese state-owned companies taking equity positions in energy resource suppliers, particularly in 'rogue' or politically unstable states such as Sudan, Angola, Venezuela, Thailand and Papua New Guinea. China has also encouraged extensive cross-investment by major exporting companies in the Chinese energy sector to reinforce long-term ties with suppliers.[12] In contrast, India's major oil companies (which paradoxically appear to be under closer state control than China's) have been subject to bureaucratic restrictions that have inhibited their ability to acquire equity oil.[13] As a result of China's aggressive approach, between 2004 and 2006 Chinese companies outbid Indian companies to acquire major stakes in oil and gas fields in Angola, Kazakhstan, Nigeria and Burma. This prompted an agreement in 2006 between India's

ONGC and China's CNPC oil companies to make joint bids on projects, leading some to be optimistic about the prospects for Sino-Indian cooperation in the development of supplies, particularly in Iran and Central Asia.[14] Bill Tow, an Australian commentator, argues that China's strategy has been to compete with India for control of energy supplies while remaining open to cooperation with India where such involvement is advantageous. He believes that it is unclear to what extent joint collaboration in securing supplies will overcome their legacy of geopolitical competition.[15]

Concerns over energy security have been a prime factor in China and India's increased focus on the SLOCs across the Indian Ocean, and particularly the chokepoints in the Straits of Hormuz and Malacca. While approximately 80 per cent of China's oil imports pass through the Strait of Malacca, China is not able to provide SLOC protection there, raising what Chinese President Hu Jiantao referred to as China's 'Malacca Dilemma'. China's concerns about protecting energy supplies is now a key factor in the expansion of its interests in the Indian Ocean region. Yoshihara and Holmes, analysts with the US Naval War College, claim that the maintenance of the SLOCs from the Persian Gulf and Africa to China has become a matter of 'surpassing importance' to China's communist regime.[16]

Sino-Indian maritime rivalry in the Indian Ocean region

Naval competition between India and China in the Indian Ocean region is becoming a significant factor in the strategic relationship and is a major factor driving India's maritime security ambitions both in the Indian Ocean region and Southeast Asia. While the Indian Navy's immediate strategic objectives involve countering Pakistan and enforcing control over India's exclusive economic zone (EEZ), the potential for China to project naval power into the Indian Ocean has become its principal long-term source of concern.

China began implementing plans for a blue water navy in the mid-1980s. Although focused on protecting China's interests in the western Pacific Ocean, in particular the Taiwan Strait, it also had long-term implications for India. China's naval capabilities now exceed India's by a considerable margin in both quantitative and qualitative terms.[17] While, as noted above, China's leadership perceive the security of China's SLOCs across the Indian Ocean as a vital interest, the Chinese navy's ability to project power into the Indian Ocean is severely restricted by its limited naval and air power projection capabilities, the distance from ports in southern China and its lack of logistical support in the Indian Ocean, as well as China's need to deploy to the Indian Ocean through chokepoints, including the Strait of Malacca.

China's attempts to mitigate these strategic limitations in the Indian Ocean region have been called its 'String of Pearls' strategy.[18] Until recently there has been virtually no Chinese naval presence in the region other than a handful of port calls to Pakistan and Burma. However over the last decade or so, China has been developing political relationships and commercial interests throughout the Indian Ocean region which include the supply of military equipment to, and the development of port facilities in, several of India's neighbours. According to Indian-sourced reports, China is or was involved in the development of some military-related facilities in the region, including electronic monitoring facilities in Burma's Coco Islands and possibly at Gwadar in Pakistan.[19] China has been involved in the funding and construction of a number of commercial port facilities in the region, including in Pakistan (Gwadar), Sri Lanka (Hambantota), Burma (Kyaukpyu) and Bangladesh (Sonadia) (announced in 2010) and it is often assumed in New Delhi that China has secretly negotiated naval access rights as part of these developments.[20] Despite the highly strategic locations of ports such as Gwadar (which sits near the Strait of Hormuz) and Hambantota (which sits midway between the Strait of Hormuz and the Strait of Malacca), China has been careful to avoid any overt military presence or even any explicit commercial role in their operation.[21] Since early 2009, China has also stationed several naval vessels in the Gulf of Aden area to protect Chinese ships from Somali pirates, which have received logistical support out of Djibouti. These operate in parallel with the US-sponsored Combined Task Force 151.[22] A senior Chinese naval official has also recently proposed the establishment of a permanent base in the Gulf of Aden to provide support for Chinese ships carrying out anti-piracy patrols.[23]

Despite the somewhat ambiguous nature of China's interests in the Indian Ocean region, many in New Delhi firmly believe that the so-called 'String of Pearls' is a coordinated military strategy aimed at India. The reactions of many in the Indian security community have been characterised by Yoshihara and Holmes as 'alarmist' and 'panicky'.[24] China's relationships in the Indian Ocean region are frequently assumed to be military in nature and are generally not perceived in the Indian security community as being a legitimate reflection of Chinese interests in protecting its SLOCs across the Indian Ocean. Rather, many perceive China's regional relationships as being directed against India: either as a plan of maritime 'encirclement' of India or otherwise intended to keep India strategically preoccupied in South Asia. Although few have suggested that any Chinese military threat to India is likely to be primarily seaborne, many in New Delhi see a significant risk that India and China will, as Admiral Arun Prakash put it, 'compete and even clash in the same strategic space'.[25] Further, as Admiral Suresh Mehta, Indian Chief of Naval Staff (2006–10), claimed on Indian television:

> [China] is shaping the maritime battlefield in the region. It is making friends in the right places. It you don't have the capability to operate in these waters, for a length of time, then you need friends who will support your cause, when the time comes, so definitely China is doing that, as there are Pakistan, Bangladesh, Myanmar, Sri Lanka and down below Africa. So it is a known fact that we are ringed by states which may have a favourable disposition towards China.[26]

Others in New Delhi who might acknowledge China's interests in SLOC security argue that China is overstepping the mark in developing influence in the Indian Ocean region, creating a security dilemma for India. As Commander Gurpreet Khurana (joint director of the Indian Navy's Maritime Doctrine and Concept Centre and author of the 2004 Indian Maritime Doctrine) describes it, China and India's vital security interests have been dilating from their immediate peripheries to regional extremities and beyond, leading them both to stretch their maritime strategic footprint across the entire Asian region.[27]

While China clearly recognises that it has vital interests in the Indian Ocean region, its strategy is not at all clear. Some non-Indian analysts believe that many Indian-sourced claims about the Chinese presence in the northern Indian Ocean are exaggerated, particularly claims of a Chinese military presence in Burma and the Andaman Sea.[28] While China has provided military assistance to Burma it seems unlikely that it maintains any significant military presence in that country. Rather than building bases, China seems to be pursuing a strategy of developing political and commercial relationships and building infrastructure in the region that could subsequently form the foundation of an overt security presence if circumstances required. Robert Kaplan, the noted US journalist and strategic thinker, sees the development of regional relationships by China in grand strategic rather than military terms, commenting that 'China's move into the Indian Ocean constitutes less an aggressive example of empire building than a subtle grand-strategy to take advantage of legitimate commercial opportunities wherever they may arise in places that matter to its military and economic interests.'[29] Kaplan nevertheless foresees the long-term development of the Chinese navy from a one-ocean power to a two-ocean navy as part of the transformation of China from a regional power to a great power, able to project force around the whole navigable Eurasian rimland.[30] However, claims that China's very small presence in the Indian Ocean region represents even the beginnings of a two-ocean navy seem overstated at this stage. Borrowing from the terminology of nuclear deterrence, China's naval capabilities in the Indian Ocean might at the most be described as 'recessed'.[31] In any event, given the geopolitical limitations on projecting and maintaining substantial Chinese power into the Indian Ocean it is not clear whether China will seek to develop any security presence beyond its current anti-piracy operations. Arguably, the geographic constraints China faces in the Indian Ocean will for the foreseeable future place significant limitations on its ability to unilaterally protect its SLOCs against other major powers (and particularly India). As one Chinese analyst commented, given the distances separating any Chinese interests in the Indian Ocean, they look more like 'sitting ducks' than a string of pearls.[32]

India has responded to China's Indian Ocean strategy in several ways. First, by trying to pre-empt the development of China's relationships in the Indian Ocean through the development of India's own security relationships in the region. Second, by developing its capability to exert negative control over the maritime choke points between the Indian and Pacific Oceans, particularly the Malacca Strait. Third, by developing the capability to project power into the South China Sea. These last two factors have particular significance for India's strategic role in the Asia Pacific and will be discussed in detail in Chapter 9.

Political and economic rivalry in the Asia Pacific

There is a great deal of uncertainty and debate about the overall trajectory of the India–China relationship in general and in the Asia Pacific in particular. To what extent will it be primarily characterised by cooperation, rivalry or a complex mixture of the two? Mohan believes that the way New Delhi handles ties with Beijing will be the biggest challenge for Indian foreign policy in the coming decades, claiming that all the big issues in India's foreign relations, including its relationships with the United States and in Asia, are intimately tied to the China relationship.[33]

There are several streams of thinking about China in New Delhi ranging from hawkish to cooperationist. The dominant view is relatively pragmatic, recognising that India and China are strategic competitors, while trying to manage their aspirations. According to this view, China is not necessarily a direct military threat, but may pose a potential threat to India's interests, particularly if it does not acquiesce to the rise of India and the extension of Indian power beyond South Asia.[34] In recent years the Indian government has sought to keep rivalry with China within limits while it builds its national power and asserts its status as a great power. Relations improved for several years following Indian Prime Minister Vajpayee's 2003 visit to Beijing and a declaration of a strategic partnership between India and China in 2006. But there are real limits to any rapprochement, as shown by India's reported rejection of a Chinese request to conclude a 'peace and friendship treaty' prior to President Hu's visit to India in late 2008.[35] India has nevertheless sought to place the border issue on the backburner as much as possible, to largely ignore what India sees as Chinese provocations, and to focus on encouraging bilateral trade. Both have made symbolic gestures of cooperation on security issues, including exchanging ship visits and small bilateral exercises.

Mohan Malik, an Indian analyst, calls India's current strategic policy toward China as one of 'balanced engagement' that steers a path between countering a Chinese threat and appeasement.[36] Mark Frazier, a US commentator on China, argues that both sides have recognised the need to prevent tensions leading to sustained overt rivalry and that the prevailing pattern of relations has been one of 'quiet competition'. There is still a real possibility of heightened competition, particularly if a stagnant Indian economy leads India to bind itself closer to the United States, or a sustained downturn in China's economic performance changes the balance of power between India and China, which could lead to greater assertiveness by India.[37] Others see an underlying conflict between Chinese and Indian concepts of national greatness and security being played out as geopolitical competition over a broad geographic area. According to John Garver's comprehensive study of the Sino-Indian strategic relationship through the twentieth century, periods of cooperation have been 'brief and problematic' and conflict is its dominant characteristic. This would continue even if the immediate issues of the border dispute and China's support for Pakistan were resolved.[38] As has been discussed in Chapter 2, such thinking underlies a large and growing school of 'hyperrealists' in New Delhi, who strongly focus on the territorial dispute and China's 'encirclement' strategy in South Asia and the Indian Ocean, and advocate a containment-cum-counter-encirclement strategy in the Asia Pacific.

Adding to uncertainties in the relationship is an asymmetry in threat perceptions between India and China – generally high from India's perspective and generally low from China's.[39] Despite its policy of engagement, India remains focused on China as its primary strategic competitor. In contrast, the Chinese do not generally see any strategic equivalence between themselves and the Indians – they perceive themselves as a global power and any comparison with India as demeaning. They see India as weak, divided and an economic catastrophe, lacking in comprehensive national strength, but with 'unrealistic and unachievable "big power dreams" (*daguomeng*)'.[40] According to one commentator: 'China perceives India to be an ambitious, overconfident yet militarily powerful neighbour with whom it may eventually have to have a day of reckoning'.[41] However, both Tellis and Garver argue that the true perceptions of Chinese security managers differ significantly from public statements and Chinese indifference towards India is 'feigned' with the objective of delegitimising India's security concerns.[42]

India and China have very different perspectives on the legitimacy of an Indian strategic role in the Asia Pacific. Several observers have commented that China sees Asia as being compartmentalised into separate regions: Northeast Asia, Southeast Asia and South Asia, with China having a central role in the first two and playing an important balancing role in the third.[43] Some also claim that China has sought to reinforce its centrality in Asian strategic affairs by destabilising Northeast and South Asia through its security relationships with Pakistan and North Korea and then seeking a role as an impartial, regional arbiter in those regions.[44] As will be discussed later, a division of the strategic affairs of East and South Asia is also consistent with long-running perceptions among many that India really does not belong in East Asia.

Theorists tend to divide Asia into different regions for strategic purposes. Barry Buzan believes that for geographical and historical reasons Asia could be split into three distinct security regions: Northeast Asia, comprised of China, the Korean peninsula and Japan; Southeast Asia, comprised of a large number of secondary states in the Southeast Asian peninsula and archipelago; and South Asia, comprised of India and Pakistan as major regional rivals and a number of smaller states that are geographically and civilisationally part of the region.[45] Until recently each of these regions had their own security dynamics and operated with relative indifference towards each other. Although there are longstanding cultural and religious ties between South and Southeast Asia, until recently, an independent India has declined to play any significant political and security role in Southeast Asia. There has also been little political or security interaction between South Asia and Northeast Asia. Until the 1950s, Tibet served to insulate South Asia from China, but since China absorbed Tibet it has played a relatively active role as an outside power in South Asia mainly through an alliance with Pakistan. In contrast, there has been a greater level of security interaction between Northeast Asia and Southeast Asia (i.e. regions not including India), partly due to attempts by China and Japan to dominate Southeast Asia in both modern and pre-modern times.

However, according to Buzan, since the end of the Cold War, the distinctions between the security regions in Asia have been changing – the Northeast and Southeast Asian security regions have been effectively merging with each other and, to a lesser extent, also with South Asia. The increased level of security interaction between South and East Asia in recent times has partly been driven by changes occurring in South Asian security, including the decline of Pakistan's claim to be a regional pole of power and the intensification of India's rivalry with China. Buzan argues that the South Asian security region is trending towards unipolarity, allowing India to gradually transcend its longstanding confinement to South Asia and carve out a wider role as an Asian great power. The greater economic and political role of China in Southeast Asia has also led the ASEAN states to try to 'pull' India into the region as a balancing force. Without doubt, there are increasing concerns among Indian policy-makers about the growing economic power of China and the potential for China to dominate the whole Asia Pacific region. Some see India's Look East policy primarily in terms of India competing with China for regional dominance.[46]

Consistent with its view of Asia in compartmentalised terms, China is a long way from accepting that India has any 'leadership' role in East Asia. Beijing's response to India's claims to membership of East Asian regional arrangements has often been to treat it as an outsider. In the late 1990s, China refused to allow India into the ASEAN + 3 grouping, apparently seeking to create an 'inner circle' of East Asian states in a close relationship with ASEAN that China hopes to eventually dominate. As a result, India was forced into a separate summit meeting with ASEAN. In 2005, China unsuccessfully sought to exclude India from participation in the East Asia Summit, and led moves during the Summit to cast India as an 'outsider', placing it in the back seat in developing any future East Asian economic grouping to be 'driven' by ASEAN within the 'vehicle' of ASEAN + 3. As Chinese Premier Wen Jiabao claimed, the East Asian Summit 'should be led only by East Asian countries'.[47]

Beijing may believe that India's own structural inadequacies are likely to limit its influence in the Asia Pacific.[48] However, over the last several years

China has shown increasing concern about the links developing between India and the United States and its Asia Pacific allies, which have been compared by some Chinese analysts to the United States and China finding common cause against the Soviet Union in the early 1970s. Some believe that there may be a hardening of China's stance on a whole range of issues as India draws closer to the United States and other East Asian maritime powers. An October 2010 editorial of the *People's Daily* harshly criticised visits by Indian Prime Minister Manmohan Singh to Tokyo and Hanoi, calling them 'missionary visit[s]' to find allies against China. It also criticised India's Look East policy as trying to repeat India's failed Cold War strategy of 'playing both ends against the middle' by playing China and Japan off against each other.[49]

There is little doubt that China would prefer to see a continuation of the long-running strategic divide between East and South Asia, thereby placing itself at the core of East Asian security while also continuing to play a major balancing role in South Asia. However, with the strategic compartmentalisation breaking down, it is not yet clear how China will seek to mould India's increasing security engagement in the Asia Pacific. Some have argued that India and China could each accommodate the other's great power ambitions through a mutual understanding of each other's sphere of influence, that is, India over South Asia and China over Southeast Asia. However, there is no indication that either China or India would be willing to accept such an arrangement.

The China factor in India's strategic relationships in the Asia Pacific

How does the China factor affect India's key bilateral relationships in the Asia Pacific? As will be discussed in detail in subsequent chapters, the China factor plays quite different roles in different relationships. China plays a central role in India's strategic relationship with Japan. Although Japan does not see India as having a direct strategic role in Northeast Asia, it does regard it as a potentially important offshore balancer against China, certainly in terms of regional economic and political institutions. In contrast, Australia has generally tried to avoid China becoming a major factor in its relationship with India, a perspective which may reflect Australia's economic relationship with China, its geographical distance from China and its close and stable security alliance with the United States.

The China factor has a more complex role in India's strategic engagement with Southeast Asia. Arguably, for more than a millennium Southeast Asia has been the primary area of (indirect) cultural and economic interaction between India and China or, as some would have it, overlapping spheres of interest. Nehru once called Sino-Indian rivalry in Southeast Asia the 'basic challenge' of security in the region.[50] Certainly, the region is fast becoming a key area of economic and political rivalry. Tellis believes that of all geographic areas where Sino-Indian rivalry is likely to materialise, Southeast Asia will likely be one of the most important. However, he sees the rivalry as asymmetric, in that China has positive objectives in the region while India's objectives are largely negative. According to Tellis, India has three broad strategic objectives in Southeast Asia, which are largely aimed at China: first, to prevent China from acquiring a forward presence that could threaten the Indian homeland and its freedom of action in South Asia; second, to prevent China from gaining sufficient regional influence so as to be able to coerce regional states into supporting policies that undercut Indian security; and third, to develop strategic relationships with key states that give India freedom to operate in the region, including providing support to regional partners.[51] However, as will be seen later, these 'reactive' dynamics are important in India's engagement with Southeast Asia; India's engagement is also to a significant extent driven by its own 'active' search for great power status in the region.

Through much of the Cold War, the political and economic influence of both China and India in Southeast Asia was limited: China was generally seen in Southeast Asia as an ideological and security threat, while India abstained from assuming a significant role in the region. Since the early 1990s China's economic and political influence in Southeast Asia has grown markedly and it is now regarded within Southeast Asia as a key economic and political partner, albeit one which still needs to be brought fully within the international order.

China's head start in economic liberalisation and its longstanding economic and cultural links with the region has given China a role far in excess of India's. Bilateral trade between China (excluding Hong Kong) and ASEAN states grew from US$8 billion in 1993 to US$192 billion in 2008.[52] In contrast, bilateral trade between India and ASEAN states grew from US$2 billion in 1993 to US$47 billion in 2008[53] (although the rate of growth in India–ASEAN trade now exceeds the rate of growth of China–ASEAN trade). The disparity is paralleled in investment, which arguably is a better long-term gauge of economic influence and interdependence than trade. Net Foreign Direct Investment (FDI) from China to ASEAN aggregated US$5.1 billion between 2000 and 2008 as compared with FDI from India to ASEAN of US$1.3 billion in the same period.[54] FDI from ASEAN to China aggregated US$52 billion up to 2008 (mostly in the manufacturing sector),[55] while FDI from ASEAN to India aggregated US$7.9 billion between 2000 and 2008 (mostly in real estate and services).[56]

China has followed a concerted strategy of developing strong institutional trading arrangements in the region. During the 1997 Asian financial crisis, China's offer of financial support to Thailand and its pledge not to undertake competitive currency devaluations won it significant goodwill.[57] China signed trade agreements with ASEAN on goods and services in 2004 and 2007. China's approach in giving ASEAN early access to the Chinese market in certain areas as well as concessional tariffs on agricultural items magnified China's image as a benevolent and responsible power.[58] An ASEAN–China free trade area which commenced in 2010 for the six original ASEAN states provides for zero tariffs on around 90 per cent of manufactured products and reduced tariffs on agricultural products. Some argue that this has significant potential to undermine any future multilateral Asia Pacific free trade area by 'dividing and conquering' ASEAN states.[59] China also hopes that the Chinese yuan, which is currently largely only used in border trade, will grow to play a significant role as a regional currency, partially replacing the current role of the US dollar.[60]

In contrast, India has been relatively slow to develop formal economic linkages with ASEAN. India signed a trade agreement with ASEAN only in August 2009. Negotiations were reportedly hampered by a lack of strategic vision on the part of India and disagreements within the Indian bureaucracy, leading to India's insistence on extensive exceptions and anti-dumping measures.[61] While India has made considerable progress in developing economic links with Singapore, it has had significant problems in negotiating bilateral trade agreements with less developed ASEAN members (including potentially important regional partners such as Vietnam and Indonesia), where the Indian government is under strong domestic pressure to maintain its protectionist policies over the import of agricultural products from Southeast Asia.

In parallel to its economic links, China is developing good political-security relationships in the region. With the end of the Cold War China has actively pursued relations in Southeast Asia, at both bilateral and multilateral levels, moving past its previous distrust of multilateral institutions. China now participates in numerous regional arrangements including the ASEAN Regional Forum from 1994, as an ASEAN Dialogue Partner from 1996 and in the ASEAN + 3 grouping from 1997, which China has sought to position as the main 'vehicle' for Asian economic integration. ASEAN + 3 has become institutionalised to a significant degree, with 57 bodies now implementing ASEAN + 3 coordination over an increasing range of political, security and economic issues. China's strong institutional links in Southeast Asia are undermined by China's aggressive territorial claims in the South China Sea, which has resulted in territorial disputes with six ASEAN states. Tensions over the South China Sea were reduced considerably by the multilateral 2002 Declaration on the Conduct of Parties in the South China Sea and China's accession to the ASEAN Treaty of Amity in October 2003. In December 2004, ASEAN and China announced a five-year Plan of Action to implement a China–ASEAN Strategic Partnership, focused heavily on defence and security cooperation, including confidence-building measures, consultation and joint exercises. At the same time, China has also pursued bilateral security dialogues with Indonesia, Malaysia, Philippines, Singapore, Thailand and Vietnam. However, China's periodic actions to bolster its territorial claims in the South China Sea continues to raise concerns in the region, as does China's military modernisation and capacity building.

While China has sometimes obstructed an enhanced role for India in Southeast Asia, it has not generally seen India as an impediment to its overall regional strategy. China's main regional rivals remain the United States and Japan whose economic (and, in the case of the United States, also political and military) influence exceed China's by a considerable margin. Some believe that in the future China may see benefit in cooperation with India in Southeast Asia to help balance the overwhelming influence and unilateralism of the United States and contribute to a multipolar Asia Pacific.[62]

India is highly sensitive to China's overwhelming advantage in any competition for influence in Southeast Asia, leading it to downplay any suggestions of rivalry in the region. Former Indian foreign ministry secretary, Sudhir Devare, warned that: 'India does not and should not seek closer military ties with Southeast Asia as a bulwark against China or Pakistan' and that such an approach would be 'flawed conceptually as well as disastrously politically'.[63] According to Mohan, despite the 'exaggerated debate' about India's rivalry with China, New Delhi is acutely conscious of its limitations in Southeast Asia and therefore wishes to expand India's strategic weight in the region while avoiding creating overt rivalry with China.[64] India will therefore attempt to build security ties with Southeast Asia outside of the matrix of Sino-Indian strategic competition.[65]

Southeast Asian responses to Sino-Indian strategic competition

Southeast Asian states may respond to perceived Sino-Indian strategic competition in several ways. First, and most obviously, is in the economic sphere. As Indonesian President Yudhoyono commented in 2004, the economic challenge for ASEAN can be described in two words: China and India.[66] While there are concerns about China and India in terms of potentially crowding out ASEAN's share of global trade and investment, ASEAN leaders generally see economic competition between China and India within Southeast Asia in positive terms, and in particular will continue to use it as an opportunity to encourage Indian economic integration into ASEAN and to open the Indian market to Southeast Asian products and investment. As will be discussed in Chapter 7, Singapore has been the most active in positioning itself as an entrepôt and services middleman to both the Chinese and Indian economies.

Second, the ASEAN states and India have a common interest in seeking to limit the growth of China's political and military power in Southeast Asia. India is generally seen in Southeast Asia in benign terms, in contrast to which China is still regarded by many as a potential security threat whose power needs to be balanced. Consequently, ASEAN has facilitated India's links with the region to help balance China (as well as the United States and Japan). This should not be seen as an attempt to create a balancing coalition in a neorealist sense. Rather, it is an attempt to enmesh both China and India in a web of cooperative relationships while using each to limit the power of the other.

Third, ASEAN states will likely try to mitigate any overt rivalry between India and China in and around the region. While many ASEAN states are encouraging India to play a greater security role in Southeast Asia, without a major change in the security environment they will also want any Indian security presence to be discreet. For the same reasons, although ASEAN states (particularly Singapore, Indonesia and Malaysia) have avoided criticising China's growing interests in the Indian Ocean they are likely to encourage China to also be circumspect in developing such interests.

Fourth, is the potential for ASEAN to use Sino-Indian rivalry to maintain and enhance the organisation's strategic influence. ASEAN's role in future regional security arrangements is unclear, particularly in light of perceived inadequacies in the effectiveness of the ASEAN Regional Forum. Some believe that India now has an important stake in the continued relevance of ASEAN in countering domination of the region by the United States or China.[67] Arguably, ongoing strategic rivalry between India and China may lead them both to seek to deepen institutional relationships with ASEAN, reducing the likelihood of its marginalisation.

Finally, there is potential for Sino-Indian rivalry to be a factor in intra-regional relations in Southeast Asia, something that receives relatively little attention. During the Cold War, rivalry between the Soviet Union, China and the United States were significant factors in stoking intra-regional tensions. It is already possible to discern incipient Sino-Indian rivalry along potential fault lines within ASEAN: in Indochina between Cambodia (traditionally sponsored by China) and Vietnam (a longstanding political partner of India); and in maritime Southeast Asia between, on the one hand, Malaysia (China's most vocal supporter in the region) and, on the other, Singapore (India's primary regional partner) and Indonesia. India and China could therefore become significant factors in existing intra-regional rivalries to the extent that ASEAN is not able to effectively manage tensions within a regional framework.

4 The United States and India's strategic role in the Asia Pacific

The United States is drawing India into a strategic role in the Asia Pacific. The relationship between them was long distant and strained as India tried to maintain its strategic autonomy. But with the rise of China, the US now wants to help India become a major world power. It is encouraging India to extend its reach into the Pacific Ocean and form strategic partnerships with its Pacific allies. But while India is being drawn closer to the United States, it still remains wary of compromising its freedom of action.

Developments in the India–US strategic relationship in recent years

The end of the Cold War led to a fundamental change in India's strategic relationship with the United States which in many ways has underpinned India's emergence as a major power. For most of the Cold War, India's relationship with the United States was distant and often strained. India essentially refused to accept a predominant role for the United States in the international system, and the United States would not cede to India predominance in South Asia. India's strategic partnership with the Soviet Union from the late 1960s only served to further estrange the United States, giving rise to a view in Washington of India as a Soviet 'fellow traveller'. From the early 1970s, many in India's strategic elite increasingly saw the United States as seeking to obstruct India's destiny to become a great power. Among other things, the United States was regularly accused of conniving with China and Pakistan against India, meddling in India's domestic affairs and trying to encircle India in the Indian Ocean. Although relations steadily improved during the latter years of the Cold War, particularly following the Soviet intervention in Afghanistan, only the end of the Cold War removed the political and psychological obstacles that prevented significant improvements in the relationship.[1]

Economic relations, which had been severely constrained by the closed nature of the Indian economy during the Cold War, surged with the liberalisation of the Indian economy in the early 1990s. The United States played a major role in providing assistance during the Indian economic crisis in 1991 and US investment has been a material factor in the development of the

Indian economy since then. The political relationship between India and the United States also improved during the 1990s, although it was limited by the Clinton administration's criticism of India over human rights abuses in Kashmir and by continuing US insistence that India give up its ambitions to become a declared nuclear weapons state. The United States successfully pressured India to abandon nuclear tests in 1995 when it learned of their preparations.

India was able to conduct nuclear tests in 1998 without prior knowledge of the United States. These caused a major – if short-lived – rupture in the relationship when the United States and its regional allies imposed punitive economic sanctions on India. However, this development also removed a psychological obstacle to US acceptance of India's emergence as a major power and led to intensified and sustained political engagement between the United States and India.[2] Despite US opposition to India's overt nuclear status, India pursued the US relationship aggressively, with Prime Minister Vajpayee calling India and the United States 'natural allies' whose relations 'constitute the key element in the architecture of tomorrow's democratised world order'.[3] The United States demonstrated its credentials as a useful diplomatic partner to India during the 1999 Kargil crisis when the United States supported New Delhi and pressured Pakistan to withdraw its insurgents from beyond the Line of Control in Kashmir. This went a long way to dispelling a decades-long view that the United States would always support Pakistan over Kashmir.[4] India was able to return the gesture following 9/11, when it offered its 'unconditional and unambivalent support' to the United States,[5] offering Indian military facilities in support of the Afghanistan campaign and providing naval escorts for US shipping through the Malacca Strait.

US efforts to engage with India accelerated under the Bush administration, which saw benefits in developing India as a counterweight to the rising power of China. The relationship was given particular impetus with the appointment of Condoleezza Rice as US secretary of state in 2005. The Bush administration appears to have decided to facilitate India's emergence as a great power rather than hinder it and to make every effort to tell India of its importance.[6] A Central Intelligence Agency report called India 'the most important swing state in the international system'.[7] In March 2005, the Bush administration announced that it would 'help India become a major world power in the 21st century', adding that: 'We understand fully the implications, including the military implications, of that statement.'[8] Condoleezza Rice portrayed India as 'a rising global power that can be a pillar of stability in a rapidly changing Asia'.[9] As a senior US official in New Delhi put it: 'India as a global power is in an early, formative phase. The United States' job for the next 5 to 10 years is to promote, assist and shape that process.'[10]

The Bush administration was relatively open about placing its relationship with India in the context of China's rising power. As Condoleezza Rice explained:

I really do believe that the US–Japan relationship, the US–South Korean relationship, the US–Indian relationship, all are important in creating an environment in which China is more likely to play a positive role than a negative role. These alliances are not against China; they are alliances that are devoted to a stable security and political and economic and, indeed, values-based relationships that put China in the context of those relationships, and a different path to development than if China were simply untethered, simply operating without that strategic context.[11]

The Bush administration approached the India relationship with an uncharacteristic degree of sensitivity, particularly in relation to India's objective of strategic autonomy. While encouraging India to develop strategic perceptions closer to those of the United States, Washington did not, in general, expect public support from New Delhi in international fora in the manner of the diplomatic support expected from US allies. Bronson Percival, a former US State Department official, comments that US policy is to support India without an expectation of immediate returns and automatic reciprocity. In future years time, the United States will likely look to India for more assistance in maintaining stability on the Indian Ocean littoral.[12]

The Indo-US civilian nuclear agreement, known as the '123 agreement', finalised in July 2007 (although not signed until October 2008), represented an important threshold in the development of the relationship and provided a strategic foundation on which many other elements of the security relationship can be built. Under the agreement, the United States effectively recognised India as a *de facto* nuclear weapons state and allowed India access to civil nuclear and US defence technology.[13] As Stephen Cohen put it, US willingness to rewrite the international non-proliferation regime in India's favour signalled a commitment from Washington to New Delhi that is unprecedented not only in US–India relations, but also in the history of arms control.[14] Despite the obvious benefits of the deal to India, it was highly controversial in India and it took the Singh government more than a year to gain parliamentary approval over objections of both the left and right. Although full implementation of the 123 agreement is yet to occur it has facilitated a further expansion of the military-to-military relationship and opened the door for the supply of US defence technology to India.

The Obama administration has continued much of the rhetoric about the India relationship, with President Obama calling India 'an indispensible partner'[15] and the relationship as 'One of the defining partnerships of the 21st century'.[16] However the Democrat administration is widely seen in New Delhi as much less sympathetic towards India than was the Bush administration. Many recall the previous Clinton administration's 'meddling' in India's affairs over Kashmir and nuclear weapons and many now have suspicions about the current administration's approach towards China. Certainly, in some respects Washington has taken a more accommodating approach with China, particularly in southern Asia where it has sought greater cooperation from Beijing over Afghanistan and Iran. Some in New Delhi have also detected a softening of the US position over China's territorial claims over India's northeastern state of Arunachal Pradesh.[17] Much to the infuriation of New Delhi, Beijing has also secured US acknowledgement of a role for it in South Asian strategic affairs. In a joint US–Chinese statement made during President Obama's visit to China in November 2009, the United States and China committed to 'support the improvement and growth of relations between India and Pakistan' and to 'strengthen communication, dialogue and co-operation on issues related to South Asia and work together to promote peace, stability and development in the region'. The statement incensed New Delhi in apparently recognising a legitimate strategic role for China in South Asia, including suggestions that it may play some sort of honest broker role between India and Pakistan. The Indian Foreign Ministry announced that a role for China in the Indo-Pakistan dispute 'cannot be envisaged'.[18] Prime Minister Singh, during a US visit later that month, 'emphatically reiterated' to his hosts that China has no role in South Asia.

For its part, Washington claims that India should not be threatened by improved US–China relations and has sought to move the US–India relationship away from its perceived focus on China and into a worldwide partnership that focuses on common interests beyond South Asia. According to one administration official, 'the security of Asia's two dominant powers [China and India] can no longer be viewed as a zero sum game. A safer, more secure India that is closer to the United States should not be seen as a threat to China, *and vice versa*.' (emphasis added).[19] Whereas the Bush administration largely focused on bilateral ties, the Obama administration seeks to push the strategic partnership into global fora. US Undersecretary of State for Political Affairs, William J. Burns, commented that the United States wanted an India that doesn't think small and that 'self-hyphenates' (i.e. allows itself to be perceived primarily in the context of Pakistan). Burns also lamented that India sometimes has a hard time realising how far its influence and its interests have taken it beyond its immediate neighbourhood.[20] Similarly, Teresita Schaffer, the former US Deputy Assistant Secretary of State for South Asia, believes that although the bilateral relationship is 'highly developed' there is 'relatively little reach into the wider world'.[21] Schaffer identifies two areas – East Asian regionalism and Persian Gulf security – where Indian and US interests are quite similar but where 'serious consultations' are needed to turn this general convergence into parallel or coordinated policies.[22] Consistent with this approach, in November 2010 President Obama announced US support for India's permanent membership of the UN Security Council. He also indicated US support for bringing India into various ad hoc non-proliferation groupings, including the Nuclear Suppliers Group, the Wassenaar Agreement (export controls on dual use technologies), the Australia Group (which deals with chemical and biological weapons proliferation) and the Missile Technology Control Regime. It has been argued that the acceptance of India into the Australia Group could be a starting point for a broader acceptance of India into non-proliferation groupings.[23]

The US Department of Defense's Quadrennial Defense Review (QDR 2010), released in February 2010, provided an opportunity for the Obama administration and the Pentagon to situate India within US strategic thinking. The QDR 2010 assumes that India will act as a guarantor of the existing liberal order, describing India as having a 'commitment to global stability' and being 'a net provider of security in the Indian Ocean and beyond'.[24] This contrasts sharply with its treatment of China and Pakistan, which are treated as sources of instability. Although the QDR 2010 foresees India as having a security role beyond the Indian Ocean region, it is not clear where or what that role might be. The QDR 2010 also lists Indian military capabilities that the US will seek to improve, including long-range maritime surveillance, maritime interdiction and patrolling, air interdiction and strategic airlift.

However, India's political culture remains a significant obstacle to US–Indian strategic cooperation. Indian public perceptions of the United States have moved well beyond the 'bogey-man' image that was often applied to it by the strategic elite during the Cold War. Many wealthy and middle class Indians now have educational and familial links with the United States and US culture has penetrated Indian society far more than in previous years, particularly among younger generations. The unusually warm welcome that President Obama received in his November 2010 visit to India demonstrated the extent of positive feelings for the United States among the general population. Nevertheless, the relationship remains a politically difficult one for the Indian government. The United States is still widely perceived as a potentially unreliable strategic partner that may ultimately seek to dominate India. Any public manifestations of cooperation with the United States – even arrangements that are obviously to India's benefit – are fraught with claims from both the left and the nationalist right that India is subordinating its national interests to the United States. As a result, any agreements with the United States relating to security or military issues are treated with an extraordinary degree of caution and suspicion that would hardly be found anywhere else in the world. While the Singh government (and the Vajpayee government before it) have embraced strategic cooperation with the United States, in practice it often seeks to keep it beyond the public gaze, and to the extent possible, far from India's shores.

US–Indian military cooperation

Over the last decade or more the US–Indian relationship has had a strong focus on military-to-military cooperation. The level of cooperation between them has been described by Admiral Michael Mullen, Chairman of the US Joint Chiefs of Staff, as 'stunning'.[25] The US focus has been on assisting in a build-up of India's conventional naval and air force capabilities to complement the US presence in the Indian Ocean. The Hawaii-based US Pacific

Command (USPACOM) took the lead in engaging with the Indian military in the early 1990s, establishing Executive Steering Groups to coordinate cooperation between each of the Indian and US armed services. A 1995 defence agreement was renewed and expanded in 2005 providing for intelligence sharing and training, technology transfers and missile defence cooperation. Strategic dialogue has been institutionalised through the Defence Policy Group, a consultative mechanism jointly chaired by the US Secretary of State for Defense for Policy and the Indian Defence Secretary. This sits over the Executive Steering Groups for military to military dialogue and a Defence Procurement and Production Group.

USPACOM retains a leading role in the US security relationship with India. Because USPACOM's Area of Responsibility ends on the western border of India, the arrangement is seen by the United States as beneficial in reducing potential operational frictions arising from US military support for Pakistan, which falls within the ambit of the Florida-based US Central Command (USCENTCOM). However, this administrative separation also serves to complicate Indian–US military relationships in the Indian Ocean region, where India has to deal with USPACOM, USCENTCOM and increasingly also US Africa Command. Indian military officials see it as involving an irrational division of India's strategic spheres in South Asia and the broader Indian Ocean region.[26] While Indian military relations with USPACOM are good, with an Indian liaison officer posted to USPACOM headquarters (a position only previously offered to Japan, South Korea and Australia), New Delhi is reportedly unhappy in having to deal with US officials of a lesser regional status and is increasingly dealing directly with Washington.[27]

The United States and India began conducting joint military exercises in 1992, which have since increased significantly in frequency, scale, complexity and jointedness.[28] India conducted more than 50 military exercises with the United States between 2003 and 2010, significantly more than with any other country. The US–India Executive Steering Group reportedly planned nine joint army exercises in 2010–11 with similar programmes for air and naval exercises. Major US–Indian exercises in 2010 included Exercise *Yudh Abhyas 2010*, a special forces exercise in Alaska to test extreme cold weather capabilities, and Exercise *Habu Nag 2010*, an amphibious exercise in Okinawa.

The annual 'Malabar' naval exercises have particularly increased in scale and complexity, including the controversial Exercise *Malabar 2007* in the Bay of Bengal which involved three carrier battle groups and other ships from India, the United States, Japan, Australia and Singapore. The presence of two US carrier task forces in the Bay of Bengal was particularly symbolic for New Delhi where the 'intrusion' of the USS *Enterprise* into the area during the closing days of the 1971 Indo-Pakistan war is still remembered darkly. Exercise *Malabar 2007* was also seen by many as having particular strategic significance, involving US allies and friends in a putative maritime *entente* aimed at containing China. However, in contrast with the Bush administration, the

Obama administration has placed less reliance on US–Indian naval exercises as a means of expanding Indian naval cooperation with US Asia Pacific allies. Neither the Japanese nor Australian navies were invited to Exercise *Malabar 2010* despite a strong desire by both to participate, while the United States suggested that China might be invited to the Malabar exercises as an observer and perhaps even a future participant (a suggestion that New Delhi appears not to have pursued).[29]

In addition to regular military exercises, the United States has also sought to enter into agreements with India to facilitate cooperation and interoperability of their armed forces. These include a proposed Acquisition and Cross-Servicing Agreement (ACSMA)[30] that would facilitate increased use of shared logistical services; a Basic Exchange and Cooperation Agreement for Geospatial Cooperation (BECA), that provides for mutual logistical support and enables exchanges of communications and related equipment; and a Communications Interoperability and Security Memorandum of Agreement (CISMOA) that requires equipment supplied to India be compatible with other American systems. These last two agreements would reportedly ease the transfer of sophisticated US communications technology to India, including in P-8 and F-35 aircraft. Although the United States has signed similar agreements with many of its allies, both are highly controversial in India due to their implications for the integration of India into the US global military network (including fears that the United States could use Indian bases to conduct regional interventions). As of early 2011 they had not been signed. Nevertheless, the Indian Navy is a party to a Fuel Exchange Agreement with the US Navy which has allowed it to lower the operational costs of its deployments in the northwestern Indian Ocean. The Indian and US navies have for some time been occasionally exchanging information related to the Merchant Shipping Information System (MSIS) which provides for tracking of maritime traffic movements and in 2010 held discussions to regularise information exchange on shipping movements, at least in the northwest Indian Ocean. These arrangements are all the building blocks for enhanced operational cooperation across the Indian Ocean and into the Pacific.

Defence trade is one of the least developed aspects of the relationship, largely due to bureaucratic and legal impediments. Progress in this area has been slow, reflecting US legal hurdles and the ponderous nature of the Indian defence acquisitions process. A crucial End-User Verification Agreement was signed in 2009, while other agreements required under US domestic law for the transfer of sensitive defence technology (including a CISMOA) are still under negotiation. The United States has the objectives of both improving India's power projection capabilities, particularly in the maritime sphere, and supplanting Russia as India's primary defence supplier, although that is likely to take many years. Only a few acquisitions of significant size have been finalised to date, including the sale of the USS *Trenton* (a 16,000 tonne amphibious landing ship), six Hercules C130J aircraft (for use by special forces) and 24 Harpoon Block II missiles.[31] However, some very large acquisitions are in process or have been proposed. The United States has approved the sale of eight P-8 long-range maritime surveillance aircraft for US$2.2 billion, 10 Boeing C-17 transports for $5.5 billion and 107 General Electric aircraft engines for India's Tejas lightweight fighter. The United States has also reportedly offered a naval version of F-35 aircraft to the Indian Navy.[32] According to Rahul Bedi, the India-based correspondent for *Jane's Defence Weekly*, in the 1990s the Pentagon established a target of meeting 25 per cent of India's defence hardware acquisitions by 2015 although the elimination of US F16s from India proposed acquisition of 126 fight jets may make this target difficult to achieve.[33] Although there was speculation in early 2009 regarding the acquisition by India of US ballistic missile defence technology, given the desire of the Indian Defence Research and Development Organisation to develop an indigenous system it seems unlikely that there will be significant US technology transfer this area.[34]

India and the United States have very different views on how military supply fits into the broader relationship. For the United States developing military-to-military relations (including enhancing interoperability and institutional relationships) is a normal way of building a broader security relationship. The use of US-supplied equipment creates linkages up and down the chain of command through training and other joint activities. In contrast, many in New Delhi regard unfettered access to US defence technology as an end in itself as well as a litmus test of a broader strategic partnership.[35] New Delhi sees the United States as merely one of several competing suppliers (including Russia and Israel) and many in the Indian military do not expect that the use of US-supplied equipment will have a significant effect on training or doctrine.[36]

US–Indian naval cooperation

The central role of naval cooperation in the security relationship was formalised in the 2006 *Framework for Maritime Security Cooperation* which commits India and the United States to 'comprehensive cooperation in ensuring a secure maritime domain'. Expanding navy-to-navy ties proved to be a politically low-cost way of strengthening the overall strategic relationship during the high-profile controversies over the nuclear deal.[37] But while there has been a significant expansion in naval cooperation in recent years, India is still generally unwilling to be seen as joining any US-led naval coalition.

The US–Indian naval relationship should be seen as part of an overall US strategy to encourage the expansion of India's naval ambitions and capabilities throughout much of the Indian Ocean region. According to the US Secretary of the Navy, Donald Winter, the United States welcomed India 'taking up the responsibility to ensure security in this part of the world'.[38] The United States has given particular encouragement to India to increase its naval presence in the northeast Indian Ocean including the development of facilities at India's Andaman Island naval base. The United States also seems to have indicated its acquiescence in a direct security role for India inside the Malacca Strait. In contrast, the northwestern Indian Ocean region remains an area where the United States has been less forthcoming in encouraging an enhanced Indian naval presence – reflecting both US naval predominance in that region and a relatively high level of naval cooperation between the US and Pakistan.

A significant factor in US interest in India's naval capabilities has been a desire by the United States to build India as a regional counterweight to China. India has similar motivations for naval cooperation with the United States. According to a former senior military official on India's Integrated Defence Staff: 'India principally wants the [United States] to partner it in shaping the strategic space in the region, which could otherwise be usurped by other regional players.'[39] Robert Kaplan believes that the US Navy will quietly leverage the sea power of its closest allies – India in the Indian Ocean and Japan in the western Pacific – to set limits on Chinese expansion while also using every opportunity to incorporate China's navy into international alliances.[40] However, Kaplan suggests that the United States may ultimately play a balancing role in relation to Sino-Indian naval rivalry.[41]

The United States may see Sino-Indian rivalry in the Indian Ocean region as not being contrary to its interests and may, in some cases, even seek to promote such rivalry. As previously discussed, the term 'String of Pearls', which describes China's putative strategy in the Indian Ocean, originated in the Pentagon and found a ready audience in India. On several occasions over the last few years the United States has actively stoked public concerns over China's intentions in the Indian Ocean. As Admiral Mike Mullen told the Indian press in July 2010:

> [in] the Indian Ocean, the Pacific region, the maritime piece – China seems to be asserting itself more and more, with respect to the kinds of territorial claims in islands like the Spratlys, but really, they seem to be taking a much more aggressive approach with respect to the near-sea area . ... I just worry about, from the military's perspective, where they're going. And from my perspective, we need to work with India in that regard.[42]

Similarly, an undiplomatic jest by a Chinese naval officer to his US counterpart that the United States should take responsibility for security in the eastern Pacific and China should take responsibility for maritime security in the western Pacific and the Indian Ocean was dutifully reported to the Indian press by USPACOM's Admiral Keating, which unsurprisingly raised many hackles in New Delhi.[43]

It has been argued that the approach of the United States in encouraging the development of India as an emerging regional naval power with a particular responsibility for the Indian Ocean while the US focuses resources on

China in the western Pacific is analogous to Britain's strategy in the late nineteenth and early twentieth century. When Britain found itself challenged by the growth of German naval power it forged partnerships with emerging naval powers, the United States in the western hemisphere and Japan in the Pacific, allowing them a measure of regional hegemony, while Britain concentrated its naval resources in the North Atlantic against the greater threat presented by the rise of Germany.[44] This analogy, while far from perfect, captures some of the factors present in US thinking. However, others have downplayed the China factor in the US naval relationship with India, claiming that the links between US maritime security policies in East, Southeast and South Asia will remain tenuous unless and until China has a navy that can be deployed, sustained and protected in Southeast Asia and the Indian Ocean. Percival claims that US policies are currently focused primarily on bilateral relationships with countries in specific regions and that concerns about China's growing power do not currently drive US naval policy in South and Southeast Asia. According to Percival, the US Navy faces very different challenges off China's coast as compared with policing maritime choke points in Southeast Asia and in strengthening its Indian naval partnership in the Indian Ocean.[45]

Enhanced US–Indian naval cooperation fits well with a more cooperative approach adopted by the United States throughout the world in an effort to leverage its naval power. This strategy, which involves a recognition of a long-term strain on US naval resources globally as well as a greater recognition of the value of naval partnerships, has been described as positioning the United States as a 'systems administrator' for the international security system. This approach was adopted by the US Navy in its 2007 *Cooperative Strategy for 21st Century Seapower* which reiterates the US naval commitment to the Pacific and Indian Oceans, while recognising that the US Navy must establish enduring partnerships in order to leverage its presence. It notes that although US forces can be surged, 'trust and cooperation cannot be surged'.[46] The overall approach of the 2007 *Cooperative Strategy* and its prioritisation of improved integration and interoperability with partner navies and enhanced maritime domain awareness has reportedly been well received among Indian naval strategists.[47] In accordance with this strategy, over the last several years the US Navy has promoted its 'Global Maritime Partnership' initiative (which was initially marketed as the 'Thousand Ship Navy'). This is described as an 'evolving concept' for cooperation among friendly navies to combat non-state security threats. Although sponsored by the United States, the US also claims to encourage other states to assume leadership roles in addressing local and regional problems regardless of US involvement.[48] India responded favourably, if tentatively, when invited to join the initiative in 2006. One senior Indian officer compared the Global Maritime Partnership favourably to the Proliferation Security Initiative (discussed below), calling it a cooperative arrangement that is 'workable since it will just require the different navies to be networked on one common information grid'.[49]

In practice, the United States sees India as playing an important role in the 'burden sharing' (if not outsourcing) of certain maritime security needs in the Indian Ocean. According to a Pentagon report, the US military sees India as a capable partner that can take on more responsibility for low-end operations in Asia such as peacekeeping, search and rescue, disaster relief and high-value cargo escort, allowing the US to focus on high-end operations. They also perceive a strong security relationship with India as providing training opportunities and the potential for basing to expand US power projection.[50] From USPACOM's perspective, the Indian military is an ideal partner in low-end missions because of its relatively sophisticated military capability, its proximity to unstable areas and its experience in peacekeeping operations.

Sea lane protection in particular, is identified by both the US and Indian militaries as the most promising area of service-to-service cooperation. An oft-cited if short-lived example of Indian naval cooperation with the United States occurred between April and September 2002 when at the request of the United States the Indian Navy contributed offshore patrol vessels to the US-led Operation *Enduring Freedom* to escort 'high-value' non-combatant shipping (e.g. oil tankers) transiting through the Malacca Strait. The US request was clearly driven by a desire to expand India's strategic footprint eastwards (in contrast to which USCENTCOM ignored Indian offers of assistance in Afghanistan). US military officials saw India's participation in Operation *Enduring Freedom* as potentially legitimising an expanded military role in Southeast Asia. However, Indian officials rejected any idea that India's cooperation with the United States would confer legitimacy on Indian actions.[51] Nevertheless, India recognised it as an opportunity to demonstrate its value as a security partner to the United States in the months following 9/11, as well as advancing its case as a maritime security provider in the Malacca Strait. As will be discussed in Chapter 7, since 2002 India has continued to press its case to be a maritime security provider in the Malacca Strait.

However, India has been less enthusiastic about participating in the US-led naval coalition in the Gulf of Aden to combat piracy. Since October 2008, the Indian Navy has deployed one or two vessels in anti-piracy patrols off Somalia. However, India has refused to join the US-sponsored Combined Task Force 151 (CTF 151), to which some 20 countries have contributed naval assets.[52] India provides escort services primarily to Indian flagged vessels (although other vessels may join Indian escorted convoys). India participates in the Shared Awareness and Deconfliction (SHADE) meetings with the Combined Maritime Forces and other independently operating maritime security providers (e.g. China and Russia). However, in practice, the Indian-escorted convoys have been barely coordinated with CTF 151. The Indian government has been reluctant to join CTF 151 for several reasons, including its sponsorship by the United States and the participation of the Pakistan Navy in the task force.[53] The Indian Navy made the deployment only after overcoming significant opposition from the Indian Foreign Ministry which, according to some, repeatedly turned down requests from the navy to conduct interceptions. It is not clear to what extent these tensions merely reflect bureaucratic caution or a more fundamental disagreement over the Indian Navy's regional strategy.[54]

Another key area of naval cooperation is humanitarian intervention. The December 2004 tsunami which devastated littoral states of the northeast Indian Ocean led to the creation of an informal coalition or 'core group' of India, the United States, Japan and Australia, coordinated by the United States, to provide disaster relief involving significant reliance on naval and air forces. The Indian Navy's experience in the tsunami led it to see the significant political-diplomatic value of contributing to international disaster relief operations and an understanding of its own limitations in that area. As a result, with the encouragement of the United States it has enhanced its amphibious operations capabilities, including through the acquisition of the amphibious landing ship, USS *Trenton* (now INS *Jalashva*). The successful experience of the Indian, US, Japanese and Australian navies cooperating during the 2004 tsunami was also credited by many with inspiring the multilateral *Malabar 2007* naval exercises in the Bay of Bengal.

India has taken tentative steps towards greater naval cooperation with the United States. However, its refusal to join the Proliferation Security Initiative (PSI) is indicative of India's continuing ambivalence about operational cooperation. The PSI, first proposed by the United States in 2003, is an arrangement under which the US and its partners could aggressively search and seize 'suspicious' ships on the high seas. Although lacking UN endorsement, the PSI is now supported by 90 states, with the notable exceptions of China and India. From one perspective, India has every reason to contribute to an international regime that would help mitigate WMD proliferation in South Asia and the Indian Ocean. India has itself been involved in the interdiction of North Korean vessels in its territorial waters suspected of transporting illicit cargo. However, the PSI faces significant Indian domestic opposition on several grounds. These include: opposition to security cooperation with the United States where India might be perceived as a junior partner; India's longstanding fears of joining cooperative security arrangements not blessed by the United Nations; the perceived historical mistreatment of India at the hands of various international non-proliferation regimes; and reports that the US attempted to mandate Indian participation in the PSI as part of the US–Indian nuclear deal.[55] While India has formally refused to join the PSI, this has not prevented India and the US undertaking PSI-style exercises (e.g. maritime interdiction and visit, board, search and seizure operations) as part of the Malabar and other bilateral exercise programmes.

From the record of US–Indian naval cooperation to date it seems that India will be an unpredictable maritime security partner to the United States and will only formally or publicly coordinate its operations with the United States on an occasional basis. India's nonaligned legacy of so-called 'merit-based' decisions on international issues means that it is little inclined to support coalition partners out of concern for the overall relationship and is likely to take coordinated action only where it sees its direct interests involved. Despite its participation in Operation *Enduring Freedom* in 2002, India will, if at all possible, seek to avoid joining any international coalition under the operational leadership of the United States or its allies. A need to demonstrate that it is acting autonomously seems strongly rooted in the Indian national psyche and may sometimes lead to India avoiding cooperation with the United States even when it is plainly in its national interests to do so. The US relationship continues to be politically controversial in India, particularly with those of a leftist or a Nehruvian strategic perspective who regard Indian relations with the United States in zero-sum terms, essentially seeing cooperation with the United States as co-option or coercion.[56] However, there may be good strategic reasons for India avoiding a perception of having too close a security relationship with the United States (whether in the maritime or other dimensions). While India derives significant leverage against China from having a good relationship with the United States, arguably that leverage may actually be reduced if the US–India relationship is perceived as moving towards an anti-China alliance.

Others see Indian naval cooperation with the United States less in terms of a tactical alliance aimed at securing Indian maritime predominance in the Indian Ocean and more in terms of a growing alignment of interests between India and the United States to secure and shape the 'global commons' (which includes not only the sea, but also outer space and cyberspace). Mohan claims that as a rising power, India is in the process of moving beyond its traditional defensive preoccupations with sovereignty and is adopting a mature and responsible role in establishing international norms and providing security in the commons.[57] If correct, this would imply that India's naval ambitions may focus less on attempting to establish semi-exclusive predominance in the Indian Ocean and more on cooperating with like-minded states in securing freedom and security of navigation in the Indian Ocean and elsewhere, such as in the South China Sea.

US–Indian security cooperation in the Asia Pacific

To what extent will the United States facilitate an Indian security role in the Asia Pacific? The United States gives conceptual support to the strategic interconnection of the Indian Ocean region and the Asia Pacific as justification for an enhanced Indian role in East Asia.[58] Over the last decade the US has generally encouraged Indian political-diplomatic engagement in East Asian regional institutions – largely to act as a partial counterweight to China.[59] Recently the US has become more vocal in supporting a greater Indian role in the security dimension in East Asia. In June 2010, William J. Burns, US Undersecretary of State for Political Affairs, commented:

> we attach great significance to India's expanding role in East Asia and welcome our partnership across the region. ... Widening economic

interests [in Asia] have reinforced India's readiness to share responsibility for securing the global commons in Asia, for safeguarding the sea and air routes on which much of the global economy depends.[60]

In October 2010, US Secretary of State, Hillary Rodham Clinton, described India's growing engagement and integration into East Asia as a 'core issue' and commented that the United States was 'expanding our work with the Indian Navy in the Pacific'.[61]

However, the practical coordination of policies in the Asia Pacific has been limited to date. In 2010, the United States organised high-level dialogues between US and Indian diplomatic, defence and national security officials to coordinate policy on East Asia as part of a series of structured bilateral consultations. Initial discussions avoided explicitly focussing on China and instead covered approaches to regional organisations such as the East Asia Summit and issues such as climate change, humanitarian assistance and disaster relief. According to Teresita Schaffer, the consultations represent a 'significant change' in bilateral cooperation on East Asia.[62] However Bronson Percival argues that while Washington welcomes India–Southeast Asian cooperation to improve maritime security, coordination of Indian and US policies in that region still 'remain fitful at best'.[63]

India and the United States now conduct regular naval exercises in the western Pacific, which seem likely to grow further in scale and complexity, including major exercises in Guam and Alaska in 2010. India also conducts periodic exercises with the United States and Japan in Northeast Asia, most recently Exercise *Malabar 2009* near Okinawa. An expansion of India's security role in the Asia Pacific has clearly been helped by the leading role played by USPACOM in the Indian–US military relationship. However other US bureaucratic divisions (e.g. in the US State Department between the Bureaus of South Asian Affairs and East Asian/Pacific Affairs) may work against an integrated strategic approach to the Pacific and Indian Ocean regions. A 2002 Pentagon report on US military perceptions concluded that many US military and policy-making organisations continue to see India not as central to 'Asia', but as lying on the periphery of important regions such as the Persian Gulf and Southeast Asia.[64] The Indian Navy was unsuccessful in its claim to be granted full membership of the Western Pacific Naval Symposium, a US-sponsored talk shop for Asia Pacific naval chiefs.[65] While some observers have claimed that the United States is seeking to coordinate its maritime strategy with India in the Persian Gulf, Southeast Asia and as far as the Taiwan Strait,[66] it is not clear as yet to what extent the United States would support a direct security role for India north or east of Singapore. Nor has India shown that it has a clear idea about how the India–US strategic relationship should translate into the Asia Pacific. Most of India's key security partners in the Asia Pacific are formal or informal allies of the United States. However, India will, where possible, seek to make these relationships as independent as possible from the United States. Nevertheless, it seems likely there will be a significant degree of political and diplomatic coordination between India and the United States and its allies in the Asia Pacific.

In general, there are significant commonalities in strategic perspectives between India and the United States in the Asia Pacific and few obvious sources of friction. This can be contrasted with West Asia where US and Indian perspectives on Pakistan, Iran and Saudi Arabia are likely to raise some difficult issues in coming years. According to some Indian analysts, the United States has also been more reluctant to allow India to expand its strategic role in the Persian Gulf. However, there are also some important differences in US and Indian perspectives in the Asia Pacific. In Burma, where India has sought to improve its relationship with the military regime to mitigate the expansion of Chinese influence, the United States has unsuccessfully argued for New Delhi to give greater priority to human rights issues. Differing perspectives on Taiwan and Korea are also likely to limit Indian cooperation with the United States in Northeast Asia. US support for the autonomy of Taiwan has a central place in the US–China relationship, while India, which recognised the PRC's sovereignty over Taiwan in 1949, has only low-level political and security relationships with Taiwan. Further, although India has little sympathy with North Korea it has generally avoided involving itself in Korean security issues. In the event of a major security crisis on the Korean peninsula or in the Taiwan Strait, India would likely maintain a low profile and, depending on the circumstances, would not be inclined to provide anything more than muted diplomatic support for the United States. However, an implosion of the Burmese military regime might see a significant degree of cooperation between India and the United States (in order to minimise Chinese influence), notwithstanding the current differences in their policies.

5 Northeast Asia
India's peer relationship with Japan

Japan holds the key to any major expansion of India's strategic influence in the Asia Pacific. Until recently, the two countries all but ignored each other, reflecting an almost complete separation of political and strategic dynamics between South and North East Asia. Now, both are being drawn closer by a shared concern over China. How far can this relationship develop and how much will Japan be willing to recognise a role for India in the western Pacific?

The strategic separation of South and Northeast Asia

The strategic history of Asia has often been more one of disjunction than of regional interaction, particularly so between South Asia and maritime Northeast Asia. Although this strategic separation is breaking down it is likely to continue to severely constrain India's strategic role in the Asia Pacific for the foreseeable future. There are several reasons behind this disjunction. First, Northeast Asians have traditionally viewed 'Asia' foremost in terms of East Asia. While Indians have often considered themselves part of a broader Asia, they have nevertheless felt a strong cultural divide between themselves and the Sinic world which predominates in East Asia. A second major factor is China. Historically, the size and power of China has served to strategically divide Asia rather than unite it, although this perception is now changing. Third is the Cold War, in which India adopted ideological and strategic alignments very different from Japan and most other states in East Asia. As a result of these factors, during most of the second half of the twentieth century there was little political or economic interaction between South Asia and maritime Northeast Asia: each region was largely preoccupied with local conflicts, and China was perceived in each region in very different terms.

Different concepts of Asia

Underlying some of these longstanding differences in strategic perspective are different concepts of 'Asia'. From a Japanese standpoint this was reflected in a particular cultural and geographic understanding as to where Asia began and ended. For many Japanese, 'Asia' has historically meant East Asia. India was seen as occupying a wholly separate cultural, economic and geo-strategic sphere to Japan, which was defined as primarily Northeast Asia, but in broader terms, East Asia and the Pacific. As the distinguished Indian journalist, Durgas Das, noted: 'A majority of [Japanese] bureaucrats prefer to exclude India from the Asian personality, which according to them ends on the borders of Burma and Malaysia.'[1] In 1967, the Japanese delegation to an Australian conference, organised to explore the possibility of a trilateral Australian–Japan–India strategic relationship, pondered the question of whether India was an Asian country at all.[2]

For its part, India has had a longstanding self-perception of its cultural centrality to Asia. Until recently, however, this has not been translated into the strategic dimension. In the years following independence many Indian scholars wrote about a 'Greater India' to describe what they saw as India's 'commanding' cultural influence over South and Southeast Asia. Some also saw great significance in India as the birthplace of Buddhism, which was carried to China and then Japan.[3] Despite these claims, throughout the Cold War India's strategic perspectives were almost exclusively focused in South Asia and India actively disclaimed any positive strategic role in the Asia Pacific.

Underlying these 'geo-strategic' perceptions is what many observers see as a particular cultural and social incompatibility between Indian and East Asian peoples, and particularly so between Indian and Japanese. Nakane Chie, a noted Japanese anthropologist, commented that while the Japanese were able to cope in social terms in China and Southeast Asia, there was a 'fantastic difference between the two sets of cultural values' of Japan and India that makes Indian culture 'almost incomprehensible' to Japanese people. He concluded that the boundary between East and West lies not between Asia and Europe, but somewhere between India and Burma.[4] This dissonance goes well beyond the cultural or social sphere and is an important underlying factor in the failure of India and Japan to develop any meaningful economic or political relationship throughout most of the twentieth century.

Some claim that Japanese perceptions about India's role in Asia are changing. Comments by Japanese Prime Minister Shinzo Abe in 2007 that the India–Japan relationship 'will be the most important bilateral relationship [for Japan] in the world'[5] would have been unthinkable 10 years earlier. Former Japanese Ambassador to India, Yasukuni Enoki, claims that 'For many decades, Asia has been, to the Japanese mind, almost identical with East Asia,' but that the 'scope of Asia' was now changing in the Japanese mind to include South Asia.[6] Others doubt that a significant change has occurred in Japanese perceptions and that Japanese will remain almost wholly focused on Pacific Asia without extending to the Indian subcontinent in any substantial way.[7] Certainly while Tokyo has in recent years come to see India as an important participant in certain regional groupings, it has arguably still not yet demonstrated a clear understanding as to how it sees India fitting into the Asia Pacific.

The role of India in Japan's East Asian empire

A perceived separation of the strategic dynamics of East and South Asia has a long history. Even at the height of the Pacific War, when Japan sought to build an Asian empire, both Indian and Japanese leaders saw a clear separation in their strategic spheres. In May 1942 a victorious and apparently invincible Japanese army stood at India's eastern border. The British army, routed in Malaya and Burma, seemed unlikely to stop the Japanese advance. The British Eastern Fleet had fled to Africa the previous month, leaving India's east coast virtually undefended. Despite its apparently overwhelming strategic position, the Japanese army halted on the Burmese border in 1942 and by the end of the war would never occupy more than an insignificant portion of Indian territory. Although the Japanese army made incursions into India's northeast territories in 1944, these were motivated by a need to disrupt Allied supply lines to Chinese Nationalist forces in southern China and to protect the Japanese flank, and not by any plan to conquer India.

In fact, Japan had little interest in conquering India during the Pacific War. There were good practical reasons for this: India was seen in Tokyo as too big and ungovernable, there were concerns about overstretch of Japanese forces and there were geographic obstacles to invasion. However, underlying Japan's decision to halt at India's border was a sense that India did not fall within what Japan considered its strategic environment – India was seen as not belonging within Japan's empire, the so-called Greater East Asia Co-Prosperity Sphere. Tokyo's plans about Japan's imperial expansion had little to say about India. While some Japanese strategic planners assumed that India would eventually become associated in one way or another with Japan's new sphere of influence in East Asia, Tokyo was also willing to trade away a sphere of influence over India to other powers. In September 1940, in negotiating the Tripartite Pact with Nazi Germany (with which the Soviet Union was then associated), Tokyo was primarily interested in obtaining recognition of its sphere of influence in East Asia and was willing to concede India and Iran to the Soviets as the price of directing Soviet attention away from East Asia. According to Milan Hauner's comprehensive study of relations between Japan and its Axis allies, Tokyo saw India as a pawn for future diplomatic bargaining in order to win Soviet partnership, or at least neutrality, against the Anglo-Saxons.[8]

During the Pacific War, Tokyo made few practical efforts to encourage Indian national aspirations, although the Japanese Army mobilised captured Indian soldiers to serve Japanese forces as armed auxiliaries under the banner of the Indian National Army.[9] Some Indian nationalists hoped that this might become the basis for an armed revolt against the British. However, Japan did very little in practice to encourage the Indian nationalist movement.[10] The Japanese Foreign Ministry was very concerned about the governability of an 'independent' India under Japanese suzerainty and the ability of the Indian nationalist movement to establish an orderly state if the British were driven out.[11]

For their part, the great majority of Indian nationalist leaders also had little appetite for cooperation with Japan in their struggle for Indian independence: Japan was generally regarded as presenting a greater danger to Indian freedom than the British Raj. The apparently imminent invasion by the Japanese in early 1942 provided Indian nationalists with an opportunity – if they wished to use it – to effectively destroy any British-led defence of India through violent protest, mutiny, strike or civil disobedience. However, the prospect of Japanese forces at India's borders also focused their minds as to the consequences of a British military withdrawal. The compromise arrived at by the Indian National Congress by mid-1942 was to seek a handover of power by the British while also seeking British military protection from the Japanese. While they would not give the British administration their positive cooperation, neither would they do anything to 'embarrass' a British-led defence of India against the Japanese. Nehru, in particular, threatened 'guerrilla warfare' and 'a scorched earth policy' should the Japanese ever try to enter India.[12] This decision allowed Britain to raise a huge volunteer Indian army which made a significant contribution to the defeat of Japan in Southeast Asia.

Cold War perspectives

During the second half of the twentieth century, the strategic separation of South and East Asia was reinforced by differing Cold War alignments and by very different perceptions of China. For much of the Cold War, New Delhi saw Japan as little more than a US puppet (if perhaps one to be admired for its economic success), while Tokyo saw India's nonalignment policy as untenable and India's economic policy as unattractive.

The first significant strategic interaction between an independent India and Japan occurred during the 1962 Sino-Indian war when India sought international support for its defence against what it saw as Chinese aggression in the Himalayas. As discussed previously, the conflict with China was a pivotal event in India's modern history. The United States and its Western allies gave substantial diplomatic and military support to India against what they saw as communist aggression. However, despite being pressed by the United States to condemn China in the strongest terms, Japan refused to clearly support India over the conflict. Japanese Prime Minister Ikeda refused to express any opinion as to whether the Chinese actions amounted to aggression[13] and later took the opportunity in the Japanese Diet to chide India over the unreality of neutrality between the West and Communism.[14] Japanese leaders were even more critical of India in private. Kenjiro Shiga, the Director General of the Japanese Defence Agency, told US Assistant Secretary of State, Averill Harriman, of the 'arrogant attitude' of the Indians in refusing Beijing's offers to negotiate the dispute, adding that most Japanese felt 'considerable resentment' against India.[15] Japanese Foreign Minister, Masayoshi Ohira, later told an 'astonished' US Secretary of State, Dean Rusk, that 'India had got its just deserts' at the hands of the Chinese Army, and that the United States 'should leave Communist China alone'.[16] While Tokyo had domestic political reasons for not supporting India over the conflict, more importantly it saw the conflict as an unwelcome hindrance to the normalisation of its economic and political relations with China. Japan and China were at this time in the final stages of negotiating a 'private' trade agreement that would create the foundation for normal relations. As Prime Minister Sato was to later put it, 'China wanted to isolate India and tempt Japan with trade.'[17] Nevertheless, the reaction of the Japanese leadership to the conflict indicated a deep empathy towards China and indifference towards India. For New Delhi, Japan's publicly equivocal stance merely confirmed their suspicions about Japan's 'amoral' policies.

During the second half of the 1960s, concerns about the growing belligerence of China and the possibility of British/US retrenchment from the region led to several proposals for new regional security arrangements to be anchored by India and Japan. India and Japan rejected these proposals. In early 1967, Australia, concerned at the prospective British withdrawal east of Suez, proposed a trilateral alliance among Japan, India and Australia aimed at containing China. The United States, contemplating a reduction in its own military commitment in Asia, also made several proposals involving regional powers taking a greater share of responsibility for the containment of China. This included a September 1968 proposal in which Australia, Japan and India should work together with other Southeast Asian nations to develop a regional security arrangement in which the United States would be limited partner.[18] The Soviet Union also proposed a regional collective security system in 1969 to be anchored by India and Japan, aimed at containing China. The Soviet proposal involved a cooperative system involving all of South, Southeast and East Asia to be guaranteed by the Soviet Union and the United States. Neither Japan nor India showed any interest in any of these proposals. Japan rejected them relatively discreetly, while India made publicly clear that any Western-sponsored arrangements were 'out of the question'.[19] As Hedley Bull, an Australian strategist, commented, the Australian and US-inspired proposals merely reflected a desire of the external powers to rationalise their own withdrawal and that India, Australia and Japan do not share a common perception of external threats to their security.[20]

Attempts by India during the same period to promote a purely economic arrangement involving Japan, India and Southeast Asian states (essentially involving Japan sponsoring India's economic development) were also rejected by Japan. In June 1969, Japanese Prime Minister Sato, with uncharacteristic forthrightness, told Indira Gandhi that Japan did not welcome Indian proposals for an India–Japan economic axis that would include Southeast Asia.[21] Japan regarded its area of interest as ending at Burma. It did not wish to be involved in India's quarrels in South Asia and saw India as a potential regional rival rather than as a partner.[22] Tokyo did give considerable thought to the Chinese 'threat' and its impact on regional security. However, concerns about the potential of any regional containment arrangement, however it was presented, to lead to confrontation with China far outweighed any possible benefits that a relationship with India might offer.[23] Tokyo came to the view that Japan could itself add little to regional security apart from promoting regional economic development.[24] From late 1966, Japanese Foreign Minister Takeo Miki began to promote a new 'Asia Pacific' policy in which Japan would act as a bridge in fostering regional economic cooperation, a policy that might now be described as 'open regionalism'. While Tokyo made clear that any Asia Pacific regional organisation should have an open membership, including even China, it did not consider that its new concept of the 'Asia Pacific region' included India.[25] The Japanese focused on the creation of East Asian-based arrangements to promote economic cooperation and free trade, including the Ministerial Conference for Economic Development of Southeast Asia (MEDSEA) and the Pacific Trade and Development forum, forerunners of the modern-day APEC. At the same time, Japan opposed India's participation in regional fora, including in MEDSEA and subsequently in APEC and the ARF.

The political and economic relationship between India and Japan remained largely frozen for the rest of the Cold War. The strategic realignments of the early 1970s, with China joining with the United States and Japan to oppose the Soviet Union, and India joining with the Soviet Union against China, cemented the strategic estrangement. Underlying these differing Cold War alignments was also a deeper divergence of strategic goals: Japan's preparedness to cede strategic autonomy to the United States while pursuing economic development stood in stark contrast with India's policy of strategic and economic autonomy, often at the cost of its economic development. From the 1970s, India pursued a model of economic autarchy, with a closed economy based on import substitution, licensing to inhibit competition and a major role for the state-owned sector. Although India made regular pleas for foreign investment, it was not interested in pursuing the model for economic development followed by many Southeast Asian states. In contrast, Japan, while sheltering under the US security umbrella, pursued a policy of economic mercantilism in which Japanese companies sat at the top of an export production chain covering much of East Asia. This allowed Japan to become the second largest exporter in the world. Japanese investment was largely channelled to Southeast Asia and China, where investors generally found cooperative governments and compliant workforces.

Japan and India's 1998 nuclear tests

Although the end of the Cold War and the collapse of the Soviet Union removed some obvious impediments to strategic engagement between them, during most of the 1990s neither India nor Japan saw any clear benefits from a close relationship. Instead, Japan's interest in India during the 1990s was largely defined by attempts to persuade India to forgo the nuclear weapons capabilities it had held since 1974 and become part of the international nuclear non-proliferation order. In particular, Japan sought political leverage from its aid contribution to India and the nuclear question became a central issue in the relationship.

The Japanese response to India's Pokhran II nuclear tests in May 1998 was unusually sharp and represented Japan's most active foreign policy intervention in South Asia since the Pacific War. Japan demanded that India suspend its further nuclear development programme, froze aid, recalled its ambassador, and used its position in the World Bank and the Asian Development Bank to block multilateral loans to India. Japan also took a leading role in organising the international community against the development, in the G-8 and the UN Security Council. Most controversially, Japan offered to host an international conference on Kashmir and to mediate between India and Pakistan on the issue. However, Japan's diplomatic intervention against India fell flat, doing significant damage to its relations with India. India resented the actions of Japan and other US allies, such as Australia, who were seen as sheltering under the US nuclear umbrella. However the strongest hostility was reserved for Japan's attempts to involve itself in the Kashmir dispute, with one Indian diplomat reportedly commenting:

> We understand Japanese special sentiments against nuclear weapons. But if Japan tries to bring the Kashmir issue into an international stage like the UN, India would regard Japan as an enemy and Japan would stay such for many years to come.[26]

Some have argued that Japan's strong reaction to the tests was motivated by the prospect that India, through its acquisition of nuclear weapons, would leapfrog Japan to major power status.[27] However a quite different explanation is more likely. In fact, Japan cared little about India's strategic requirements or its claims to major power status. Rather, Japan was primarily motivated by concerns about India's actions in encouraging North Korea to become a declared nuclear weapons state (which, in fact, occurred in 2006).[28] The nuclear tests also allowed the Japanese to exhibit their commitment to anti-proliferation and provided an opportunity for them to demonstrate international leadership. Japan felt it was in a position to take such an activist line against India precisely because it had so little of concrete interest in South Asia – the Japanese had little to lose in terms of bilateral relations and potentially much to gain in international prestige if they gained a leadership role on non-proliferation and the India–Pakistan conflict.[29]

The strategic partnership between India and Japan in the twenty-first century

India's declaration as an overt nuclear power in 1998 marked a major turning point in its relationship with Japan, fundamentally altering the balance of the relationship that had existed since the 1950s. Japan's response to the tests represented a significant defeat for Japanese diplomacy and a failure to understand the limitations in its own strategic position. After 1998, Japan, like the rest of the world, was forced to treat India as a major strategic player in Asia and give more rigorous consideration of India's place in the broader strategic environment. This led to a major realignment of Japanese strategic thinking about India. According to a senior Indian diplomat in Tokyo, 'For all its downside, it provided a much needed reality check which, by briefly stripping our ties of false sentiment, allowed for a serious engagement, perhaps for the first time.'[30]

The initial steps to mend the relationship after India's 1998 nuclear tests were made by Indian Foreign Minister Jaswant Singh during a visit to Tokyo in December 1999. The Japanese responded quickly, realising that their failed stance against India over its 1998 nuclear tests risked leaving Japan isolated from India's growing engagement with the region.[31] As early as January 2000, Indian Defence Minister George Fernandes commented that: 'after more than 50 years of aloofness on these issues, India and Japan have decided on a security and defence related dialogue on a regular basis.'[32] In August 2000, Japanese Prime Minister Yoshiro Mori visited New Delhi to declare that Japan and India had become 'global partners', and Japan used the aftermath of 9/11 to lift its post-Pokhran II sanctions against both Pakistan and India. The political relationship between India and Japan has improved steadily from that time, although generally in parallel with developments in India's relationship with the United States. A so-called 'strategic partnership' was announced in 2005 and in 2006 agreements were concluded providing for the expansion and formalisation of defence ties, particularly in the area of maritime cooperation.

The 2007 Quadrilateral initiative

This process moved into top gear in 2007 under the leadership of Japanese Prime Minister Shinzo Abe and his Foreign Minister, Taro Aso. Abe believed that India would play a key role in Japan's future, claiming that the India–Japan relationship 'will be the most important bilateral relationship [for Japan] in the world'.[33] Aso also sought to provide an ideological basis for the relationship through his 'Arc of Freedom and Prosperity' initiative which proposed that Japan should pursue 'value-oriented diplomacy', justifying closer cooperation by Japan with others holding 'shared values' such as India, Australia and NATO states.

In early 2007 Prime Minister Abe proposed the so-called 'Quadrilateral' initiative, under which India would join a formal security dialogue with Japan, the United States and Australia. Abe's proposal was vague and would remain so, although some saw it as essentially suggesting the extension of the US–Japan–Australia Trilateral Security Dialogue to include India. In April 2007, the first ever trilateral naval exercises were held between the United States, Japan and India in the western Pacific. In August 2007, the annual India–US *Malabar* naval exercise was transformed into large-scale multilateral exercises in the Bay of Bengal involving ships from the United States,

India, Japan, Australia and Singapore. These developments reached a crescendo with the visit of Abe to India in August 2007, when in an address to the Indian parliament he spoke of a 'broader Asia' partnership of democracies. Abe suggested that the India–Japan partnership would 'evolve into an immense network spanning the entirety of the Pacific Ocean, incorporating the US and Australia'.[34] These developments, taken together, were seen by some as the beginnings of a formal four-way coalition between the United States, India, Japan and Australia, aimed at balancing or containing a rising China.[35]

However, by late 2007 these developments had lost much of their momentum. Reactions from Chinese official and semi-official sources to the Quadrilateral initiative and naval exercises in 2007 were very negative, including criticism that the initiatives resurrected 'a cold-war mentality' and marked 'the formation of a small NATO to resist China'.[36] In May 2007 China issued diplomatic *demarchés* to India, Japan, the United States and Australia requesting explanations about the Quadrilateral proposal and in the following month Chinese President Hu Jintao pressed home the point by seeking 'clarification' of India's position in a face to face meeting with Indian Prime Minister Singh.[37]

During the course of 2007, Australia, India, the United States and even Japan became increasingly hesitant about the Quadrilateral initiative. Canberra had serious misgivings over the proposal, which was seen by many as undefined and unduly provocative. Australia declined to participate in meetings on the initiative after May 2007, although its withdrawal was only announced in early 2008. Washington was divided over the proposal and did not make any public statements in support of it. The Indian government also faced significant domestic political pressure against any perceived alliance involving the United States. In Japan there was criticism of the proposal from within the governing coalition, the bureaucracy and the opposition, with many considering a formal multilateral political coalition as 'too provocative' towards China. The resignation of Abe as Japanese Prime Minister in September 2007 removed a strong proponent of a security relationship with India and by the end of 2007 proposals for a formal multilateral security relationship involving Japan, India and the United States had, it seemed, been quietly shelved. However, the emphasis shifted towards the development of the bilateral relationship between India and Japan.

The 2008 India–Japan Security Declaration

In October 2008, the Indian and Japanese Prime Ministers concluded the India–Japan Joint Security Declaration, asserting that the strategic partnership between the two countries would become 'an essential pillar for the future architecture of the region'.[38] This was the third security declaration made by Japan (after joint declarations with the United States in 1996 and Australia in 2007) and the first such declaration by India (and was followed by a further joint security declaration by India with Australia in 2009). Both Japanese and Indian leaders made repeated denials that the Declaration was 'aimed at' China[39] and Taro Aso (then Prime Minister) downplayed suggestions that Tokyo was still pursuing the idea of a security relationship involving India, Japan and the United States. China's reactions to the Security Declaration have been restrained.[40]

While the Security Declaration is more symbolic than substantive, it is nevertheless an important step in creating a framework for the further development of the security relationship.[41] The Declaration identifies shared security interests and outlines consultative mechanisms to be implemented between them. Key areas of cooperation include the creation of a new Asian security order, bilateral cooperation within multilateral regional frameworks, a continuing defence dialogue, cooperation between coastguards, transport safety, the fight against terrorism and transnational crimes, sharing of experiences in peacekeeping and peace-building, disaster management and disarmament and non-proliferation. The Security Declaration gives significant emphasis to cooperation within existing regional multilateral frameworks and in the creation of a new Asian security order. The emphasis on political cooperation is an inevitable consequence of Japan's inability under the current interpretation of its Constitution to engage in anything that smacks of collective defence or to make a military contribution to regional security beyond Japan's immediate environs.

The Declaration mandates bilateral consultation and cooperation at multiple levels, including consultation among Foreign and Defence Ministers (although not in the so-called 2+2 format as currently occurs between Japan and the United States and Australia) and the respective permanent secretaries and national security advisors. The Declaration also prescribes a range of military to military cooperation and exchanges, navy to navy staff talks, coastguard cooperation, a Joint Working Group on counterterrorism and cooperation on money laundering. A December 2009 Action Plan added further agreements on consultation and cooperation including an annual subcabinet/senior officials 2+2 meeting (foreign affairs and defence), the institutionalisation of the annual maritime security dialogue and annual bilateral naval exercises, discussions of direct cooperation in anti-piracy operations, institutionalisation of cooperation on UN reform (particularly on permanent membership of the UN Security Council for both India and Japan) and the development of detailed plans for cooperation in disaster management both in India and regionally. The level of detail devoted to these consultative mechanisms portrays an apparent determination of both to undertake a prolonged and multifaceted engagement and to build a broad-based relationship across multiple agencies.

Developments in India's other security relationships in maritime Northeast Asia

Before examining the India–Japan relationship in further detail, it is worth placing it in the context of developments in India's other security relationships in maritime Northeast Asia. In parallel with improved relations with Japan, since the turn of the century India has upgraded its security relations with South Korea and, in a much more restrained way, with Taiwan.

Historically India was even more estranged from South Korea than it was from Japan – throughout the Cold War, India largely avoided any dealings at all with South Korea. In the early 1950s, during the Korean War, India had made a brief attempt at mediation between the great powers which earned it few friends, and for the remainder of the Cold War effectively pursued a policy of mutual indifference towards South Korea. However, in recent years India and South Korea have developed a strong economic and a good political relationship.[42] This has been facilitated by some commonalities in their mutual relationships with the United States and China. China's security relationships with Pakistan and North Korea, and its role in facilitating nuclear and missile proliferation to those states, have also created a number of strategic parallels for India and South Korea as they deal with their often threatening and recalcitrant 'breakaway' neighbours. Some have argued that China's relationships with Pakistan and North Korea are essentially proxy strategies aimed at India and Japan (and to a lesser extent, South Korea). Mohan Malik argues that China has played what he calls a 'double game' in South Asia and Northeast Asia, having earlier contributed to their destabilisation by transferring nuclear and missile technology to its allies (North Korea and Pakistan) and later offering to help contain the problem of nuclear/missile proliferation in South Asia and on the Korean peninsula. According to Malik this buttresses China's 'centrality' in regional security issues and allows China to essentially use North Korea andPakistan as proxies to threaten Japan or India while also allowing it to act as an impartial, regional arbiter.[43] However, it is not clear to what extent these mutual or parallel concerns have led India and South Korea to see the benefit of strategic cooperation.

Although security cooperation between India and South Korea is still relatively undeveloped, South Korea sees India as a major potential customer for its defence and civil nuclear technology and as an important maritime security provider in the Indian Ocean. Although Seoul reportedly requested India to use its influence with Pyongyang in the Six Party Talks, India has avoided any involvement in Korean security issues.[44] Despite its improved relationship with Seoul, Tokyo and Washington in recent years, India has often withheld or muted criticism over provocative or aggressive actions by North Korea.[45] To some extent this has reflected Indian domestic politics and its traditions of nonalignment in which it would usually refrain from criticising even the worst totalitarian regimes, particularly those that claimed to be socialist. However, underlying New Delhi's reticence is also a view that northeast Asia falls beyond India's strategic sphere.

India has for many decades also avoided any involvement in Taiwanese security issues, showing considerable sensitivity towards the PRC's claims to sovereignty. India recognised the PRC's claims over Taiwan in 1950 (being one of the first non-communist states to do so). Since then, at the request of China, it has repeatedly affirmed and reaffirmed its unambiguous adherence to the One China policy, most recently during the visit of Prime Minister Manmohan Singh to China in January 2008. India has thus shown greater sensitivity to Beijing over Taiwan than say Tokyo or Seoul. Despite India's difficulties with China since the late 1950s, India never contemplated reviving its ties or even seriously engaging with Taiwan. It was not until after India and China's rapprochement in the early 1990s that India began to open ties with Taipei. Today, official relations are coordinated through their respective Economic and Cultural Centres and India remains very touchy about official political-diplomatic contacts with Taipei, although non-official and non-public security contacts have been increasing in recent years.[46]

Over the last decade, India has been slowly developing unofficial political and security links. In 2002 India and Taiwan exchanged military personnel to act in the capacity of unofficial military attachés and there were reports, officially denied by India, that top Indian air force officers had visited Taiwan. In 2004, the former Indian Defence Minister George Fernandes visited Taiwan and in 2007 India consented to an 'unofficial' visit to India by Ma Ying-jeou, then opposition KMT presidential candidate and now Taiwan president. This was perceived by some as an indication of New Delhi's displeasure over Chinese actions on the border.

Despite calls from more hawkish Indian strategic commentators to use Taiwan to place pressure on China or to develop Taiwan as India's strategic gateway to the Asia Pacific, India remains cautious about developing links. New Delhi has an interest in the maintenance of the status quo on the Taiwan Strait, as a resolution of Taiwan's status would potentially allow China to shift military resources to Tibet or Xinjiang. However, India would also be concerned about the potential to provoke further Chinese support of separatist movements in India. As Jiang Yili, a Chinese South Asia expert, commented: 'As India is facing disputes with Pakistan and the independence movement in its northeast area, India would [tend to] be concerned with our attitude and not go too far on the Taiwan issue.'[47] Some commentators have optimistically suggested that the Indian Navy could become a strategic factor in the Taiwan Strait, although that assessment disregards India's limited power projection capabilities.[48] Some security links have developed in recent years, primarily motivated by India's needs for intelligence on China, including signal intelligence.[49] According to Antonio Chiang, former deputy secretary general of Taiwan's National Security Council, Indians 'have been eager to learn more about China and Taiwan is the easiest way', adding that what India could offer Taiwan was 'more limited'.[50]

Taiwan's perspective on India is if anything even more reserved than India's. The economic links are tenuous and seem unlikely to develop in a hurry. According to the Chairman of the Taiwan Merchants' Association, 'India is not attractive at all. We can't speak the language and have a different lifestyle.'[51] Although there is recognition of India's increasing regional importance, there is also political reserve. Taiwan continues to support the PRC's territorial claims in the Himalayas and in 2007, it made a point of denying visas to two Indian sportspeople from Sikkim on the basis that they 'looked Tibetan'.

Japanese perspectives on a security relationship with India

While India has moved to upgrade other security relationships in maritime Northeast Asia, it is India's security relationship with Japan that will have the most strategic significance. India's relationship with Japan, one of Asia's major powers and the greatest maritime power in Asia, will have broad-ranging consequences for India's perceived role throughout the western Pacific. Arguably, the relationship could lead to a long-term strategic alignment, something that would have a significant effect on the regional balance of power. Changes in the relationship in recent years reflect a convergence of Japanese and Indian strategic perceptions and expectations on several levels.

Japan's security environment is dominated by two factors: its security alliance with the United States and its relationship with China. While the US alliance is generally regarded as central to Japan's security there are also widespread anxieties in Japan about the future of the alliance. This has led to attempts to draw closer to the United States simultaneously with a desire to reduce Japan's reliance on it. Japan is also painfully aware of the decline in its power relative to China and perceives potential risks in the maintenance of the US alliance in the face of China's rise.[52] Comments by the now US Secretary of State, Hillary Rodham Clinton, that the US relationship with China 'will be the most important bilateral relationship in the world this century'[53] have only served to heighten these fears. Despite broadly held fears in Japan about a China 'threat' and the relative decline in Japan's strategic position, there is little consensus in Japan about an appropriate response to this perceived threat or about Japan's relationship with the rest of Asia.

Since the end of the Cold War, Japan's security policy has been hotly contested among numerous streams of thinking which commentators have tagged variously as normal nationalists, middle-power internationalists, new autonomists, neo-revisionists, realists, globalists, mercantilists, Asianists and pacifists.[54] According to Peter Katzenstein, a writer on Japanese strategic culture, a lack of consensus has contributed to a lack of direction in Japanese security policy and resulted in a high degree of policy rigidity.[55] While changes in Japanese government have led to a change in emphasis, there is generally no clear change in policy direction. According to Katzenstein, Japan's political and bureaucratic structure creates a strong bias against the forceful articulation of military-security objectives, making it difficult to discern changes in policy.[56]

Amid this debate, Japanese thinking about the substance of its relationship with India is relatively undeveloped. Nevertheless, the Japan–India relationship is unusual for the degree to which it is seen in positive terms (if not always of central importance) across several streams of Japanese strategic thinking, simultaneously fulfilling several different external policy objectives. In broad terms, the development of a relationship with an India whose relative power is on the rise while Japan's relative power is in decline is seen as one response to Japan's strategic dilemma vis-à-vis China and the United States.

Some in Japan see a closer relationship with India as part of developing better security relationships with key US security partners both inside and outside the region. They argue that the US security relationship can be *strengthened* through better embedding Japan in the broader Western alliance system. An explicit goal of improving Japan's relations with US strategic partners was first articulated as a specific strategic objective by Japanese Prime Minister Junichiro Koizumi in May 2003 and was reaffirmed in the 2004 Araki Commission Report and Japanese National Defence Programme Guidelines. Aso (then Foreign Minister and later Prime Minister) also expressly advocated strengthening relations with NATO as a means of strengthening Japan's relations with the United States. Developments in Japan's relationships with Australia and to a lesser extent India (at least during the period 2007–8) should be understood within this context.[57]

There is little doubt that Japan's relationship with India has improved as a consequence of improvements in US–Indian strategic relations in recent years. Elements of the Bush administration played an important role in encouraging Japanese proposals for the Quadrilateral, which the Abe government was keen to pursue. The idea had been proposed within the track 1.5 US–Japan–India trilateral strategic dialogues first held in June 2006[58] and then supported in the so-called Second Armitage-Nye Report issued in February 2007.[59] It was then pressed by Vice President Dick Cheney during his March 2007 visit to Tokyo.[60] While the Quadrilateral initiative did not receive wholehearted support in the Bush administration (with Secretary of State Condoleezza Rice reportedly opposed to it), the United States remains supportive of Japan developing a closer security relationship with India as part of extending its regional security role.[61] Mike Green, a leading US analyst of Asian security affairs, sees the India–Japan relationship as beneficial in continuing the movement of India towards an active stakeholder role in the international system. India could also have a positive influence on Japanese foreign policy 'by pulling Japan out of East Asia' and encouraging Japan to partner on a global basis.[62] However, as will be seen below, future Japanese governments may be inclined to extend the bilateral nature of the relationship with India while also distancing the relationship somewhat from the US aspect.

A relationship with India is also consistent with a long-running *Pan-Asianist* stream in Japanese strategic thinking. Pan-Asian ideas are common across a broad ideological spectrum in Japan, ranging from nationalists and historical revisionists (many of whom have had influence in the Liberal Democratic Party (LDP) administration over the last decade or so) to anti-militarists within the current Democratic Party of Japan (DPJ) administration. The Pan-Asianism prevalent in Japan in the years up to the Pacific War was a loose set of ideas positing egalitarianism among Asians (in opposition to the West), at the same time as Japanese superiority.[63] It grew as an idealistic/romantic antithesis to the realist foreign policies pursued by Meiji-era Japan in pursuing relationships with Western great powers. Although suppressed in post-war Japan, ideas of Pan-Asian nationalism have experienced something of a revival. In broad terms Pan-Asian thinking favours close relations with Asia over exclusive reliance on the US alliance and it is seen by some as potentially undermining the alliance.[64] Others see such thinking as not necessarily inconsistent with a simultaneous desire to continue or even strengthen the US alliance. Pan-Asianism in Japan has traditionally been confined to Japan's relations with the Sinic world (China, Korea and Vietnam) and more generally East Asia, although in recent years the Japanese concept of 'Asia' has been gradually expanding westwards.

A particular attachment to India could be found during Prime Minister Nobusuke Kishi's administration during the late 1950s, which was continued in 2007 by his grandson, Shinzo Abe, then leader of the Kishi faction in the LDP. Abe was particularly fond of highlighting examples of supposed solidarity between India and Japan against the West during the 1940s. Thus Abe on his visit to India in August 2007 made a public visit to the home of Subhas Bose, the wartime leader of the Indian National Army, a group of captured Indian soldiers who collaborated with the Japanese in fighting the British during the Pacific War. (Although, in celebrating Japan's sponsorship of the INA, Abe conveniently forgot that in early 1942 Nehru and the great majority of the Congress Party leadership had firmly resolved to assist the British in resisting Japanese imperialism.) Abe also met with the family of Radhabinod Pal, an Indian judge who in 1949 dissented from the conviction of Japanese leaders in the Tokyo War Crime trials.[65] In highlighting these episodes Abe sought to legitimise both Japan's wartime role and the supposed legacies of Pan-Asian cooperation between Japan and India. Many in the current DPJ government exhibit similar ideas about Asian regionalism (sometimes but not always with an anti-militaristic bent). This may lead to greater emphasis on key regional relationships as an intended counterpoint to Japan's relationship with the United States.

A security relationship with India would also find support among Japanese *nationalists* who hold significant (though often non-public) influence throughout Japan's political, bureaucratic and military systems. The nationalist or rightist movement is essentially revisionist in terms of Japan's foreign policy, advocating a militarily strong, assertive and independent Japan and generally identifying China as Japan's key threat. Although some nationalists find Japan's reliance on the US security umbrella 'humiliating' they do not necessarily oppose the US alliance, though they would advocate that the alliance be placed on more equal terms. Nationalists are attracted to a relationship with India in terms of finding common cause in potentially forming a balancing coalition against the perceived China threat and an opportunity for Japan to partially hedge against the risk of the United States abandoning Japan in favour of China. Some nationalists identify India as a potentially important security partner of a future Japan shorn of its current legal and political constraints on the projection of military power and having the ability to act outside the US security umbrella.

Overlaying these streams of Japanese thinking are questions about whether Japan may be about to make a major change in strategic direction. Kenneth Pyle, a long-time observer of the historical development of Japanese strategic practice, believes that Japan is currently in the process of making one of its periodical revolutionary changes of course in foreign policy strategy in response to the new strategic environment in Asia and a generational change in Japan's leadership. According to Pyle, this may involve Japan completely abandoning the Yoshida Doctrine which anchored Japan to the US security relationship during the Cold War. This will not necessarily involve a loosening of the US alliance, but is likely to involve Japan seeking to rebuild its ties in Asia and promoting multilateral institutions in Asia where it can establish leadership and compete with China for influence.[66]

While a security relationship with India has conceptual support among several different streams in Japanese strategic thinking, there is little consensus about how the relationship might be developed in practical terms. A security relationship with India is inescapably limited by Japan's self-imposed limitations on the projection of military power. Under its current constitutional arrangements, Japan is effectively unable to extend military cooperation with India much past the level of regular joint naval and coast-guard exercises,[67] anti-piracy operations,[68] joint disaster management[69] and the multilayered consultations as provided in the Security Declaration. Despite these limitations, India could still play an important role in Japan's evolving security posture in at least two key respects.

First, the key area of cooperation between Japan and India over the coming years is likely to be political and diplomatic cooperation in regional fora. Japan's efforts to include India in regional multilateral political and economic structures such as the East Asia Summit have clearly been motivated by a desire to use India to balance China within those fora. This balance may be more in the nature of a balance of power contemplated by some classical realists (i.e. the development of a preferred distribution of power) than the type contemplated by neorealists (i.e. the formation of a coalition to balance against a perceived military threat). In this sense, a relationship with India may serve simultaneously as part of a political balancing strategy in relation to China and as a political hedging strategy with respect to the United States. In cooperation with India, Japan might carve out for itself a greater political role in Asia Pacific security and play a greater role in security agenda-setting so as to potentially strengthen Japan's political hand *within* the US alliance.[70] This could help ensure that Japan's interests were not overlooked by the United States, as was sometimes perceived to be the case in the past (for example, the North Korean nuclear issue).

Developing this theme further, some have argued that India might also be a useful partner for Japan in helping to bring about a 'strategic convergence' between the United States and its allies and a future East Asian economic community which would include both China and India.[71] This reasoning rejects casting India as merely a defensive balancer against China, a role which, it is claimed, India would refuse to take in any event.[72] Instead, India would be a partner in promoting multilateral political and economic institutions that allow for the inclusion of China in a way that is acceptable to the region.

For Japan, the second key role of an India relationship is in maritime security. Many in Japan identify the India relationship primarily as a maritime coalition, particularly in connection with the security of Japan's sea lanes to the Middle East.[73] The title of Prime Minister Abe's 2007 address to the Indian Parliament, 'The Confluence of Two Seas', provides an insight into Japanese thinking about the relationship, that is, a meeting of maritime powers of the Pacific and Indian Oceans. For Japan, a key concern is the ability of India to provide maritime security to Japan in the Indian Ocean in combination with or, potentially, as a partial alternative to Japan's reliance on the United States. As the former Chairman of Joint Staff of the Japanese Defence Agency, Admiral Natsukawa, commented in 2006, 'Only India has the capability and intention for security cooperation in this huge sea area [the Indian Ocean], the west side of the Malacca Strait.'[74] Yasukuni Enoki, former Japanese ambassador to India, commented in 2007: 'Japanese energy security is dependent on the Indian Navy. ... We have only the Indian Navy which can be trusted. Other navies are not reliable.'[75] Similarly, the Japanese National Institute of Defence Studies has called India 'the sole dominant power' in the Indian Ocean.[76]

Given the current pre-eminence of US military power in the Indian Ocean region these comments are significant and suggest that Japan may wish to hedge its reliance on the United States. Japanese views on an Indian security role inside the Malacca Strait may be less enthusiastic, although it is arguable that Japan, like the United States, may see India as playing a useful role as an external security provider in the Strait given local political sensitivities.

In contrast with its enthusiasm for an enhanced role for India in the Indian Ocean there seems to be little desire in Tokyo to see the Indian Navy playing a material role west or north of Singapore.[77] India is largely seen as an Indian Ocean power without direct interests in East Asian security. Nevertheless, a tacit division of responsibilities between India providing maritime security in the Indian Ocean and Japan in the Pacific is not wholly unfeasible from Tokyo's standpoint, particularly if the United States is perceived to have a reduced presence or reliability in the Indian Ocean. Some might even go further and see a potential demarcation of Japanese and Indian maritime spheres of influence north and west of the Malay peninsular.

The unanswered question in all this is the extent to which Japan would realistically be prepared to develop a meaningful security relationship with an India that is not prepared to act substantially in coordination with the United States. Some in Japan would prefer to see India as occupying a strategic role akin to a 'France in Asia'[78] (i.e. generally acting within the US strategic sphere while maintaining a degree of political autonomy), in which India could cooperate closely with a Japan that is still deeply embedded in the US security relationship. However it seems unlikely that India would allow itself to be cast in those terms.

While the current DPJ-led government generally sees an India relationship in positive terms, the government's foreign policy stance remains unclear in many respects. In 2009, a DPJ government, led by Prime Minister Yukio Hatoyama, scaled back the previous government's goal of a global security partnership with the United States.[79] The DPJ is also generally inclined against the projection of military power (it cancelled Japan's token maritime role in the Indian Ocean in support of the Afghanistan campaign, although it has so far continued Japan's contribution to anti-piracy operations in the Gulf of Aden) and against any relaxation of restrictions on the export of nuclear technology. Nevertheless there are also DPJ 'hawks' such as the Parliamentary Vice Defence Minister Akihisa Nagoshima, who has called for the maritime coalition comprising Japan, Taiwan, India and others to contain China. However, until the current administration develops a clearer vision of Japan's role in the region it seems unlikely that there will be significant developments in the India relationship.

Indian perspectives on a security relationship with Japan

For India, the evolving security relationship with Japan is one outcome of the revolution in Indian strategic thinking since the end of the Cold War. India's nonaligned policy made it very difficult for New Delhi to consider Japan as a potential strategic partner. However, a strategic relationship with Japan is now consistent with several themes in contemporary Indian strategic thinking. As discussed in Chapter 2, these themes include the 'holy grail' of strategic autonomy and related ideas of a multipolar regional security order; concerns over the impact of China on the Asian balance of power and ambitions to make India an 'indispensible element' in that balance; thinking about India as a maritime power; as well as the development of a new strategic relationship with the United States. Japan, as a key US ally, a major Asian power and a Pacific maritime state with security needs in the Indian Ocean, stands at the intersection of many of these themes in Indian strategic thinking.

Since the turn of the century, Indian policy towards Japan has been consistent, largely reflecting a consensus within the Indian political elite on the desirability of enhancing the relationship. As Manmohan Singh commented, 'Our relations with Japan enjoy a strong national consensus in our country.'[80] A bilateral security relationship with Japan is almost universally seen as non-threatening to India's strategic autonomy. A lack of strategic or historical baggage, together with Japan's non-assertive stance in regional security affairs since the end of World War II, has contributed to a view that Japan is unlikely to act as a strategic competitor to India.

India has also shown a considerable degree of patience in developing its relationship with Japan. New Delhi is relatively sensitive towards Japan's domestic political limitations and as a result has generally allowed Japan to set the pace in developing security aspects of the relationship. Whether or not India would be prepared to enter into a multilateral relationship involving Japan and the United States (in the nature, for example, of the putative Quadrilateral), it is clear that New Delhi is very comfortable with a bilateral security relationship with Japan. Thus New Delhi acted with uncharacteristic speed in September 2008 when a new Japanese government under Taro Aso proposed the Security Declaration.[81] As Shiv Shankar Menon, then Indian Foreign Secretary, commented at the time, the Security Declaration was signed largely at the initiative of Japan and its form was largely driven by Japanese considerations.[82]

Although there is broad consensus in the Indian security community about the desirability of an India–Japan relationship, there is a divergence of views in India about how it might fit within India's evolving strategic posture. To a significant extent this reflects tension between a perceived need of India to form strategic relationships with the United States and its allies and its goals of maintaining strategic autonomy and promoting the development of a multipolar region. While there is a broad understanding in New Delhi of Japan's strategic limitations, these are not generally seen as a major impediment to India's goals except as they affect India's immediate desire to gain access to Japanese nuclear and defence technology. Paradoxically, Japan's self-imposed limitations on the projection of power also make it an attractive partner in helping to legitimise India's great power status regionally and particularly in the Indian Ocean.

Many in India see a security relationship with Japan as highly consistent with India's goal of strategic autonomy. While it is generally understood in New Delhi that the immediate trigger for improvement in relations with Japan over the last several years was the development of India's security relationship with the United States, Indian analyses tend to place significant emphasis on the 'independent' and 'equal' nature of the India–Japan relationship. This is often contrasted with the India–US relationship where there is a perceived risk of the United States building India as a junior alliance partner.[83] Although a US ally, Japan is generally not seen as threatening India's freedom of action. Many Indian strategic commentators see India and Japan as becoming 'key stakeholders' in the Asia Pacific.[84] Japan, as a major power could also anchor a series of bilateral relationships between India and its Asia Pacific partners. Some even see the Japan relationship as potentially part of an Indian-sponsored 'constellation' of Asian states linked by strategic cooperation and sharing common interests, including counterbalancing China.[85] Brahma Chellaney sees the Japan relationship as providing India with another link to the US security sphere, forming the foundation for a coalition with the United States and Australia, as well as potentially forming the foundation of an India–Japan–Russian trilateral relationship. This, according to Chellaney, would be the way to form a 'true counterbalance to China,' because it 'would effectively contain China on all sides'.[86] Others hope that Japan (presumably with India's encouragement) will one day cast off its US strategic umbrella to join with India as a new global power centre and that China will thereby afford them both 'strategic space'.[87] According to these perspectives, the Japan–India relationship is potentially of fundamental importance to India, possibly helping to place India at the pivot of future Asian security arrangements.

Although suggestions of an East Asian maritime alliance led by India and Japan lie largely within the realm of speculation by Indian commentators, the visit of Indian Prime Minister Manmohan Singh to Tokyo and Hanoi in October 2010, was seen by many as connecting regional tensions over China's aggressive stance on the South China Sea, which had come to the fore in July 2010, with the Sino-Japanese dispute over the Diaoyo/Senkaku islands, where there had been a maritime incident in September of that year. An editorial in the *People's Daily* called it a 'missionary trip' to seek new allies against China and asked why Japan would allow itself to be drawn into Vietnam's 'self-inflicted' problems with Beijing.[88]

Others in New Delhi are less enthusiastic about any suggestion that India might attempt to sponsor a separate Asian security system, but nevertheless see Japan as an important partner in India's strategic ambitions. These include the modern-day successors of the nonalignment school who see a relationship between Japan and India as potentially helping to keep India relatively equidistant and nonaligned between two poles in Asia, China and the United States.[89] Others see the possibility of India occupying a middle ground of partial attachment to the United States while retaining significant autonomy. Mohan sees the Japan relationship as springing from India's closer relationship with the United States, but also potentially as part of an issue-based coalition that India could use to maintain its strategic flexibility.[90] According to this view, while India and Japan will have interests in assisting each other in the Asia Pacific and elsewhere, neither will Japan abandon the US alliance nor will India become a 'deputy' for the United States in Asia. Mohan believes that a bilateral relationship between India and Japan (in contrast to a multilateral security relationship including the United States) would avoid alienating China, allowing India and Japan to 'create a new magnet in Asia; not a wall of separation'.[91]

One area where New Delhi recognises a strong alignment of interests with Japan is on the need to better integrate India into various Asia Pacific political and economic institutions. Japan along with others such as Singapore can provide India with crucial diplomatic support in gaining entrance to these groupings potentially against the resistance of China. New Delhi believes it imperative that India be integrated into the economic engine of East Asia and avoid being locked out of regional economic and political fora as has often occurred in the past. Japan is seen as a key ally in ensuring that India not only participates in these regional arrangements, but that it is seated at the 'top table' in the negotiation of an Asian economic community and in any future regional security arrangements.

As in Japan, many in India also see the relationship primarily in terms of maritime security. It is recognised in New Delhi that Japan's present ability to contribute to regional maritime security is limited. However, Japan can play an important role in legitimising India's ambitions in the Indian Ocean. While Japan is recognised as a major (if partly inchoate) naval power in the western Pacific, it also has few pretensions about projecting significant naval power into the Indian Ocean or in challenging the Indian Navy's vision of having a leading role there. Japan's preparedness to accommodate itself to this vision serves to legitimise India's great power ambitions. As K.V. Kesavan, an Indian scholar in Japanese affairs, puts it, 'Indo-Japanese cooperation could become a core component of the entire Indian Ocean security mechanism.'[92] (One might mischievously add, in an Indian Ocean security mechanism which recognises Indian naval pre-eminence.) Not surprisingly, the Indian Navy is at the forefront of advocating the Japan relationship, and is keen on building strong ties with the Japanese Maritime Self Defence Force and Japanese Coastguard as part of a coalition of maritime powers. There are suggestions that India and Japan could enter into reciprocal security arrangements in their respective maritime zones (e.g. allowing escorts of each other's vessels on request, or cooperation in maritime interdiction).[93] However, there is little indication of concrete Indian expectations of a Japanese role as a maritime security provider in the South China Sea for example.

Constraints on the India–Japan security relationship

Although there is desire in both India and Japan to build a broad-based consultative security relationship, any such relationship will be subject to constraints that could significantly restrict India's strategic role in the western Pacific. A major constraint is New Delhi's desire to avoid taking an active role in Northeast Asian security issues, something evident in India's relationships with both South Korea and Taiwan. Thus the India–Japan Security Declaration (unlike, say, the Australia–Japan Security Declaration) does not include reference to Japan's concerns about abduction of its citizens by North Korea and North Korea's nuclear capacity. It is not clear whether this hesitancy arises from fears of provoking China in its own backyard (leading, for example, to Chinese retaliation in Kashmir) or if India simply regards Northeast Asia as beyond its area of strategic interest. Japan may find this reticence convenient in some respects and disappointing in others. However, it does arguably point to the weakness of India's tradition of 'merit-based' foreign policy in which India feels little if any obligation to support friendly states on issues where India's direct interests are not at stake.

The most obvious factor inhibiting a *symmetrical* security relationship between India and Japan is the restrictive Article IX of Japan's Constitution which, as it is currently interpreted, prohibits Japan from entering into collective defence arrangements. However, India appears to have few expectations in this regard and arguably, like the United States, may benefit from the lack of symmetry in the relationship (which would be somewhat ironic given the decades of criticism by New Delhi of Japan's relationship with the United States). There are, however, other issues which India expects Japan will address and resolve in order to further develop the relationship, particularly the willingness of Japan to meet India's needs in civilian nuclear cooperation and defence technology cooperation. While India has shown patience on these issues, their resolution will inevitably be seen in India as a test of Japan's seriousness to further developing the relationship.

Japan's refusal to supply nuclear generation technology to India has been a significant issue. For India, the participation of Japanese companies is likely to be an important factor in the development of its nuclear industry and an important legitimisation of India's status as a nuclear weapons state. However, Japan, as a leading campaigner against nuclear proliferation, remains extremely sensitive about India's nuclear status. Japan has tacitly accepted India's status as a *de facto* nuclear weapons state outside the non-proliferation system through its conditional approval of India's 123 nuclear deal with the United States in the multilateral Nuclear Suppliers Group. However, the Japanese government's position is that progress on civil nuclear cooperation with India can only occur when India becomes a party to the Comprehensive Test Ban Treaty (CTBT) and commences negotiations on the Fissile Material Cut-off Treaty (FCMT). In April 2010, India and Japan agreed to establish a joint working group on civil-nuclear cooperation, signalling a desire by Tokyo to engage on the issue. However, the Fukushima nuclear crisis in March 2011 is likely to make it extremely difficult for the Japanese government to relax rules on the export of nuclear technology for some time to come.

Another significant security issue is Japan's willingness to supply defence technology to India. Just as India has made access to US defence technology a threshold issue in the India–US relationship, India is placing significant pressure on the Japanese government to relax its restrictions on high-technology trade. The ability of Japan to supply defence technology to India is a regular point of discussion and in March 2007 Japan agreed to the creation of a so-called bilateral Japan–India 'Consultation Mechanism for High Technology Trade' to give consideration to relaxing Japan's restrictive rules regarding arms exports to India on a case by case basis. Like the nuclear issue, any easing of the longstanding restrictions on arms exports and sharing of defence-related technology by Japan represents a major taboo and like the nuclear issue, it will essentially be for the Japanese government to decide whether the strategic relationship with India has priority over domestic political considerations.

The most glaring structural weakness in the India–Japan strategic relationship is in the economic sphere. Tokyo's courting of a security relationship with India despite the lack of significant economic links has been called 'a remarkable case of the Japanese flag preceding trade and investment'.[94]

Despite persistent attempts by the Japanese government to encourage Japanese private investment in India since the early 1990s, Japanese business is, and seems likely to continue to be, wary of doing business there. The theoretical literature indicates that a close economic relationship is not an absolute prerequisite to a good political and security relationship.[95] However, one might argue that a closer economic relationship would at least help avoid a misalignment of interests, particularly in dealing with China, as was the case in the early 1960s. An anaemic economic relationship between Japan and India when placed against the overwhelming economic significance of China to Japan and the burgeoning trade relationship between China and India could place significant limitations on the alignment of Japan and India's interests, particularly in seeking to develop 'balanced' regional political and economic institutions. The lack of a substantial economic relationship could lead to fragility in the security relationship to the extent there is a disjunction between India and Japan's political and economic interests.

Through most of the twentieth century, Japanese businesses found India an unattractive place for investment as a result of high tariff barriers, an inefficient, obstructive and often corrupt Indian bureaucracy and legal system, restrictive labour laws and severe restrictions on repatriation of capital and profits. Underlying the weak economic relationship was a disconnect between Indian and Japanese business cultures. While Japanese successfully adapted to the business environments in Southeast Asia and China during the 1960s, 1970s and 1980s, they had great difficulties in adapting to the Indian business environment. This contributed to the inability or unwillingness of Japanese business to adapt to India the assembly–export business model that was so successful in Southeast Asia and China. Japan's experience stands in notable contrast with South Korean businesses which have been better able to adapt to the local business environment. South Korea has become a major economic force in India, with South Korean companies dominating the consumer whitegoods sector and developing manufacturing operations for worldwide export. This has led to a degree of 'bottom up' alignment of economic and political interests between India and South Korea.[96]

The focus on developing Indian economic links by Japanese political leaders since the early 1990s, and particularly since the turn of the century, has so far largely failed to reverse the relatively weak economic alignments. While Japanese investment in India has increased significantly in absolute terms, it remains extremely small relative to other Japanese investment destinations. Japanese investment in India over the period April 2000 to December 2009 aggregated US$3.6 billion or 4 per cent of total foreign direct investment in India. Japanese investment in India in the 10 years to 2007 represented a mere 0.7% of all Japanese foreign investment over that period (as compared with 26% invested in China). Bilateral trade too is small in relative terms. Bilateral trade between India and Japan for 2008/09 was US$10.9 billion and is growing at a rate of around 20–30 per cent per annum. (By way of comparison, Japan–China bilateral trade was US$232 billion in the year to November 2009.)

Nevertheless, a December 2009 survey indicated that Japanese businesses expect India to become a major trading partner over the next several years.[97]

The picture for private trade and investment between Japan and India contrasts with Japanese Official Development Aid (ODA) to India, where in recent years the Japanese government has made a concerted effort to give priority to the relationship. India overtook China as the largest destination of new Japanese ODA loan commitments in 2003. The Japanese government is continuing to use its ODA programme in an attempt to expand economic ties. Simultaneously with the signing of the Security Declaration, Japan announced an ODA package of US$4.6 billion in loans to help build a Mumbai–Delhi rail freight connection, the largest amount ever provided under Japanese ODA for a single project. However, suggestions that ODA should be directed towards security-related projects such as the upgrading of port and maritime infrastructure have not been implemented.[98] While an impressive indication of political commitment from the Japanese government, the focus on ODA-driven investment underlines the lack of major private Japanese investment in India as compared with Japan's economic competitors.

Both India and Japan have sought to encourage greater economic links through a bilateral Comprehensive Economic Partnership Agreement covering trade, investment and intellectual property rights, signed in February 2011. The agreement will eliminate tariffs on goods comprising 94 per cent of bilateral trade over 10 years and will assist Japan to compete in the Indian market with South Korea in auto and electronics sectors. However, given the history of the economic relationship over the last 60 years there may be doubts whether a free trade agreement would in itself make a major difference to economic relations between India and Japan.

The continuing weakness in the economic dimension of the relationship has led to the India–Japan relationship being described as having a 'top heavy security component (albeit, at present, more in intent than content)'.[99] Indian Prime Minister Manmohan Singh made no bones about this problem in an October 2008 visit to Tokyo, reminding his hosts of the paucity of Japan's economic links with India in comparison with its competitors. Singh pointed out that the *increase* in India's bilateral trade with China in the past year alone is more than the whole of India's *total* annual trade with Japan. Indian Foreign Secretary, Shiv Shankar Menon, described security and political cooperation as the *second* leg of the bilateral relationship and made it clear that the *first* leg, economic cooperation, was yet to realise its full potential.[100]

One Japanese initiative that could substantially alter the dynamics of the India–Japan economic relationship is the so-called Delhi–Mumbai Industrial Corridor (DMIC), which was the centerpiece of the visit of Prime Minister Yukio Hatoyama to India in December 2009. This ambitious project involves an attempt to create 24 new integrated industrial areas across six states between Delhi and Mumbai over the next 30 years in which major Japanese companies would be cornerstone investors. Initial construction will be undertaken by four consortiums selected by the Japanese government and led by

Toshiba, Mitsubishi, Hitachi and JGC. The DMIC is intended to involve the transfer of substantial Japanese manufacturing capacity to India, essentially as a hedge against overreliance by Japan on investments in China. One of the focuses of the project will be on 'digital' manufacturing, which marries India's software expertise with precision manufacturing. Connected with the DMIC is a dedicated rail freight corridor to run between Delhi and Mumbai. In March 2011, India proposed the establishment of a US$9 billion fund, jointly funded by India and Japan, as part of a projected total US$100 billion investment in the project. The Indian Commerce and Industry Minister, Anand Sharma, commented that once the project is completed, it would double India's industrial production and quadruple exports. Prime Minister Singh has claimed that the DMIC project will have a 'transformational impact' on both the Indian and Japanese economies.[101] However, the success of this massive project would not only require Japanese investors to overcome the longstanding cultural constraints that have inhibited the economic relationship, but would also require a major transformation of India's traditionally weak SME manufacturing sector necessary to support the large-scale manufacturing enterprises.[102]

Despite important weaknesses in the relationship, after many decades of strategic indifference the India–Japan relationship has developed remarkably over the last five years. Whereas India and Japan saw little reason to engage during the second half of the twentieth century (even if others may have sometimes discerned good reasons), they now perceive many reasons. This reflects a virtually simultaneous change in both India and Japan's strategic positions at the end of the twentieth century: Japan now sees itself as strategically vulnerable, with good cause to develop new relationships; India has a newfound confidence that has opened up its strategic options. A security relationship between them now has strong conceptual support within several constituencies in both Japan and India and has the potential to fulfil multiple strategic goals for each.

China looms large in the relationship and mutual perceptions of a 'China threat' are clearly strong motivations to develop the relationship as a regional balance. However the United States looms equally large. For Japan, a relationship with India could help strengthen its US alliance (through broadening Japan's relationships in the US security sphere) as well as potentially providing it with greater bargaining power within that relationship. For India, the relationship with Japan has been facilitated by its closer relationship with the United States. However, a security relationship with Japan, either embedded in the US security relationship or, as some in New Delhi dream, loosened from it, can potentially increase India's influence and help in achieving India's objectives of strategic autonomy and a multipolar region.

Despite some differences in objectives, a growing alignment of interests has broken through their history of strategic indifference. One might argue that the foundations exist for a potential 'grand bargain' between India and Japan. This could potentially involve a loose coalition to balance against China, a partnership to develop regional economic, political and security structures and possibly even an implicit recognition of spheres of influence in the Indian and Pacific Oceans. Although Japan currently seems to have little clear strategic direction, there is good reason to believe that the relationship will continue to develop.

6 Indochina
India's political partnership with Vietnam

Southeast Asia is the main focus of India's strategic ambitions in the Asia Pacific. For many centuries Indian civilisation was a leading cultural and religious influence in Southeast Asia as the names of Indochina and Indonesia attest. In modern times, India has claimed a special role in Indochina. For more than 40 years, India has stood with Vietnam, its 'most trusted friend and ally',[1] in resisting external domination. Over the last decade, India has been seeking – with only limited success – to use Vietnam as a key partner in its security ambitions in the Asia Pacific. But while Vietnam wants to develop India as political and economic balance to China, it does not yet see India as a credible security partner.[2]

The long-running political partnership with Vietnam

The political relationship between India and Vietnam over the last half a century or more was built on an ideological foundation of pan-Asian nationalism reinforced by shared struggles against US and Chinese hegemony over Indochina. During the 1940s, Indian and Vietnamese nationalists were at the forefront of independence struggles in Asia and in the immediate post-war years, Ho Chi Minh looked to Nehru and the Indian leadership for support. This was forthcoming in moral if not material terms.[3] Although Nehru's support for the Vietnamese nationalists was initially tempered by his suspicions of communism, Nehru was the first foreign leader to visit Hanoi on the establishment of the separate North Vietnamese state in October 1954 and his public embrace of Ho Chi Minh reportedly provided him 'incalculable prestige'.[4]

In the 1950s, India saw itself as having an important role to play in securing the independence of Vietnam through the negotiation of the French withdrawal from Indochina. Although not an official party to the Geneva Peace talks in 1954 (largely due to US opposition), the Indians made significant efforts to insert themselves into the discussions, and the role of Indian Foreign Minister Krishna Menon in the talks has been described as 'ubiquitous'.[5] The Indians saw it as essentially a process of applying to Indochina the principles of *Panchsheel* (the five principles of coexistence or non-interference developed by

Nehru, which later came to form the basis of nonalignment). The Indians sought, as far as possible, to limit the roles of China, the United States and France in the region. India took the job of overseeing the implementation of the Geneva agreements through the International Control Commission which had the job of supervising the separation of rival forces, dealing with refugees and overseeing proposed nation-wide elections.

India's relationship with North Vietnam during the 1950s and 1960s was not entirely smooth. Arguably, New Delhi saw its primary interest as limiting Chinese influence in Indochina in priority to resisting the United States. In his memoirs, US Vice President Hubert Humphrey claimed that during a visit to New Delhi in 1966, Indira Gandhi admitted to him that although domestic politics required her to criticise the United States, she was glad the Americans were there to resist China.[6] However, as the 1960s progressed, the Indians increasingly believed that the administration in the South would collapse without American support, which would one day be withdrawn. It was therefore prudent and sensible to cultivate relations with the North rather than the South.[7] As a political rift developed between Beijing and Hanoi through the 1960s, Hanoi leaned more and more towards New Delhi and India reciprocated, viewing Vietnam as a major long-term regional actor because of its intrinsic moral and material strength. During the late 1960s, Indira Gandhi, aware of the increasing divergence of North Vietnamese and Chinese views, took the opportunity to draw North Vietnam into the anti-Chinese camp. However, the relationship was still driven more by a mutual desire to keep Indochina free from superpower alignment and from shared ideals of Asian nationalism than by overt hostility to China.[8] By April 1975, when the fall of Saigon was greeted with thunderous applause in the Indian Parliament, New Delhi and Hanoi had developed a mutually supportive political relationship that has continued for several decades.

China played a significant role in India's strategic calculations in Indochina. Indira Gandhi reportedly believed that if India were to become the paramount power in South Asia, it must prevent a Chinese advance into Southeast Asia. According to Gandhi, a strong, anti-Chinese Indochina, led by Vietnam, would guard the flank of India's sphere of influence in South Asia.[9] During the 1970s and 1980s, there were influential calls in New Delhi to create an India–Vietnam axis to contain China, in the nature of the 'all-weather friendship' between China and Pakistan. In 1979, India's long-time senior diplomat and foreign secretary, T.N. Kaul, was dispatched on a 'private' visit to Hanoi and later argued that India should enter into Soviet-style 'Friendship Treaties' with Vietnam and other Indochinese states in order to 'protect' Indochina from great power rivalry.[10] However, India shied away from developing any security relationship with Vietnam and also refused to provide it with assistance in developing an indigenous arms manufacturing capability.[11] Whether or not a close security relationship may have been possible during the 1970s and 1980s, India did not pursue the opportunity and security relations were limited to information sharing arrangements.[12] Indian support for Vietnam remained firmly at a politico-diplomatic level even after the Chinese invasion of Vietnam in February 1979.

India's diplomatic support for Vietnam, in opposing US hegemony in Indochina in the 1960s and 1970s and Chinese hegemony in the 1970s and 1980s, came at a significant cost in India's political relations with the United States, China and much of Southeast Asia. Indian support for Hanoi during the Vietnam War was an important factor in the development of a hostile relationship between India and the United States during the 1960s and 1970s. As early as 1965, India's position on Vietnam led to US President Johnson postponing the planned visit to the United States by Indian Prime Minister Shastri, and a decade later New Delhi's glee at the fall of Saigon in 1975 led to the cancellation of a planned visit by President Ford. India's later support for Vietnam over Cambodia merely confirmed India's place in US policy perspectives as a Soviet fellow-traveller.

As mentioned, India's support for Vietnam also came at significant cost to its relationship with China. In late 1978, following a series of provocations, Vietnam invaded Cambodia to remove the Chinese-backed Pol Pot government and install its own regime. Although Vietnam was not without some justification, its actions were seen by many as a bid by Hanoi to dominate Indochina. In February 1979 China responded by conducting a month-long limited invasion of Vietnam, claiming it wished to 'teach Vietnam a lesson' over Cambodia. The Chinese invasion, which occurred during the visit of Indian Foreign Minister Vajpayee to Beijing, had a profound effect on Sino-Indian relations. For New Delhi, China's actions evoked bitter memories of India's defeat by China in 1962, which Chinese Premier Zhou Enlai had famously claimed was to 'teach India a lesson'. The Indian Prime Minister, Morarji Desai, expressed his 'profound shock and distress' at the invasion and the Indian press described it as 'perfidy' and 'studied insult' by China.[13] Whether the timing of the invasion during Vajpayee's visit was intended to achieve tactical surprise,[14] was a reminder of Chinese military power or an attempt to create suspicion between India and Vietnam, it seems unlikely to have been a coincidence, particularly given the care with which the Chinese had given prior notification of the attack to the Americans. In all events, it pointed to the extraordinary disregard held by the Chinese for their relations with India. The Indian visit was cut short and Vajpayee returned to Delhi, humiliated. The planned return visit by Chinese Foreign Minister Huang Hua to New Delhi, scheduled for August 1980, was also postponed by almost a year after India recognised the Vietnamese-backed Cambodian government a few weeks earlier.[15] In January 2001, Vajpayee, now Prime Minister, repaid the diplomatic insult from 1979 by pointedly keeping Chinese Premier Li Peng waiting for two days in New Delhi while he completed an official visit to Vietnam.

India's support for Vietnam also came at significant diplomatic cost in Southeast Asia, where Vietnam's actions were seen by many as part of Soviet-inspired designs on the region. In 1980, in the face of considerable ASEAN hostility to Vietnam's adventure in Cambodia, India cancelled discussions over India's elevation as a full ASEAN dialogue partner and days later officially recognised the Vietnam-installed Cambodian government (becoming the first non-communist state to do so). India's support for Vietnam was widely interpreted in Southeast Asia as proof of it toeing the Moscow–Hanoi line. Whether this was true or India was primarily concerned with resisting Chinese influence in Indochina, it was not able to convince the ASEAN states that China represented a greater threat than Vietnam. For their part, Indian policy-makers viewed ASEAN's stance on Cambodia as not based on real fears of Vietnamese expansionism, but as merely playing an anti-Soviet card to curry favour with the United States. Undoubtedly, as a result of its relationship with Vietnam, India's opportunity to form a 'special' relationship with ASEAN was lost and its relationships in Southeast Asia remained cool for most of the 1980s. India's unsuccessful attempts during the 1980s to facilitate a Vietnamese withdrawal from Cambodia, without strengthening China's regional position, continued to place it at odds with most ASEAN states which, by and large, feared Vietnam as a Soviet regional proxy more than China. It was only with the collapse of the Soviet Union that India's relationship with Vietnam has become a potential asset in its political and security relationships in the Asia Pacific.[16]

India's attempts to develop a post-Cold War security relationship with Vietnam

It took almost a decade after the end of the Cold War for India and Vietnam to seek to revitalise and extend their bilateral relationship beyond their Cold War and anti-colonial camaraderie. This occurred only after both India and Vietnam had taken significant steps to develop other economic and political relationships in the region.

The end of the Cold War forced a major change in Vietnam's strategic thinking. For Vietnam, like India, the collapse of the Soviet Union meant the loss of its major arms supplier and its strategic guarantor against China. However, the end of the Cold War also facilitated a resolution of the impasse over Vietnam's occupation of Cambodia and consequent room for improvement of relations with ASEAN states and China. Vietnam moved quickly in the new strategic environment to stabilise its regional security relationships, beginning with Southeast Asia. Vietnam signed the ASEAN Treaty of Amity and Cooperation in 1992 and was invited to join ASEAN in 1995. Beginning in the early 1990s, Vietnam also made efforts to repair relations with China. A 'good neighbourliness' treaty was signed in February 1999, leading to the resolution of their land border dispute in December 1999, and an agreement delimiting the maritime boundary in the Gulf of Tonkin in December 2000. Boundary disputes in the South China Sea remain a major source of disagreement, with periods of heightened tensions, largely in response to Chinese actions.

Despite significant progress in stabilising its relations in the region, sharp ideological divisions remained between Vietnamese reformists and conservatives over whether China should be viewed as Vietnam's last remaining socialist friend, and the extent of Vietnam's relations with non-socialist states.[17] Vietnam's policy of re-engagement with China also reflected the centuries-long pendulum between obeisance and outright hostility towards China. As one Vietnamese official remarked, 'Remember, after defeating the Chinese we always sent tribute.'[18] In the late 1990s, the balance had swung towards paying 'due respect' towards China and acceptance of a position as 'Little Brother' in the relationship. Vietnam's leaders took the view that strategic stability was a precondition to economic development and that it would be better to settle territorial disputes sooner rather than later, given the continuing rise of China's power. As one observer put it: 'Economics has replaced security as the central concern of the normalcy era.'[19] The increased importance placed on 'economic security' within the context of national security would also be played out in Vietnam's relationship with India.[20]

In April 2001, a new Vietnamese Communist Party General Secretary, Nong Duc Manh, re-emphasised a policy of seeking a diversification of international relations. Vietnam had already moved to revitalise its relationship with Russia, declaring a 'new strategic partnership' between them in 1998, and now also sought (if hesitantly) to improve relations with the United States, Japan and India. An enhanced relationship with India may have been seen as not just helping to provide a measure of balance with China, but also in providing a balance between the conflicting pressures coming from the United States and Russia.[21] However, in hedging its relationships, the Vietnamese have avoided any explicit discussion of any threat from China and continued to pay public respect towards its socialist brother.

Consistent with moves towards a diversification of international relations, the Vietnamese military were also looking for diversification in arms procurement and training beyond its traditional partner, Russia. Despite a significant amount of military-to-military contact between the Vietnamese and Chinese militaries since the end of the Cold War, China was not considered an appropriate weapons procurement partner at least until 2005.[22] While Russia and former Soviet republics would remain Vietnam's predominant arms suppliers, India, with its large inventory of Soviet-designed weapons and indigenous defence industry, also seemed to be a good source of weapons and training. The Vietnamese military had been pursuing a defence supply and training relationship with India since the mid-1990s and was eager to develop closer military-to-military relations.[23]

The first significant steps in expanding India–Vietnam relations beyond the traditional political relationship were taken in 2000 at the instigation of the right-wing BJP-led government under Indian Prime Minister Vajpayee. During a visit by Vietnamese Prime Minister Phan Van Khai to New Delhi in January 2000, the Indian Defence Minister, George Fernandes, called for a renewed political relationship with a strong security focus, describing Vietnam in rather extraordinary terms as India's 'most trusted friend and ally'.[24] The Indians proposed to develop India's naval presence in the South China Sea through access to the Cam Ranh Bay naval and air base (discussed later) and joint defence training and the supply of advanced weapons to Vietnam. The Indians and Vietnamese formalised a wide-ranging defence cooperation agreement providing for regular exchange of intelligence, joint coastguard training to combat piracy, jungle warfare and counterinsurgency training for the Indian army (something particularly useful in dealing with the Naga insurgency in northeast India), repair of Vietnamese MiG aircraft, training of Vietnamese pilots and Indian assistance on small and medium arms production. Fernandes declared that India could supply Vietnam with not only warships, but also anti-ship and air defence missiles.[25] Pursuant to the agreement, Hindustan Aeronautics and Bharat Electronics were contracted to repair and overhaul up to 125 of the VPAF's Russian-built MiG-21s, including new avionics and radar to support Russian anti-aircraft missiles.[26] The Indian Navy also supplied much-needed spares for Vietnamese Osa II-class missile gunboats and other Russian-built warships and the Vietnamese requested submarine training for its navy.

While Hanoi made steps towards closer security relations with New Delhi, they remained cautious, concerned not to upset the newly found stability in relations with China. It was only in early 2003 that the General Secretary Nong Duc Manh yielded to pressure from the integrationist camp within the Vietnamese Communist Party to enter a 'strategic relationship' with India.[27] This resulted in the 'Joint Declaration on the Comprehensive Cooperation Framework' in May 2003, which included commitments to regular high-level meetings, close cooperation in international fora and gradual steps to expand cooperation in security and defence. At the same time, the Vietnamese decided to pursue what they called a 'reliable partnership' with Japan and later that year made significant steps to improve political ties with the United States. In recent years, Vietnam has increasingly used the United States to balance China. However, the Vietnam–India relationship has developed at a much slower pace than India had hoped.

For its part, India has turned out to be a less than reliable weapons procurement partner, proving itself often uncompetitive, bureaucratic and politically hesitant in supplying weapons to Vietnam. While Vietnam was initially keen on sourcing spares for Soviet-vintage equipment from India, the Indians found themselves undercut by cheap suppliers from Belarus, Ukraine and Russia. Other deals have been lost through payment-related problems and Indian bureaucratic bottlenecks. One Indian observer complained of excessive bureaucracy coupled with highly complex and uncoordinated procedures required to export military goods.[28] There was also a significant element of political caution on the part of India, particularly in relation to the supply of advanced missile technology. Vietnam has formally requested the supply of Indian Prithvi intermediate range ballistic missiles and BrahMos anti-ship cruise missiles (both of which can be supplied under the Missile Technology

Control Regime).[29] The supply of BrahMos missiles was blocked by India's Russian partners. Although the Indians reportedly agreed 'in principle' to the sale of Prithvi missiles, they have since stalled.[30] The Vietnamese are believed to have indicated their displeasure at delays in the supply of Prithvi missiles through the purchase by the Vietnamese Ministry of Public Security of a small number of small arms from Pakistan in 2007 and 2009, despite 'discreet' protests from India.

As will be discussed later, bilateral discussions after 2003 have increasingly placed greater emphasis on political and economic aspects of the relationship and less on security aspects. The Congress-led Indian government, elected in May 2004, was much less assertive in regional security matters than its BJP predecessors and the Vietnamese too sought greater focus on an economic partnership. As a result, the joint statement following the October 2004 visit to Hanoi by Indian Foreign Minister, Natwar Singh, did not include the references to security and defence cooperation that were so prominent in the 2003 Cooperation Framework. India and Vietnam have nevertheless generally continued their tradition of mutual political support. Vietnam has continued its support of India's position on Kashmir, India's status as a nuclear weapons state, and India's bid for a permanent seat on the UN Security Council. Vietnam took the lead in blocking Pakistan's bid for membership of the ASEAN Regional Forum.[31] India also supported Vietnam in its recent successful bid for a non-permanent Security Council seat. However, Vietnam's unwillingness to publicly support India's membership of the East Asia Summit in 2005 – leaving it to Singapore and Indonesia to give their public support – left some Indian diplomats questioning the depth of the relationship.

The Indo-Vietnamese relationship has been complemented by India's relationships elsewhere in Indochina. India has longstanding links with Laos, which has been historically close to Vietnam although increasingly under Chinese economic influence. This has included Indian assistance in training the Laotian army and air force.[32] It also has nascent security links with Cambodia, which has traditionally been backed by China.[33] In November 2000, India and Thailand sponsored the establishment of the Mekong Ganga Cooperation with the ostensible purpose of promoting greater east–west transport connectivity between South Asia and Indochina, as well as regional tourism, culture and education. Its members include India, Burma, Thailand, Vietnam and the other Indochinese states. China, a major Mekong river state, was conspicuous by its absence. Indian Foreign Minister Jaswant Singh claimed that the initiative 'was not aimed at China or a means of increasing India's power projection'.[34] China has shown interest in joining the grouping several times, but has made no formal request (presumably reflecting a desire by the majority of members not to include China). The Indians continue to emphasise the non-security and even non-economic focus of the MGC grouping, describing it as 'engaging India's civilisational neighbours'.[35] Although it has had few concrete achievements, it remains for both India and

Vietnam a potentially useful regional talk shop among China's southern neighbours. China has also taken steps to cultivate a separate grouping of Mekong River states;[36] however, no formal Indochina regional grouping which includes China has yet been established.

Despite slow progress in a number of areas and reduced priorities in overhauling the Vietnamese armed forces, both the Indians and the Vietnamese are continuing to develop their security relationship. A 'New Strategic Partnership' was declared during a July 2007 visit by Vietnam Prime Minister Nguyen Tan Dun to New Delhi and the third bilateral Strategic Dialogue held in November 2007 decided to step up training of junior-level officers, hold annual security dialogues and share other expertise. This was followed by a flurry of official visits to Vietnam by the Indian Defence Minister A.K. Antony and senior Indian officers and to India by Vietnamese signatories. In July 2010, Russia announced the sale of 20 Sukhoi aircraft and six Kilo class submarines to Vietnam. If those acquisitions proceed, it is likely that India will play a significant role in the provision of training and maintenance services for these platforms.

The role of Vietnam in India's strategic ambitions in the South China Sea

One of the most interesting and intriguing aspects of India's recent attempts to create a security relationship with Vietnam involves India's request in 2000 for rights to the Cam Ranh Bay naval and air base. Indian strategists have long recognised the potential role of Vietnam in controlling the South China Sea and blocking Chinese naval penetration of the Indian Ocean,[37] and this was not the first time that the Indians had sought to establish a naval presence in the South China Sea. In the early 1990s, there had reportedly been preliminary talks between Indian and Vietnamese officers about the use of Cam Ranh Bay by Indian warships[38] and/or an Indian naval squadron of Bear maritime reconnaissance aircraft.[39]

When George Fernandes visited Vietnam in March 2000, he proffered India's capabilities not only in policing sea lanes of communication in the South China Sea but, significantly, also India's capability in 'containing' local conflicts. In referring to the South China Sea, he stated: 'A strong India, economically and militarily well endowed, will be a very solid agent to see that the sea lanes are not disturbed and that conflict situations are contained.'[40] He was, of course, referring to the longstanding disputes between Vietnam and other littoral states with China over maritime boundaries in the South China Sea. The disputed maritime boundaries in the South China Sea remain one of Asia's military flashpoints, and represent a clear and continuing strategic divide between China and Vietnam. As recently as 1988, the Vietnamese and Chinese navies had clashed in the Spratly Islands, when several Vietnamese naval vessels were sunk. There were further naval confrontations in the mid-1990s and in 2007, the Chinese PLA navy sank an 'armed' Vietnamese fishing boat as part of a dispute about the grant of oil exploration blocks. China has increased its assertiveness over its claims in recent years, including pressuring oil companies not to conduct exploration in Vietnamese-claimed waters and establishing an administrative body for the Spratly and Paracel islands.

However, it should have come as no surprise to the Indians when the Vietnamese turned down their request to use Cam Ranh Bay. It is widely understood that the Vietnamese consider Cam Ranh Bay as a strategic trump card of great domestic and international political sensitivity. The Soviets were granted rights to Cam Ranh Bay in 1978 as part of the Vietnam–Soviet Friendship Treaty, which was signed by Vietnam only when it became clear that they would require significant Soviet assistance in dealing with both Pol Pot and an increasingly threatening China. While the base was provided as *quid pro quo* for considerable Soviet military and economic support, the Vietnamese quickly decided that they gained insufficient benefit from the Soviet presence. By the early 1990s, the Vietnamese were actively trying to evict the Russians, and saw their complete departure in 2002.

If the Indians believed in the early 1990s or in 2000 that they might be the natural post-Cold War inheritors of the strategic mantle of the Soviets in the South China Sea, they were mistaken. Since the late 1980s, Vietnam has sought to use Cam Ranh Bay in what has been called a 'subtle game' of balancing relations with the United States and China and seeking to increase Vietnam's strategic options.[41] During this period the Vietnamese have tried to use Cam Ranh Bay as leverage in its relations with the United States and Japan including as a carrot to normalise relations,[42] obtain aid and to extract promises in relation to their support of local opposition groups.[43] Even before the final departure of the Russians, the US navy was flirting with the possibility of returning to Cam Ranh Bay, and the idea of US access or prepositioning rights (in the style of US access rights in Singapore) has been a regular item on the agenda of US–Vietnamese discussions.

In August 2010, China's elevation of its maritime claims to be a 'core national interest' on par with Taiwan and Tibet, significantly altered the security dynamics in the South China Sea. Vietnam responded principally by turning to the United States. At an ASEAN Regional Forum meeting in Hanoi in July 2010, US Secretary of State, Hillary Rodham Clinton, vigorously opposed China's claims. At the same time, a US–Vietnam agreement on civil nuclear cooperation was announced, along with a visit by US aircraft carrier USS *Washington* to Vietnamese waters. In October 2010, Vietnam announced that facilities at Cam Ranh Bay would be available for use by all navies on a commercial basis and in June 2011 announced that the Indian Navy would be permitted to dock at the small port of Nha Trang in southern Vietnam (some 40 km north of Cam Ranh Bay). This is seen as an effective way to improve Vietnam's strategic position vis-à-vis China without being overly provocative, in that it would attract several navies that would help keep China's strategic ambitions in check. There was no suggestion that Vietnam would allow any on-shore physical presence. Russia will assist in partially upgrading facilities at Cam Ranh Bay. An agreement with India was also announced in which India could make use of facilities, along with other navies, in return for assistance in naval logistics capabilities. While India is likely to make regular port visits to Cam Ranh Bay, it will be very much a secondary player in the South China Sea.

The dragon is scratching away and the elephant must move fast: economics comes to the fore

Over the past several years, the India–Vietnam relationship has also increasingly focused on mutual economic interests, particularly so following the announcement of a 'New Strategic Partnership' between them in July 2007. The shift of the relationship primarily into the economic dimension reflects India's increasing economic integration into the Asia Pacific, as well as a response to widely held fears of Chinese economic dominance of Vietnam and the wider region. It is something that the Vietnamese have been emphasising to the Indians for some time. As one senior Vietnamese Foreign Ministry official commented, 'The dragon is scratching away and the elephant must move fast.'[44]

Although Vietnam began its process of economic liberalisation and globalisation later than India, its recent economic performance has been impressive, with annual economic growth of around 7–9 per cent and annual export growth of around 25 per cent. Economic growth has been driven to a significant extent by economic integration with ASEAN and trade with China. Its location in the Asia Pacific in proximity to Japanese and South Korean markets, low wage rates and an autocratic political system make it an attractive destination for foreign investment. Nevertheless, Vietnam remains relatively poor and many years behind India in economic development. As a result, India's economic relationship with Vietnam is in many ways the opposite of its relationship with capital-rich East Asian states such as Japan, South Korea and Singapore. Vietnam looks to India as a potential investor and provider of technology and manufactured goods. India–Vietnam bilateral trade is growing strongly (though from a low base) from a nominal US$72 million in 1995 to over US$2 billion in 2008. In the reverse of India's normal trading position in Asia, the India–Vietnam balance of trade is strongly in favour of India. The Vietnamese are impatient to gain greater access to the Indian market through a reduction of tariff barriers over agricultural and manufactured goods.

Indian FDI in Vietnam is growing, with announced investments over the last several years including a US$5 billion steel plant to be built by Tata Steel. It is uncertain whether this and other announced projects will come to fruition. India and Vietnam have targeted increased future Indian investment in the Vietnamese energy sector, including in the strategically sensitive oil and gas sector and in nuclear power generation. Some of the proposed and targeted investments have strong political overtones, including the grant to Indian state-owned ONGC Videsh Limited of major gas production blocks in areas of the South China Sea claimed by China. The proposed acquisition announced in 2010 by ONGC of BP's Vietnamese energy assets (including its offshore gas exploration and production fields and pipeline and electricity generation assets), if finalised, will further embed Indian interests in Vietnam's territorial claims in the South China Sea.[45] India has also been a strong supporter of the development of civil nuclear technology by Vietnam since the 1970s, and in 2002 funded the establishment of a joint nuclear research centre in southern Vietnam.[46] However, India's participation in the development of a civilian power industry is likely to be limited and non-exclusive.[47]

The Vietnamese have given consistent diplomatic support for Indian economic integration into the Asia Pacific, reflecting their concern about regional economic dominance by China. The Vietnamese are anxious about Chinese domination of multilateral arrangements, and were reportedly privately unenthusiastic about the China–ASEAN Free Trade Area, established in 2010.[48] There were also concerns about a proposed East Asian economic community which would not include India. Vietnam publicly supported India's alternative 'Arc of Advantage and Prosperity' proposal for an Asian economic community that included India. However, it is apparent to many that an Asia-wide free trade area is many years away. Of more immediate concern, particularly to Vietnam, is to put in place a bilateral free trade agreement with India, including access to the Indian market and facilitation of Indian FDI. In July 2007, the Vietnamese proposed negotiations on a bilateral free trade agreement, but the Indians, as beneficiaries of the trade imbalance, have since stalled.

Some might see the failure of India to open its markets to Vietnam and actively pursue an economic partnership as being short-sighted in view of India's broader ambitions in the South China Sea. While a long-term political partnership is likely to continue, the experience this century suggests that the relationship needs to be placed on a more comprehensive footing. Vietnam is enjoying a relatively stable security relationship with China and, at least in the short term, is likely to give priority to economic development over the development of new security partnerships.

Perspectives on India's strategic relationship with Vietnam

The story of the attempt by India to inject a significant security dimension into the India–Vietnam relationship is an interesting one. For decades, the political partnership between India and Vietnam has provided a limited exception to the strategic separation between East and South Asia. It seems likely in the long term that the relationship will grow in significance – if nothing else as a result of India's closer engagement with the region as a whole. The relationship is underpinned by more than six decades of anti-colonialism, pan-Asian nationalism and fiercely independent foreign policies. Their shared concerns about Chinese hegemony are derived from their past experience of Chinese military aggression and fears of future economic domination. These shared perspectives provide a potentially strong foundation for the relationship. However, the failure of India to develop a substantive security relationship with Vietnam over the last decade also highlights some of the limitations of New Delhi as a regional security partner, including its reliability as an arms supplier, its limited credibility in projecting naval power beyond its immediate neighbourhood and its failure to fully understand the security dynamics of East Asia.

There can be little doubt that a substantial factor in India's strategic calculus was to strengthen Vietnam's military power as a partial balance to China. Numerous Indian strategic commentators have pointed to the parallels between China's strategic relationships with Pakistan and Burma, and India's relationship with Vietnam. Bharat Karnad, a noted Indian nuclear strategist, claims that 'by cultivating a resolute Vietnam as a close regional ally and security partner in the manner China has done Pakistan, India can pay Beijing back in the same coin.'[49] These views contrast sharply with those of Hanoi. Although Vietnam is seeking to diversify its international relationships, it is usually only willing to do so in a context of overall deference towards China. As C. Raja Mohan commented, 'An acute sensitivity to the changing balance of power in Asia guides the current Vietnamese strategy of befriending the US and Japan and intensifying security cooperation with India without antagonizing China.'[50] According to Mohan, Vietnam has the history and self-confidence to play the game of *realpolitik*, something which by implication India is less able to do. During the heightened tensions in the South China Sea in 2010, Vietnam moved decisively to involve the United States, a clear signal that Hanoi sees the United States as the key player in limiting China's assertiveness in the South China Sea. Nevertheless, it is also careful to act to avoid unnecessary provocation towards China. In seeking Vietnam as a balancing partner against China, India may have underestimated the influence of the long tradition of formal deference that Vietnam has shown to China and failed to understand that Vietnam's relationship with the Soviet Union during the latter half of the Cold War was an exception to this tradition. India must take this into account in its dealings with Vietnam and elsewhere in Southeast Asia.

It seems that India's relationship with Vietnam will always have a strong political element, although to what extent that is translated into a direct security relationship remains to be seen. India may see its interests as best served in focusing on an economic partnership with Vietnam which promotes Vietnam's economic development and India's influence in the region.

7 Archipelagic Southeast Asia
India's strategic relationships with Singapore, Malaysia and Indonesia

Archipelagic Southeast Asia, which principally consists of Indonesia, Malaysia and Singapore, forms the gateway between the Indian and Pacific Oceans. Over the last two decades, India has sought to develop a strategic role in the area as a counterweight to China and to provide it with a strategic stepping stone into the Pacific Ocean. Singapore has quickly positioned itself as the hub of India's strategic engagement in the region. India has also been trying, with varying degrees of success, to improve its relations with Malaysia and Indonesia. What are the future trajectories of these relationships? What are the potential implications for an Indian sphere of influence that reaches into Southeast Asia?

India's hesitant strategic role in archipelagic Southeast Asia

India has long been seen as having a potentially important strategic role in archipelagic Southeast Asia. However, for decades following independence, India's relationship with the region was characterised by indifference and lost opportunities. In renewing its role in the region, India is still making up for these lost opportunities.

In colonial times the British took an expansive view of India's strategic role throughout the Indian Ocean and Southeast Asia. The British Raj administered British possessions from the Persian Gulf to Singapore and employed Indian troops to enforce *Pax Britannica* from Beijing to Singapore to Africa. Singapore, in particular, was identified as a key connection with British imperial interests in the Pacific and as an eastern bulwark for the security of British India. Early Indian strategists such as K.M. Panikkar also had a clear understanding of the significance of Southeast Asia in the security of India. Panikkar advocated that a newly independent India should create a 'steel ring' of naval bases throughout the Indian Ocean and proposed that India and Indonesia, as the local maritime powers, would need to take joint responsibility for the security of Singapore.[1]

These perspectives on the importance of archipelagic Southeast Asia were largely lost at India's independence. Nehruvian strategic doctrine eschewed a direct security role for India outside South Asia. India also refused to recognise the legitimacy of colonial-era security linkages between South and Southeast Asia. Instead it saw its regional interests as limited to (largely ineffective) efforts to minimise the intrusion of other major powers into Southeast Asia. Nehru gave relations with Southeast Asia a particularly low priority and in the Indian diplomatic service all regional postings there were classified as 'category C', the least desirable and important in the diplomatic service hierarchy. Nehru had particular contempt for Western-leaning governments of Southeast Asia, calling them 'Coca Cola governments', and he discouraged attempts to engage with them over their security concerns.[2] While Nehru resented the growing US strategic and cultural influence in Southeast Asia, he was also unwilling to take active steps to counter it through cultivating India's own relationships in the region. As a result, India abdicated any leadership role in the area and only really sought to exert its influence in negative terms, such as its emphatic rejection of SEATO and other Western-sponsored security arrangements.[3] Although Nehru's disdain for the concerns of Southeast Asian states was progressively moderated under Indira Gandhi and successive Indian leaders, the basic temper of the relationship had been established and would to some extent remain until the early 1990s.

Consistent with its nonaligned principles, India refused to participate in any regional security arrangements in Southeast Asia throughout the Cold War. Through the late 1960s, there were several proposals (including from Singapore and Malaysia)[4] for India to join in collective defence arrangements to counter Chinese subversion and fears of a 'power vacuum' following the British withdrawal east of Suez. Following the first Chinese Lop Nur nuclear test in October 1964, Singapore's Chief Minister, Lee Kuan Yew, reportedly suggested to visiting Indian dignitaries and journalists that India should also explode a nuclear bomb, 'at least for the sake of Southeast Asia, even if she wanted to throw it into the sea later'.[5] Lee later proposed that India should adopt an 'Asian Monroe Doctrine' to prevent 'poaching' in Asia.[6] New Delhi disregarded all these proposals. To Southeast Asians, India's persistent downplaying of regional concerns and statements about the uselessness of military alliances seemed callous, incredible and unrealistic.[7] Lee reportedly told friends that India was 'living in a dream world'.[8]

While New Delhi opposed security alliances or treaties *a priori*, there were also important differences in perceptions of the ideological or military threat posed by China – many in Southeast Asia saw a Chinese threat primarily in terms of ideological subversion, while the Indians saw Chinese expansionism primarily in territorial terms, driven by an unfortunate distortion of Chinese nationalism. New Delhi saw China as a conventional military threat to India, but not to Southeast Asia. The Indians also saw themselves as hardly capable of providing for their own security, let alone acting as a regional security provider. As the junior Indian Foreign Minister, B.R. Bhagat, argued in the Indian parliament in April 1968:

> If there was a defence agreement [with Southeast Asia] it would only mean India committing her manpower to the defence of areas which is

beyond our capacity at present ... If we dispersed our efforts and took on responsibilities that we are not capable of shouldering, it would not only weaken our own defence but would create a false sense of security and might even provoke a greater tension in the area.[9]

Some Southeast Asian states, such as Singapore, also reportedly tried to encourage India to join ASEAN upon its formation in 1967, perhaps with a view to finding a balance with large states within that grouping. However, others such as Indonesia were not in favour of India's inclusion, possibly for the same reason. India, suspicious of a possible security dimension to ASEAN, declined any tentative approaches regarding its participation.[10]

India's move towards a security relationship with the Soviet Union in the late 1960s further reduced its interest in the security of maritime Southeast Asia, although it continued to regard Indochina as within its sphere of influence. At about the same time, the balance of strategic and economic interests of many Southeast Asian states also shifted decisively towards the Asia Pacific and the United States. As has been discussed previously, Indira Gandhi's refusal in 1980 to oppose what many saw as aggression by Vietnam in Cambodia brought India's standing in Southeast Asia to its lowest point. Singapore and Thailand, in particular, took a hardline stand on the Vietnamese actions, seeing them as a major test of the principle of sovereignty of small states, even if run by a despised regime such as the Khmer Rouge. India's support for Vietnam and its relationship with the Soviet Union would bedevil political relations between India and ASEAN states throughout the 1980s.

While India was widely perceived as not contributing to the security of Southeast Asia through the Cold War, it was rarely seen as a potential security threat. In the late 1980s however, India's naval expansion plans prompted concerns from several ASEAN states over its intentions. These concerns were heightened following Indian military interventions in Sri Lanka (1987) and the Maldives (1988). In the 1970s, Indonesia had extracted an informal promise from India that it would not provide the Soviet navy with facilities in the Andaman Sea. However, by the mid-1980s there was open concern in Indonesian military circles both about India's naval expansion programme and the possible use by Soviet submarines of Indian naval facilities at Great Nicobar Island (which lies about 150 km from Sumatra). An Indonesian military commander claimed that there had been 20 sightings of Soviet submarines roaming in Indonesian waters and that they came from the Indian base at Nicobar island. This prompted an angry response from the Indian Ambassador to Indonesia that there were no 'Soviet bases' on Indian territory.[11] Singaporean Prime Minister, Goh Chok Tong, publicly questioned India's intentions in Southeast Asia following reports of India's naval expansion plans. The Malaysian Defence Minister, Tengku Rithauddeen, commented that

> we would still like to see an Indian assurance that it will not use force against neighbouring countries ... [Malaysia] hoped that New Delhi would

not go to the extent of flexing its military muscle beyond the Indian Ocean or attempt to control the gateway to the Straits of Malacca.[12]

According to some reports, the Indonesian Chief of Naval Staff visited New Delhi in 1989 to raise concerns about the proposed expansion of facilities at Great Nicobar Island, and this may have contributed to New Delhi shelving its plans.[13] Some in New Delhi saw Southeast Asian concerns as inspired by Australia and intended either to obstruct India's efforts to improve relations in Southeast Asia or to justify increases in its own defence spending.[14]

The collapse of the Soviet Union in 1991 led to a major reassessment by India of its political and economic relationship with Southeast Asia. India's 'Look East' policy, announced in 1992, quickly focused on convincing Southeast Asians that India was now a welcoming environment for foreign investors. ASEAN states were largely receptive to India's approaches and welcomed India into many regional organisations. Although the engagement was initially focused on economic links, India made it clear that it also sought a closer security engagement with ASEAN. As Indian Prime Minister Rao declared in 1994:

> India would like to be part of the evolving security framework in the region to assuage doubts about arising [sic] from its potential military might as to contribute to the security edifice that was being crafted by the Asia-Pacific powers.[15]

As will be discussed later, with the support of Singapore and Indonesia, India was invited into several ASEAN-centred institutions, including the ASEAN Regional Forum in 1996. ASEAN has now acknowledged India's 'important role in maintaining the peace, stability and prosperity of the region'.[16] From the early 1990s, the Indian Navy also tried to address regional concerns about India's naval expansion plans through confidence-building measures with their regional counterparts. It began some basic bilateral exercises with both Indonesia and Singapore and from 1995 hosted the biennial MILAN 'gathering' of regional navies at Port Blair in the Andaman Islands, primarily intended as a social networking opportunity among senior officers. By 2010 this has grown to an event involving representatives of 12 regional navies.

India's special relationship with Singapore

Over the last two decades, Singapore has been positioned as the hub of India's economic, political and strategic relationships in Southeast Asia.[17] The close relationship dates from when Singapore was founded by the British East India Company as a trading post for its China trade. For almost the first 50 years of its settlement Singapore was under the direct administration of British India and to a great extent Singapore inherited its political, legal and administrative systems from the Raj – it was under the authority of the Indian legislative council, the jurisdiction of the Supreme Court of Calcutta and its civil service was established by the Indian civil service. Even after Singapore was placed under separate colonial control it was assumed that British India would be primarily responsible for its security. This reflected not only the availability of Indian imperial forces, but also a broadly held acceptance that the 'natural' strategic sphere of British India ran to Singapore and beyond. Leading thinkers from Lord Curzon to K.M. Panikkar recognised the strategic importance of Singapore to India as the eastern anchor of India's maritime security. Singapore's importance to India was highlighted with the fall of Singapore to the Japanese in February 1942, which involved the surrender of some 40,000 Indian troops. Soon after, India's Andaman Islands were captured by Japan and the British Eastern Fleet was evacuated to Africa, exposing India's entire eastern seaboard to attack. However, the Japanese were unwilling or unable to properly exploit their position.

Nevertheless, Singapore continued to recognise a legitimate role for India as a regional security provider. In Singapore's 'survival phase' during the years following independence in 1965, it saw itself in a precarious strategic position, threatened by Communist Chinese-supported internal subversion, a hegemonic Indonesia and a potentially revanchist Malaysia. Within minutes of Lee Kuan Yew's declaration of Singapore's independence in August 1965, in what was probably his first act as leader of an independent Singapore, Lee wrote to Indian Prime Minister Lal Bahadur Shastri requesting assistance in training the newly established Singaporean army. The Indians declined to even respond to the request, apparently not wishing to be seen as taking sides against Malaysia.[18] (The United States, Britain and Egypt also reportedly declined Singapore requests for assistance in military training, leading Singapore to turn to Israel for military advisors.) In following years, Lee continued, unsuccessfully, to lobby New Delhi to involve itself in Singapore's security, with the idea that India would in some way take over Britain's role as a 'protecting' power. Lee believed that India's presence was necessary to deter Malaysia's plans to continue to control Singapore after independence and to guarantee against Indonesia going 'berserk'. At the same time, Malaysia actively campaigned in New Delhi against any Indian assistance to Singapore, with Malaysian Prime Minister Tunku Abdul Rahman arguing to Indira Gandhi that India should not 'do anything to hurt Malaysia'.[19] In May 1968, following the announcement of the withdrawal of the British navy from Singapore, Lee again unsuccessfully tried to encourage an Indian military presence in Singapore, proposing to Indira Gandhi that the Indian Navy should take over the Royal Navy's regional security role, including using Singapore's naval dockyard facilities for the building and repair of ships.[20] When, during a visit to India in 1970, Lee asked Indira Gandhi whether India intended to extend its naval influence into Southeast Asia, the Indian Foreign Minister Swaran Singh responded that India's greater interest was in keeping its *western* sea lanes open.[21]

Although the political relationship between India and Singapore went into abeyance for much of the 1970s and 1980s due to India's relationships with the Soviet Union and Vietnam, there was ongoing military-to-military contact between the Indian and Singapore armed forces. However, it took the realignments following the end of the Cold War for the a comprehensive relationship to blossom.

When India announced its Look East policy in 1992, Singapore, which was undergoing a foreign policy reorientation of its own, responded with enthusiasm. Despite fears in the early 1990s that a superpower withdrawal from the region might lead to unhealthy rivalry between Japan, China and India, Singapore had concluded by 1993 that India's strategic presence in Southeast Asia would, as it said, 'help stabilize the region by counterbalancing the other political heavyweights'.[22] Singapore was concerned not only about a more assertive China (which in 1992 claimed much of the South China Sea as its own), but also by the modernisation of the Malaysian and Indonesian armed forces and fears of the possible formation of a Kuala Lumpur–Jakarta political axis directed against it.[23] At about the same time, the Singapore government also concluded that for its relatively mature economy to develop further in spite of its severely limited size and resources, it needed to create an 'external economy' within the region as a 'second wing' to its onshore economy.[24] India, with its large labour force and relatively undeveloped markets, was identified as a key target for the development of an external economy for Singapore.

Singapore quickly positioned itself as India's *de facto* regional sponsor and became central to India's multilateral engagement in Southeast Asia. With the support of Singapore and Indonesia, India was soon elevated to be a full ASEAN dialogue partner in December 1995 and following Singapore's hard lobbying of reluctant ASEAN members, India joined the ASEAN Regional Forum (ARF) in 1996. India's entry into the ARF reportedly involved a significant diplomatic effort by Singapore to overcome fears of importing the India–Pakistan dispute into the forum, the reason why India's membership had been rejected in 1993.[25] When India was refused membership in the ASEAN + 3 grouping in 2000, Singapore successfully lobbied for a separate India–ASEAN summit, which was held in November 2002.[26] In 2005, Singapore (along with Indonesia, Japan and others) supported the inclusion of India in the first East Asia Summit, with Lee arguing that it 'would be a useful balance to China's heft'.[27] Unsurprisingly, Lee also supported the inclusion of India in any Asian Economic Community, arguing that it would help 'expand the market' and lead to 'more specialisation and division of labour'.[28] While acting as India's regional sponsor, Singapore also worked hard to develop the bilateral relationship. Despite scepticism among many ASEAN partners about the ability of India to deliver economic development comparable to China, the Singaporeans have shown considerable tolerance of and patience with Indian systemic problems, often seeking to bypass New Delhi and work directly with Indian state authorities, while nudging the centre towards economic and institutional reform.[29]

Singapore now unquestionably plays a pivotal role in India's ambitions in Southeast Asia and the broader Asia Pacific. As Indian Defence Minister Pranab Mukherjee commented in 2006, Singapore has become 'the hub of its political, economic and security strategy in the whole of East Asia'.[30] Singapore is India's regional advocate, its economic and political gateway into Southeast Asia and its most enthusiastic security partner.

The new economic and security partnership between India and Singapore

Economics plays a leading role in most of Singapore's bilateral relationships, including its relationship with India. Although Singapore benefits from its role as an economic gateway between China and Southeast Asia, India could present an even greater opportunity. In contrast to China, which has the benefit of longstanding direct trading links with many Southeast Asian economies (including through the large Chinese ethnic communities in many states), India's direct economic ties with the region are much less established. As well as acting as India's gateway to Southeast Asia, the Singaporeans also believe that they can become a trade and financial intermediary between India and China.[31] More generally, they believe they can assist in India's development as an 'economic balancer' to China.

Singapore has aggressively pursued economic ties with India since the opening of the Indian economy and the announcement of its Look East policy in the early 1990s. It has now become the largest investor in India among ASEAN states and in 2006/07 was the third largest foreign investor overall. In 2007, Singapore FDI in India aggregated US$2.9 billion for the year, much of it in the infrastructure sector, including ports and roads, while cumulative Indian FDI in Singapore aggregated US$8.8 billion. Bilateral trade has grown from US$2.34 billion in 2000/01 to approximately US$23 billion in 2010 (with the balance of trade in India's favour). Nevertheless, Singapore–India bilateral trade is a fraction of Singapore–China trade and is likely to remain so for some time.

In June 2005, India and Singapore signed an extremely broad-ranging Comprehensive Economic Cooperation Agreement (CECA), the first such arrangement India has entered into with a developed country. The CECA is unusually comprehensive, covering not just trade in goods, but also services, investment and tax. It provides for significant tariff reductions on goods covering approximately 80 per cent of Singapore's exports to India and for Indian exports to Singapore tariff-free – thereby promoting Singapore's role as a logistics hub for the export of Indian goods to Asia and the United States. However, the most significant aspects of the CECA are its treatment of services, investment and tax. It provides for the removal of many restrictions on services, something of particular significance for India with its large number of well-trained English speakers. The CECA also extends to financial services, giving specified Singaporean banks unrestricted access to the Indian market (and Indian banks to the Singaporean market) and provides special arrangements for Singaporean companies (and in particular the Singapore state-controlled investment companies, Temasek and GIC) to invest in India. The significance of the tax treaty arrangements should also not be underestimated, providing special concessions to Singaporean companies that place them on par with investors from Mauritius and Cyprus, historically the two primary gateways for foreign investment into India. As a result of the CECA, more than 2,800 Indian-owned companies now operate out of Singapore.[32] In aggregate, the CECA gives Singapore a gateway role with respect to India – particularly in relation to financial services and investment – that it could never realistically hope to achieve with China. The China–Singapore Free Trade Agreement, which was signed in October 2008, is significantly more limited in scope. The Singaporeans certainly have high hopes for the CECA as a key element in India's regional economic integration and Prime Minister Goh Chok Tong suggested that the agreement would eventually lead to an Asian Economic Community linking South Asia, Southeast Asia and Northeast Asia.[33]

The successful India–Singapore economic agreement contrasts with the slower progress on India's other regional free trade arrangements. Whereas clear complementarities in the Indian and Singaporean economies have assisted in the creation of economic links, the negotiation of free trading arrangements with other ASEAN states is hampered by greater competition in low-end manufacturing and agriculture. As a result, the multilateral India–ASEAN Free Trade Agreement, signed in August 2009, is much narrower than India's agreement with Singapore and excludes from its scope important manufacturing sectors such as textiles, chemicals, automobiles and steel, as well as agricultural products and services. If anything, the limited scope of the multilateral agreement may well reinforce Singapore's role as India's economic gateway in Southeast Asia.

Closer security links have paralleled the economic relationship. India and Singapore held annual bilateral naval exercises since the early 1990s. From around the turn of this century, in what has been called the second phase of its Look East policy, India has become more proactive in developing the security relationship. In October 2003, Singapore and India entered into a defence cooperation agreement providing for comprehensive annual defence policy dialogues between defence secretaries, joint exercises, intelligence sharing and cooperation in defence technology. This facilitated extensive and broad-based defence cooperation. Intelligence cooperation was formalised through the establishment in 2003 of a Joint Working Group for Intelligence Cooperation on Combating Terrorism and Transnational Crime and cooperation in defence technology was formalised through the establishment in 2006 of a Defence Technology Steering Committee. India has become the largest recipient of Singapore arms exports, although a US$1 billion purchase of Singapore howitzers was cancelled in 2010 following bribery allegations.

In addition to extensive joint maritime exercises discussed below, since 2004 the Indian and Singaporean air forces have conducted annual exercises (generally hosted by India, but hosted by Singapore in 2006). Commencing in 2005, India has hosted the annual 'Agni Warrior' artillery and 'Bold Kurukshetra' armoured exercises (which by 2007 included joint planning of brigade-level armoured operations). Singapore has been granted access to Indian facilities to conduct its own air and army training.[34] The security relationship was taken to a new level when, in October 2007, India gave the Singapore Air Force long-term use of the Indian Kalaikunda air base (near Kolkata). In August 2008, India also agreed to the stationing of a small number of Singaporean army personnel and artillery and armoured vehicles at its Babina and Deololli firing ranges for an initial five-year term. While of obvious benefit to Singapore, India also gains benefits from being able to conduct extended training with Singapore forces.[35]

Training on foreign soil is certainly nothing new for Singapore which, due to severe constraints on domestic land and airspace, has for decades had numerous overseas training establishments for its air force, army and navy.[36] In fact, the Singaporeans, as ever, have made a virtue out of necessity. In what has been called a 'second wing' to its defence,[37] Singapore has used its overseas establishments to give its armed forces (and particularly its Air Force) strategic depth as well as an opportunity to develop closer relationships with its informal allies. The opportunity to train with Indian forces deploying Soviet/Russian equipment and non-Western military doctrine also provides a significant tactical benefit to Singapore, particularly given the extent of Soviet/Russian equipment deployed by the Malaysian armed forces (and, perhaps, also given India's role in providing training to the Malaysian Air Force).[38] It is possible that the growing relationship with India may also eventually replace Singapore's existing training arrangements with Taiwan which, naturally, are an ongoing irritant to Singapore–China relations.[39]

In contrast, the long-term use of Indian territory by foreign military defence forces represents a major shift in Indian policy. Since 1947, India has opposed any foreign military bases in Asia. It has fiercely opposed any foreign bases on its territory and has until recently refrained from establishing its own military bases elsewhere. In the early 1960s, in the wake of the Sino-Indian war, the Indians refused to allow US forces to be based in India to assist in its defence against China, and in the early 1970s largely resisted pressure from the Soviets to be granted limited naval basing rights to support the Soviet Indian Ocean fleet. It appears that these 'sacred cows' of Indian politics are quietly dying – at least so far as Singapore is concerned – as the announcement of these arrangements seems to have created little political stir in India.

Given the position of Singapore at the head of the Malacca Strait, between the South China Sea and the Indian Ocean, maritime security will inevitably be at the heart of any security relationship between India and Singapore. Since the end of the Cold War, the Singaporean and Indian navies have exercised together frequently and the tempo of joint training has increased in recent years. Singapore and India have held annual bilateral naval exercises since 1993 (which later became known as the SIMBEX exercises), making Singapore India's longest-running naval exercise partner in Asia and India's only regular bilateral exercise partner in the region. The exercises started primarily with an anti-submarine focus and over the years have expanded in both size and scope to include maritime interdiction and air defence. In the future they may be expanded to combine exercises of all three services. While most of their joint maritime exercises have been held in the Bay of Bengal, in 2005 and 2009 exercises were held in the South China Sea (which, according to the Commanding Officer of the Indian Navy's Eastern Fleet, 'was not a signal to be given to somebody').[40] The Indian Navy also provided Singapore with training onboard Indian submarines, as well as providing Singapore's navy with access to Indian naval facilities and firing ranges. In 2007, the annual Malabar exercises with the United States were expanded to also include Singapore, Japan and Australia.

The extent to which India might seek to use its relationship with Singapore to extend its naval power into the South China Sea remains to be seen. However, any credible Indian naval presence in the South China Sea would require the cooperation of a local partner such as Vietnam or Singapore. This could involve non-exclusive arrangements for the use of Singapore's Changi Naval Base, just as it is currently used by the United States navy. It has been reported that an arrangement allowing for 'frequent' visits of Indian naval vessels to Changi Naval Base is already in place, and the development of a semi-permanent Indian logistical presence seems not beyond the realms of possibility.[41]

From India's perspective, Singapore, in terms of its size, economic role and geographic position, makes it an almost ideal partner for extending India's strategic influence into Southeast Asia. Singapore's role as the key trading and services hub in Southeast Asia gives India an expeditious way of expanding its economic presence while it improves direct bilateral trading and investment links with the major regional economies. In political terms, Singapore's clear-sighted approach to its own diplomatic and strategic needs and those of the region allows the relationship with India to develop without the historical or ideological baggage that could be a factor in some of India's other relationships in the region. In strategic terms, access to Singapore's port and air facilities, in combination with India's bases in the Andaman Islands, places India in an excellent position to potentially control the Malacca Strait and project power into the South China Sea.

There are, however, some important limitations to the relationship. The ease and convenience for India of the Singapore relationship may to some extent have delayed India's imperatives to develop its own close bilateral security relationships in the region. Indeed, India faces the risk of Singapore shaping its agenda for the entire region, especially in light of India's very limited diplomatic resources. In the longer run, Singapore's small size and its omnidirectional foreign policy means a relationship with Singapore can only be a stepping stone for India to develop stronger economic, political and security relationships with larger states if India wishes to have a major strategic role in the region. India has been seeking to develop its strategic relationships with other key ASEAN states such as Malaysia and Indonesia with varying degrees of success.

India's strategic relationship with Malaysia

Malaysia, through its political and economic influence in Southeast Asia and its geographical position, is important to India's strategic ambitions in the region. However, for a number of reasons, the security relationship is likely to remain limited for some time.

During the 1950s and 1960s, India had a strong political relationship with Malaya/Malaysia. India provided it with considerable diplomatic support in the years following its independence and during the *Konfrontasi* era with Indonesia. However, the relationship has become strained over the last few decades, particularly after Malaysia began emphasising its ties with Muslim countries, and there are now a number of political and diplomatic irritations in the relationship.

Islamic politics has been a significant factor in the relationship. Malaysia was outspoken over the destruction of the Babri Mosque in Ayodhia by Hindu fundamentalists in 1992[42] and actively campaigned for Pakistan to be admitted to the ASEAN Regional Forum despite India's concerns that Pakistan would simply use it as a forum to attack it. The relationship is also clouded by political unrest among the Indian ethnic community in Malaysia, unhappy with their perceived economic and political marginalisation.[43] A further source of irritation has been Malaysia's relatively close economic, political and ethnic links with China, which have led Malaysia to be cool about the expansion of East Asian regional organisations to include India. Malaysia opposed holding a separate ASEAN–India summit (which was first held in 2002) and also quietly supported China's attempts to exclude India from the first East Asian Summit in 2005.

Over the past several decades, Malaysia has also not been welcoming of India's strategic ambitions in Southeast Asia. India's attempts to promote itself as the leading maritime security provider in the Andaman Sea and gain a role inside the Malacca Strait have provoked suspicion in Malaysia, which closely guards its prerogatives as a littoral state on the Malacca Strait. Despite numerous invitations, Malaysia has declined to hold regular bilateral naval exercises or conduct 'coordinated patrols' with the Indian Navy in the Andaman Sea (in the nature of the patrols the Indian Navy conducts with Indonesia and Thailand). It has also been the most vocal opponent of India's attempts to gain a security role in the Malacca Strait, although it recently agreed to Indian assistance in 'capacity building' in the Strait, while emphasising that the primary responsibility for the security and safety aspects of Malacca lie with the littoral states.[44] Cooperation in connection with

Malaysia's Russian-built equipment has also yielded mixed results. India did not distinguish itself as a defence cooperation partner under a 1993 agreement for maintenance and training in relation to Malaysia's MiG-29 fighter aircraft, when it was perceived to be more concerned about commercial profits from the arrangement than the long-term strategic benefits. India seems to have performed better under a 2007 agreement for training of the Malaysian Air Force's Russian-built SU-30 MKM aircraft.

Despite difficulties in the relationship, it now seems to be on the upswing, and the Malaysian government under Prime Minister Najib appears to have fewer strategic concerns about India than previous governments. There are many longstanding economic links between Indian and Malaysian small to medium-sized enterprises. While they have not been fully exploited, these links could make the India–Malaysia economic relationship qualitatively different to India's economic relations with Singapore or other Southeast Asian states. India and Malaysia signed a Comprehensive Economic Cooperation Agreement in February 2011 and there are expectations of a significant increase in two-way direct investment.

Malaysia may also come to see India as a useful balance against China. Like other ASEAN states, Malaysia is in dispute with China over territorial claims in the South China Sea (although the areas of dispute are comparatively small) and it also has concerns about the level of Chinese influence in Burma. According to one Malaysian analyst:

> There is a fear that the Chinese are coming in to Southeast Asia from the other side, via the Indian Ocean. This will give them access to the Straits of Malacca. If China has access through that area, it will give Beijing a better basis for power projection.[45]

However, the extent to which Malaysia would view a broader strategic or security role for India in the Asia Pacific in positive terms has yet to be seen.

India's strategic relationship with Indonesia

India's relationship with Indonesia, though relatively undeveloped, is likely to be the key to its strategic role in maritime Southeast Asia in coming years. While India's security engagement with Southeast Asia over the last two decades has given priority to improving multilateral links with ASEAN and developing securities ties with Vietnam and Singapore, the importance of Indonesia in India's regional strategy is now increasing. New Delhi has long perceived Indonesia, the dominant state in archipelagic Southeast Asia along with Vietnam, the dominant state in Indochina, as being the linchpins of any strategy to constrain Chinese influence in Southeast Asia.[46] There are indications that India now sees Indonesia as an essential partner in expanding its strategic influence in Southeast Asia.[47]

For India, Indonesia has particular significance in several ways. First, it is by far the largest state in Southeast Asia and is regarded as *primus inter pares* in ASEAN. A relationship with Indonesia will help India develop its relationship with ASEAN institutions and its bilateral relationships across the region. Second, Indonesia's historical concern about China makes it a potentially important partner in balancing China's influence in East Asia, particularly in influencing the development of regional political and economic institutions favourable to India. Third, Indonesia's geographical location between the Indian and Pacific Oceans makes it key to India's aims to counter China's growing maritime interests in the Indian Ocean, to control the Malacca Strait and gain a role as a naval power in the western Pacific. Fourth, Indonesia's cooperative (though independent) security relationship with the United States fits well with India's new strategic posture. For India, a political partnership with Indonesia may be useful in increasing its freedom of action in working with the United States and its regional allies while simultaneously promoting the development of a multipolar region. Fifth, India has an important stake in the continued stability and viability of Indonesia, the world's largest Muslim majority nation, as a secular and democratic state. The modern Indian and Indonesian states share secular traditions and Indonesia's relatively tolerant (or syncretic) Islamic tradition, infused with mystical Sufi beliefs, has many links with the Islamic Sufi traditions practiced in India. A secular Indonesia can act as an important bridge for India's dealings with the Islamic world. Indonesia has generally avoided the Islamic factor colouring its relationship with India (including, for many years, opposing Pakistan's stance on Kashmir in various international fora).[48] However, the advent of an Islamist and non-secular Indonesia could have major ramifications for India's relationships in Asia and the Middle East, as well as India's internal stability. India would be likely to regard such a development in the most serious terms.

Like India, there have been significant changes in Indonesia's strategic perceptions following the end of the Cold War. Indonesia experienced a succession of economic and political crises in the late 1990s, including a major economic crisis, the fall of the Suharto regime and a transition to democracy. Together, these were a catalyst for Indonesia to readjust its relationships with major powers, including India. Since 2004 Indonesia has adopted a more active foreign policy, showing impatience with the 'golden cage' of ASEAN and seeking to develop its bilateral relationships with major powers beyond it. Although ideological differences between Indonesia and China have been reduced, Sino-Indonesian relations remain strained by their maritime territorial dispute in the South China Sea and continuing resentment in Indonesia against its economically powerful Chinese ethnic minority. Indonesia's relations with the United States have improved under the Bush and Obama administrations. Despite its rhetoric against external intervention in the region, Jakarta has indicated that it prefers a continuing US security role in Southeast Asia as a counter to China's rising power.[49] President Susilo Bambang Yudhoyono's administration has reinforced previous statements that Indonesia is looking for a new global role which includes taking the lead in the Muslim world.[50] Recently there have been influential calls in Jakarta to develop a new regional security management arrangement – a sort of regional concert of powers – that would include Indonesia alongside India, China, Japan and the United States.[51] There has also been increased interest in the Indonesian security community for promotion of democracy in the region, including the establishment of the Bali Democracy Forum in December 2008.

As Indonesia's strategic posture continues to evolve, it is also likely to see India as an attractive security partner. The growth of China's power in the region will only increase Indonesia's need for 'balancing' partnerships. Daniel Novotny's study of attitudes of India's foreign policy elite found that their comfort level with India is higher than with China and some other regional countries. The elite regards China as the main external factor that needs to be constrained and India (and Japan) whose power is seen as more benign and limited, as countries that should provide the necessary counterweight. Nevertheless, there was still considerable hesitancy about India's ability to act as a counterweight to China.[52] Improvements in the India–US security relationship have also brought India's strategic posture much closer to Indonesia's. Both India and Indonesia are now prepared to cooperate with the United States in a number of areas including the creation of 'balanced' regional institutions. A relationship with India would fit well with Indonesia's hopes to extend its reach beyond ASEAN towards other major powers and, ultimately, to sit alongside India at the top table in a multipolar regional order.[53] Indonesia may also see benefit from India playing an active maritime security role in the region, balancing not only against China but also potentially against US naval predominance. Despite considerable sensitivities over any foreign security presence in the Malacca Strait, India could be seen as a useful partner in developing Indonesia's naval capabilities both in the Strait and further afield.

Current dimensions of security cooperation between India and Indonesia

Indonesia has given significant support to India's ambitions to improve its political and security links with the region. Indonesia has long been in favour of an institutional relationship between India and ASEAN and in the mid-1990s came to see India as important to the regional balance of power. According to Lee Kuan Yew, in the mid-1990s Indonesia came to the conclusion that the region would be dominated by China or Japan after the Americans eventually left and decided to help bring India into the region.[54] Although Indonesia has generally allowed Singapore to take the lead as India's regional advocate, India has acknowledged that Indonesia's assistance has been essential at each step, including in supporting India's membership of the ASEAN Regional Forum in 1996 and helping to head off significant criticism of India over the Pokhran II nuclear tests in 1998. Indonesia also backed the creation of the annual ASEAN–India summit in 2002 and was a strong supporter of India's participation in the

East Asian Summit in 2005, 'in order to keep balance in the East Asian community'.[55]

Since the turn of this century, there have been important developments in the bilateral relationship, with the tempo of visits and meetings between Indian and Indonesian leaders increasing markedly. Much of the emphasis, particularly from the Indonesian side, has been on the development of the economic relationship with India. For Indonesia, India represents a potential source of capital and an enormous market for Indonesian agricultural products. Nevertheless, trading links have been slow to develop and to date Indian investment in Indonesia has been minimal. A bilateral Free Trade Agreement has stalled since 2005 on issues of access to Indian markets for Indonesian palm oil and other key agricultural products, although this may be given fresh impetus following the signing of the India–ASEAN FTA in August 2009. The visit of President Yudhoyono as Chief Guest at India's Republic Day in January 2011 indicates a renewed focus on the relationship. Bilateral trade, which topped US$12 billion in 2010 is targeted to reach US$25 billion by 2015. Major Indian investment plans in Indonesia were also announced in January 2011 with an aggregate value of US$15 billion, including plans by the Indian steel authority to develop a US$3.3 billion steel plant in Kalimantan.

Over the last decade there have also been important developments in the security sphere, with agreements on defence cooperation in 2001, on joint naval patrols in the Andaman Sea in 2002 and on terrorism in 2004. In 2005, the Indian Prime Minister and Indonesian President declared a 'New Strategic Partnership' which placed significant emphasis on political, defence and security cooperation, including the creation of an annual strategic dialogue between senior officials. As will be seen, maritime security is likely to remain the key focus of the security relationship.

A 2001 Defence Cooperation Agreement between India and Indonesia, although nominally dealing with the supply by India of training and defence equipment and the development of an Indonesian defence industry, was seen in Jakarta as having broader symbolic value. Indian assistance in defence technology and training could, at least in theory, be of particular value to Indonesia in light of India's capabilities in producing and supporting Russian-designed equipment and Indonesia's goal of diversifying its defence supply arrangements away from the United States. According to an Indonesian foreign ministry spokesman in 2007, defence industry cooperation with India would 'help enhance security in the region' and that 'would be a way for Indonesia to help ASEAN nations check the power of China in the region'.[56]

However, there has been little real progress in this area. Indonesia has unsuccessfully sought to acquire Indian radar systems, BrahMos cruise missiles[57] and training for its Russian-built Su-30 aircraft,[58] and has indicated interest in Indian Advanced Light Helicopters, corvettes and communications and networking technology. But the prospect of India becoming a significant supplier of defence technology and services to Indonesia is restricted both by the small size of Indonesia's defence acquisition budget and India's own limitations. The supply of radar systems and missiles was vetoed by India's European and Russian partners. At least in the medium term, it seems likely that cooperation in the field of defence equipment supply will remain limited and Indonesia's focus may shift to India's training capabilities. This too is not without problems – India is hesitant to provide training for Indonesia's SU-30 aircraft, fearing the risk of disclosure to third parties of operational information on its frontline strike fighters.

India has also been in a position to provide considerable assistance to Indonesia in countering domestic threats from Islamic jihadists. Indonesia's vulnerability in this area, and its potential as a source of regional instability, was underlined through the rise of Islamic extremist cells based in Indonesia and the Bali and Marriott bombings in 2002 and 2003. The arrest of senior members of Indonesia's Jemaah Islamiyah while training in Pakistan with the Kashmir separatist group Laskar-e-Toiba led to a Memorandum of Understanding on Combating International Terrorism in July 2004. In November 2004, Indonesia requested additional Indian assistance in countering terrorism, with an emphasis on maritime security.

Fears about the Islamic-inspired separatist insurgency in Indonesia's Aceh province (located on the western end of Sumatra, around 150 km from India's Nicobar Islands) was another focus point in developing the security relationship. For India, Aceh's significance is not only as a case of separatism or of a potential source of jihadist terrorism in the region, important as those issues are, but that Aceh also commands the western entrance to the Malacca Strait. Some fear that an independent and fundamentalist Aceh might obstruct international use of the Malacca Strait or that China might obtain port facilities in an independent or autonomous province.[59] Insurgents from the Free Aceh Movement (*Gerakan Aceh Merdeka* or GAM) were believed to have been involved in the hijacking of merchant vessels off Sumatra both as a political statement and a source of funding. New Delhi, claiming evidence of links between Aceh insurgents and Pakistan's Inter-Services Intelligence agency and the use of isolated islands in the Nicobar Island group for gunrunning to Aceh, pressed Indonesia to put in place a cooperative response.[60] This led to the IndIndocorpat Agreement under which the Indian and Indonesian navies have undertaken biannual 'coordinated' naval patrols in the Andaman Sea, in the Six-Degree Channel at the northern entrance to the Malacca Strait through which most of the traffic to and from the Malacca Strait passes. Since 2002 these patrols have comprised Indian and Indonesian vessels and aircraft, commanded out of India's Joint Operations Command in the Andaman Islands. Although token in practical terms, such joint military action has significant symbolic value.

While India has been able to demonstrate its value as a maritime security partner in the Andaman Sea, it has been less successful in nurturing concerns in Indonesia about the growth of Chinese naval influence in the Indian Ocean. As discussed in Chapter 3, since the early 1990s, Indian officials and commentators have repeatedly raised concerns about a perceived Chinese plan of maritime 'encirclement' of India through its so-called 'String of

Pearls' strategy, including repeated assertions by Indian analysts that China has established naval facilities on the Burmese mainland and islands in the Andaman Sea. India also expressed concerns to Indonesia over possible Chinese involvement in the development of a port facility in the Palau Weh islands in Aceh province, a contract which was later awarded to Malaysian interests. According to one Indian observer, while Southeast Asian countries have historically seen the 'China threat' as emerging from the east through Indochina and the South China Sea, they should now be concerned about the opening of a new 'front' through Chinese expansion into the Indian Ocean.[61]

However, there is little evidence that concerns about a Chinese naval presence in the Indian Ocean are high on Indonesia's agenda. Instead, Indonesia's maritime security concerns about China are focused on the South China Sea, including its long-running dispute with China over the oil rich waters adjacent to Indonesia's Natuna Islands.[62] It is apparent that while both India and Indonesia are generally concerned about China's power in the region, these concerns have not yet coalesced into a shared perspective on a China threat in maritime security. Nevertheless, the 'String of Pearls' continues to be a significant issue in Indian strategic thinking and is an important factor in India's relationship with Indonesia. India may, for example, encourage Indonesia to play a more mediatory role in bringing political reform to Burma – using its own experience in developing a system of 'guided democracy' – with the hope that a more open Burmese government would be less susceptible to Chinese influence. Indonesia could also help in India in creating a Recognised Maritime Picture of shipping that extends all the way from the Persian Gulf to the Malacca Strait. A further issue of immediate import in the India–Indonesia relationship is India's ambitions to act as a security provider in the Malacca Strait. As will be discussed in Chapter 9, a direct security role in the Malacca Strait represents a key strategic objective for India in Southeast Asia, and India's relationship with Indonesia is central to that objective.

Indonesia's leading role in Southeast Asia, together with its geographical position as gatekeeper between the Indian and Pacific Oceans, makes it an indispensible partner for an India which has ambitions to be an Asia Pacific great power. However, one should treat developments in the security relationship with caution. As C. Raja Mohan has commented, 'While India has a set of complementary interests with Indonesia, both countries are notorious for their inability to turn words into practical deeds.'[63] Although there are several areas where one might expect further development in the security relationship, when this occurs, if ever, will depend on the extent to which both India and Indonesia see an imperative to turn their numerous complementary interests into practical deeds.

8 India's uncertain partnership with Australia

Australia is another potentially important factor in India's ambitions in the Asia Pacific. It physically divides the Indian and Pacific Oceans and dominates the South Pacific. It is also the United States' closest ally in the Asia Pacific and plays an active security role in the region. Australia and India share many common perspectives on maritime security and regional stability which could form the basis of an active security partnership between them. But there are also important areas of divergence and India, in particular, has been slow in giving substance to the relationship. Will India and Australia be prepared to overcome these differences?

A history of divergent perspectives

Australia's strategic relationship with India during the second half of the twentieth century was characterised by long periods of indifference interspersed with occasional bouts of irritation.[1] The India–Australia relationship broadly fits the pattern of India's relations with many states in East Asia – divergent geopolitical perspectives, ideological differences and weak economic links. However there are additional factors, such as race, identity and status, which continue to colour the overall relationship.

Although Australia and India had a cordial relationship at India's independence in 1947, with the spread of the Cold War to Asia they soon found themselves on opposite sides of several political and strategic divides. India followed a path of nonalignment and avoidance of regional security entanglements, while Australia cemented the ANZUS security alliance with the United States. Australia also pursued an active security role in Southeast Asia as part of a policy of forward defence against communism, including providing troops to aid Malaya/Malaysia against communist insurgency and the Indonesian *Konfrontasi* and supporting the United States in Vietnam.

There were several public squabbles between Indian and Australian leaders through the 1950s and 1960s, particularly over the role of the United States in Asia. The differing worldviews of India and Australia were in many ways personified by the Indian Prime Minister Jawaharlal Nehru, a leader of the nonaligned world, and Australian Prime Minister Robert Menzies, a great supporter of the British Empire. According to the last Indian Governor-General, C. Rajagopolachari, Menzies represented the 'true voice of British colonialism, speaking from the grave'.[2] In general, India's attitude towards Australia during the Cold War and after might be described as disinterest together with vague feelings of resentment. Situated beyond Southeast Asia and on the other side of the Indian Ocean, Australia was well beyond India's area of strategic concern and, until recently, barely figured in New Delhi's strategic calculations. Australia was often seen as a colonial anomaly whose White Australia immigration policy placed it, for some, on a similar moral spectrum as apartheid South Africa. Its security alliance with the United States made it a US stooge.[3] To many in New Delhi, Australia would remain politically suspect and strategically inconsequential until it decided to become properly 'independent' (which was often shorthand for Australia abandoning the US alliance and becoming demographically Asian). In contrast, Australia showed little sympathy for Third World ideologies in general and for India's championing of nonalignment in particular. India was generally seen as too difficult to deal with and, increasingly, too pro-Soviet. Instead, Australia focused on relationships with anti-communist countries in East Asia.

Australia and India only began to gradually come into sustained strategic contact as they both gave greater attention to the Indian Ocean during the 1970s and 1980s. Following the 'intrusion' of the USS *Enterprise* into the Bay of Bengal in 1971, India spent much of the 1970s unsuccessfully trying to limit the military presence of the superpowers in the Indian Ocean region. India also began expanding its naval capabilities, and in 1978 the Indian Navy announced a highly ambitious 20 year programme involving building a fleet of 250–300 vessels with significant blue water capabilities. Through the 1980s, India's naval expansion included the acquisition of a second aircraft carrier and the lease of a Soviet Charlie-class nuclear-powered submarine.

Australia's interest in the Indian Ocean increased with the growing Soviet naval presence in the 1970s. In the mid-1980s, Australia adopted a new 'Defence of Australia' strategy which emphasised defence of the 'sea–air gap' around the Australian continent over the previous emphasis on expeditionary forces for forward defence. This led to a decision to relocate half of the Australian Navy's fleet to the Indian Ocean. As a result of these developments, Australia began seeing India as something more than just a South Asian power. In the late 1980s India's naval ambitions in Southeast Asia became a matter of concern to some in the Australian defence community.[4] In March 1990 Australian Air Marshall David Evans publicly chided India for its spending on defence to an audience in Beijing, commenting that, 'Perhaps it is no more than excessive nationalism that compels India to seek an almost dominant role in the Indian Ocean.'[5] The Australian government sought to defuse the controversy with the Australian Defence Minister, Kim Beazley, commenting that India's 'overall strategic context justifies a substantial navy,' and that India 'has never and does not threaten Australia'. Beazley however described India's posture as 'intriguing' and as posing 'possibilities for extensively increased Indian influence at the major eastern Indian Ocean choke points'.[6]

Although the end of the Cold War defused controversy over India's ambitions in Southeast Asia, a degree of friction between Australia and India continued throughout the 1990s, with several incidents demonstrating an aptitude for Australia to offend India. In 1990, the sale by Australia to Pakistan of 50 Mirage III jets and spares for a seemingly knock-down price of A$36 million led to significant strains in the India–Australia relationship. Although the jets were considered obsolete by Australia, they were in fact suitable for frontline deployment by Pakistan, and enhanced Pakistan's capabilities during a period of heightened India–Pakistan tensions. The affair was long resented in New Delhi.[7] Similarly, an incident in 1993 when Australian naval aircraft overflew an Indian aircraft carrier and another in 1997 when the Australian navy dropped sonar buoys near the Indian destroyer INS *Delhi*, both elicited strong protests from New Delhi.[8] These actions arguably demonstrated an element of indifference to the relationship on the part of Canberra, or as Canberra viewed it, oversensitivity on the part of New Delhi.

India's Pokhran II nuclear tests in 1998 provoked a very strong reaction from Australia, which caused significant damage to the relationship. Prime Minister John Howard publicly characterised the tests as 'a grotesque status symbol'[9] while Foreign Minister Alexander Downer called them 'outrageous acts'.[10] Australia suspended ministerial contacts, non-humanitarian aid and defence-related cooperation, and India responded in kind. New Delhi took particular offence at Australia's 'intemperate' reaction to the nuclear tests, seeing the Australian reaction as either a case of it doing the bidding of the United States or, alternatively, as trying to curry favour with the United States through outdoing US protests. New Delhi also saw hypocrisy in the Australian stance in condemning India's desire to provide for its own security while sheltering under the US nuclear umbrella. Some even sought to explain Australia's reaction to the tests on the basis of racism.[11] While Canberra believed that it was unfairly singled out by New Delhi, there is little doubt that Australia placed itself, along with Japan, at the forefront of international opposition to India. In fact, Australia's reaction to the Pokhran II tests had little to do with India itself, but was primarily driven by Australian convictions about the sanctity of international non-proliferation norms and domestic political factors.[12] Nevertheless, Australia's reaction to the nuclear tests again demonstrated an indifference to India's security perspectives.

The contemporary security relationship

The Australia–India security relationship has gained significant momentum over the last decade, primarily at Australia's initiative. Like Japan, Australia quickly realised that its stance over the Pokhran II tests had not been productive and sought engagement with New Delhi instead. There have been several visits by Australian Prime Ministers to New Delhi since the turn of this century, along with numerous ministerial-level visits. This led to several bilateral agreements on security-related matters, including a 2003 agreement on terrorism, a 2006 Memorandum of Understanding on Defence Cooperation, a 2007 defence information-sharing arrangement, and agreements on intelligence dialogue, extradition and terrorism in 2008.

In November 2009, Australia and India announced a Joint Declaration on Security Cooperation, intended to set out shared strategic perspectives and create a framework for the further development of bilateral security cooperation. At the same time, Prime Minister Kevin Rudd told an audience in New Delhi that India and Australia were 'natural partners' and should become 'strategic partners'.[13] Australia has similar Security Declarations with Japan (in 2007) and South Korea (in March 2009). Although the Australia–India Security Declaration contained little new of substance, it established a framework for the further development of the security relationship, including the formalisation of regular consultations and dialogues between foreign ministers, senior military and diplomatic representatives, and joint working groups on maritime security operations and counter-terrorism and immigration.[14]

The Declaration identified shared security interests and outlined consultative mechanisms to be implemented between them. Key areas of cooperation targeted include information exchange and policy coordination in regional affairs including within multilateral regional frameworks and cooperation in defence, terrorism, crime, disaster management, and maritime and aviation security. The Declaration also provides for the exchange of visits between foreign ministers, defence policy talks between senior officials, staff talks and service exchanges, consultation between respective National Security Advisors, consultation on counter-terrorism including through the existing Joint Working Group on Counter-terrorism and sharing knowledge on disaster prevention. In conjunction with the Security Declaration, Australia and India finalised new cooperation arrangements in intelligence, law enforcement, border security, terrorist financing and money laundering.

Overall, the Australia–India Declaration was a notable step in the development of the bilateral security relationship. However, a comparison with the Japan–India Security Declaration is instructive. It affirms their 'similar perceptions of the evolving environment in the region', while the Australia–India Declaration steers clear of even coded references to China, merely affirming a 'shared desire to promote regional and global security'. There are also significant differences in New Delhi's enthusiasm in pursuing relationships with Tokyo and Canberra. The Japan–India Declaration displays an apparent determination to undertake a prolonged and multifaceted engagement that is simply not present in the Australia–India Declaration. In addition to the consultative mechanisms prescribed in the Australia–India Declaration, the Japan–India Declaration prescribes consultation between Defence Ministers, the permanent Foreign and Defence Secretaries and Chiefs of Armed Services, navy-to-navy staff talks and a comprehensive security dialogue at the Director General/Joint Secretary level. The Japan–India Declaration also specifies a range of military-to-military cooperation and exchanges including bilateral and multilateral exercises, coastguard cooperation and cooperation between space agencies, which are not addressed in the Australia–India Declaration. While the Indian and Japanese Prime Ministers asserted that the strategic partnership between the two countries would become 'an essential pillar for the future architecture of the region',[15] India has downplayed the Australian relationship.

Australian security analysts strongly support a closer security engagement between Australia and India. The consensus is that Australia and India are natural strategic partners whose interests are essentially congruent. With the end of the Cold War and the strategic rapprochement between India and the United States, the gates are now open for Australia and India to recognise their shared perspectives and build a close strategic partnership reflecting many common interests.[16] Australia's 2009 Defence White Paper flagged the 'strong mutual interest' of Australia and India in enhancing maritime security cooperation in the Indian Ocean, commenting that, 'As India extends its reach and influence into areas of shared strategic interest, we will need to strengthen our defence relationship and our understanding of Indian strategic thinking.'[17] There may be significant scope for bilateral security cooperation, such as in maritime policing (piracy and maritime terrorism, illegal fishing, people trafficking etc.), disaster management in the eastern Indian Ocean and anti-terrorism throughout the region. Australia and India also have shared interests in the political stability of South Asia (Afghanistan and Pakistan) and Southeast Asia (particularly Indonesia) and are both keen to play an important role in any future Asian regional architecture. There could also be scope for cooperation on broader international issues such as nuclear non-proliferation and disarmament. Underlying this is a strong incentive by Australia to see India becoming a major investor in its resources sector to match other investors such as China.

By contrast, Australia does not currently occupy a major role in New Delhi's thinking about the Asia Pacific. Australia is broadly seen as an element of an extended Look East policy, although it does not have the priority afforded to India's relations with say Japan or Singapore. Some see Australia as a potentially useful junior partner along with the United States and Japan in an informal coalition to balance against China.[18] Even those who oppose the idea of any coalition against China tend to define Indo-Australian common interests in terms of building an Asian order that addresses mutual concerns about China.[19] In general however, Australia is seen to have little to offer India beyond natural resources. There is little perceived imperative to take Australia's views into consideration in formulating policy, including when making judgements about China or the Indian Ocean.

Despite the Security Declaration, naval cooperation between India and Australia is currently minimal. Although the Indian Navy conducts regular bilateral exercises (or patrols) with the United States, Russia, France, Britain, Singapore and Indonesia, the Indian and Australian navies do not undertake any regular bilateral exercises.[20] Despite invitations from Australia, India has declined to participate in Australia's *Kakadu* exercises due to participation of the Pakistani Navy. Nor was the Australian Navy invited to attend the US–Indian Exercise *Malabar 2010* hosted by India in the western Indian Ocean. In short, India does not currently view Australia as a significant Indian Ocean or Asia Pacific power on which to expend its limited resources.

Both Australia and India have been cautious about giving the relationship broader strategic significance. Australia, in particular, has been careful to avoid anything that might resemble a coalition against China. Many see Australia as having torpedoed Shinzo Abe's so-called 'Quadrilateral' proposal in 2007, under which India would have joined a security dialogue with Japan, the United States and Australia. Some saw the proposal as essentially involving the extension of the annual Trilateral Strategic Dialogue among US, Japanese and Australian foreign ministers to include India. Canberra had serious misgivings over the Quadrilateral proposal and declined to participate in meetings on the initiative after May 2007 (nor did Japan pursue the proposal following a change in leadership later that year). While Australia may have been under pressure from China not to participate, it is not clear that Canberra would in any event have welcomed the inclusion of India in the Trilateral Security Dialogue. The Dialogue is regarded in Canberra as a useful vehicle for ensuring that Australia's role as Washington's closest ally in Asia is not overshadowed by Japan's role as Washington's most important ally in Asia.[21] In particular, Australia sees the Dialogue as crucial to helping to socialise Japan into playing a more constructive regional security role in cooperation with Australia. Canberra may well have feared for Australia's goals in a wider arrangement in which it would inevitably be only a very junior partner. Whatever the mix of reasons, Australia's decision not to participate in further discussions was seen in Tokyo and New Delhi as showing too much sensitivity to China.[22] The decision of Australian Foreign Minister Stephen Smith to use a press conference with Chinese Foreign Minister Yang Jiechi in February 2008 to announce that Australia would not be proceeding further with the Quadrilateral proposal appeared to be a particularly clumsy attempt by Australia to curry favour with China. While the Quadrilateral initiative was unlikely for all concerned, the failure to develop a forum of that nature leaves a potential gap for Australia in ensuring its involvement in future discussions between India, the United States and Japan. This is a weakness Australia may need to rectify, especially if the United States, Japan and India decide to go ahead with a trilateral dialogue.

One factor of growing importance in the India–Australia relationship has been trade, and in particular Australia's attempts to develop India as a major resources and energy customer. This is driven by a general desire to expand Australia's export markets and also to balance Australia's economic relationship with China. A weak economic relationship has contributed to the lack of political alignment over the last 60 years. In 2009, bilateral trade aggregated US$16 billion after growing at around 24 per cent per annum over the previous five years. This has made India Australia's fourth largest trading partner after China, Japan and the United States. However, the balance of trade is heavily in favour of Australia and this imbalance is likely to grow. Australian exports to India are dominated by resources (primarily coal, gold and copper) and education services. Some resource exports, including coal, minerals and natural gas, are expected to grow significantly in coming years. By contrast, Indian exports to Australia, while growing in absolute terms, are actually declining as a percentage of Australia's total imports. Bilateral investment also remains very small, barely reaching US$120 million in 2008.[23] There is considerable scope for significant Indian investment in the Australian resources sector, which might balance the sometimes politically controversial Chinese investment in the sector over the last decade or so. Although an Australia–India Free Trade Agreement has been proposed, negotiations have not yet commenced and it seems unlikely that any agreement will be finalised quickly. A greater degree of economic interdependence could have a positive effect on the security relationship.

Despite improvements in relations, the overall relationship between Australia and India remains uneasy in some respects. A series of assaults on Indian vocational students studying in Melbourne in 2008–9 was taken up by the Indian media and became a major source of controversy. But the greatest irritant in the security relationship is the nuclear issue, where Australia has not yet been able to fully accommodate India's new status as a nuclear power outside the nuclear non-proliferation regime and continues to prohibit the supply of uranium to India. While Australia holds approximately 40 per cent of the world's supply of low-cost uranium reserves[24] it has also a long anti-nuclear tradition. Australia is active in international nuclear non-proliferation efforts and the supply of uranium even for power generation remains politically controversial. In 2007, in his last days of office, Australian Prime Minister John Howard announced that he proposed to make an exception for India to the longstanding prohibition on the supply of uranium to non-NPT states. However, much to the annoyance of New Delhi, this change of policy was rejected by the incoming Prime Minister Kevin Rudd. Australia supported approval of the US–Indian nuclear deal by the Nuclear Suppliers Group in August 2008, but still refused to overturn its prohibition on supply of uranium to India. Although India may want Australia as a stable, long-term supplier of uranium it has secured sufficient supplies from Russia, Kazakhstan, Gabon, Mongolia and even Canada. Australia's refusal to supply uranium to India is taken by many in New Delhi as a lack of commitment to the relationship, a refusal to fully accept India's claims to great power status and even as proof of excessive Chinese influence.[25]

Other relationships in the South Pacific

Over the last several years, India has demonstrated increased interest in extending relationships in the South Pacific – a region in which Australia and New Zealand have traditionally played dominant security roles.

India's strategic relationship with New Zealand is peripheral to both countries and is likely to continue to be so. New Zealand's primary strategic focus is on the South Pacific, although it maintains interests in East Asia. There is also little reason for India to engage strategically with New Zealand. New Zealand remains strongly anti-nuclear and a staunch supporter of international anti-proliferation norms, and was one of the last hold-outs against granting a waiver to India in the Nuclear Suppliers Group in 1998.

India's greatest interaction with the South Pacific has been in relation to Fiji, where tensions between indigenous Fijians and the large Indian ethnic community have resulted in four military coups since 1987. From the early 1980s, New Delhi voiced concerns about the effective exclusion of the Indian ethnic community from political power and began dabbling in local politics, including assisting the Indian-ethnic political party. As Prime Minister Indira Gandhi commented, she felt 'somewhat like a mother concerned about the welfare of a married daughter who has set up home far away'.[26] In May 1990 the entire Indian High Commission was expelled by the Fiji government for alleged interference in Fiji's internal affairs. According to Vice Admiral Mihir Roy, a former Director of Indian Naval Operations, the Indian Navy actively considered intervention in Fiji,[27] a possibility that was taken seriously by the Fijian government.[28] In reality any meaningful intervention by India in Fiji was well beyond the resources of the Indian Navy or other armed forces. Australia would no doubt have considered Indian intervention as unhelpful.

In recent years New Delhi has been more publicly circumspect in its dealings with Fiji although it continues to press Canberra to take a stronger stance against the Fijian military regime. India's stance on Fiji in the 1980s and 1990s also did considerable damage to its relationships with other South Pacific states (which were often broadly supportive of the goals of indigenous Fijians if not their methods), which India is still in the process of repairing. Since 2003 India has sought to re-engage with the region, announcing that the Look East policy would be specifically broadened beyond East Asia to include the South Pacific. India joined the Pacific Island Forum as a dialogue partner and now makes small aid contributions to all Pacific Island members.[29] Mohan has suggested that there is scope for cooperation between India and Australia in respect of failing states in the South Pacific, including conducting peacekeeping operations, although that would seem an unlikely use of Indian resources.[30] For most South Pacific states though, India has yet to demonstrate its relevance as a potential partner.[31]

Continuing constraints on the Australia–India strategic relationship

Underlying recent developments in the Australia–India relationship are several difficult issues that could impose significant limitations in coming years.

Much of the profound indifference in the strategic relationship between India and Australia over the last 50 years can be ascribed to differing geostrategic orientations. This may be changing, but only slowly. For much of its existence as an independent state India has focused on defending and consolidating its position in South Asia and only since the 1970s has it begun to show any real interest in the Indian Ocean. By contrast, Australia's strategic focus since World War II has almost wholly been on the western Pacific, with a primary focus on East Asia in terms of threat perceptions and economic partnership. Australia's political and economic engagement with Asia, which began in earnest from the early 1970s, was heavily focused on Southeast Asia and more broadly on China and Japan. Until relatively recently Australia's vision of an 'Asia Pacific' community did not include India (which Australia and other founding members intentionally excluded from consideration for APEC membership). Australia has traditionally shown little real interest in the Indian Ocean in terms of either threat perceptions or economic opportunity, an attitude compounded by the lack of any regional identity analogous to that in the western Pacific basin. Paradoxically, despite a lack of strategic focus towards its west, over the last two decades, Australia's armed forces have been extremely active in the Indian Ocean, undertaking several military interventions or operations, often, but not always, in conjunction with the United States.[32] However, while Australia has shown increased rhetorical interest in the Indian Ocean in recent years, the benefits (apart from engagement with India) are still perceived to be fairly meagre. But a gradual shift in Australia's economic centre of gravity towards its west coast means that relationships in the Indian Ocean will almost certainly become more important in the future.

The shared imperial heritage of Australia and India has served to divide more than unite them. On gaining political independence in 1901, Australia's white colonial heritage led it to identify closely with Britain and then the United States as essentially benign forces in international affairs. By contrast, India saw its colonial heritage in terms of an alien intrusion and for many years also saw any US strategic presence in the region in neo-imperialist terms. Differing perspectives on identity and nationalism found expression in very different perspectives on strategic autonomy. India saw any security alignments as inconsistent with its notion of 'independence'. India's Foreign Minister, V.K. Krishna Menon, characterised India's policy of nonalignment as 'the policy of independence' in which India took its decisions in its own national interests, in contrast with aligned states where decisions were placed 'in foreign hands'.[33] As a result, New Delhi often saw Australia as an imperial lackey, first of Britain and then of the United States. Australia's identification with US interests was a great irritation to Nehru, who commented that Australia 'could have no opinion of [its] own on great international issues, or freedom to express it'.[34] India showed greater frustration with Australia than with other US allies in Asia arguably because Australia's alignment with the United States went to the heart of what Australia represented in Indian eyes. According to Alison Broinowski's study of Asian perspectives of Australia:

> Indian [media] representations habitually emphasised that Australia was not, and did not want to be, fully independent of Britain or the United States; that Australia was committed to discrimination against Indians on the basis of race; and that, consequently Australia could not be relied on

as a participant in the Asian Renaissance. Australia failed to support Asian, and specifically Indian, causes because it lacked Asian identity.³⁵

In contrast, the proposition that security alignments are inconsistent with a notion of absolute 'independence' would puzzle many in Australia. Since the beginning of the twentieth century, Australia has often assumed that security alignments are a prerequisite for its national independence. In mainstream thinking there is rarely seen to be a fundamental inconsistency between security alignment and political independence. On the contrary, the US alliance is often seen as increasing Australia's strategic weight in the region and the wider world.

As has been discussed, ideas of strategic autonomy have a central role in Indian strategic thinking, leading some in New Delhi to show condescension towards states that do not regard strategic autonomy as a major objective. While India's strategic rapprochement with the United States in recent years has removed many sources of friction in the India–Australia relationship, it has not always improved New Delhi's assessment of the strategic importance of Australia. There continues to be a view in New Delhi that Australia is not an independent strategic actor on which India needs to expend significant time or resources. Why deal with Canberra when one can deal with Washington?

Another significant factor in Indian perceptions of Australia – and one that continues to have a real effect on the strategic relationship – is race. Australia's identification with Britain in imperial times and beyond often carried the strong implication that Australians considered themselves first-ranking citizens of the empire, in contrast to the 'coloured' subject peoples. This was reinforced by Australia's 'White Australia' immigration policy that restricted immigration from non-European sources. Indians widely saw this as a great affront, morally akin to the apartheid policies followed by white South Africa. According to Walter Crocker, the Australian High Commissioner to India in the 1950s, the White Australia policy created a 'depth of resentment [that] can hardly be exaggerated'.³⁶ Frank Moraes, the influential editor of the *Times of India* commented that he could see no difference between Australia and South Africa.³⁷

Although the White Australia immigration policy was largely dismantled in the late 1960s and formally ended in 1972, Indian perceptions and suspicions continue. Despite Australia's efforts to integrate itself more closely with East Asia, many in New Delhi still arguably regard Australia to some degree as an anomalous white outpost in the region. They would find Australian formulations that it can be strategically and economically inside Asia while culturally and ethnically different as difficult to accept. Accusations of racism continue to affect the political and security relationship. Australia has been accused of racist or discriminatory motives on matters as diverse as Australia's reaction to the expansion of India's naval capabilities in the 1980s,³⁸ Australia's stance on India's 1998 nuclear tests,³⁹ the safety of Indian students and Australia's refusal to supply uranium to India. Australia's racism against India, so it is argued, is now manifested in a reluctance to recognise and acknowledge

India's claims to be a great power, such as denying India's legitimacy as a nuclear weapons state. This perceived denial of rightful status may be doubly insulting to a society such as India's with a high degree of formal social stratification. Differing Indian perceptions of Australia and Japan illustrate the underlying impact of race on the relationship. Although Japan continues to be reluctant to accept India's status as a nuclear weapons state and allow the export of nuclear technology to India, Japan's policies are generally treated in New Delhi as understandable, if unfortunate, artefacts of Japanese history and not as an illegitimate refusal to accept India's rightful status. In contrast, few in New Delhi see any legitimacy in Australia's anti-proliferation policies.[40]

All of these factors – geopolitical outlook, conflicting ideas about identity and strategic autonomy, and sensitivity towards perceived racism have contributed to the relative marginalisation of Australia and India in each other's strategic thinking. These factors continue to underlie some of the controversies and political caution that characterise the current relationship.

Prospects for strategic cooperation

Prospects for cooperation in the Indian Ocean

The Indian Ocean is generally seen as an area ripe for enhanced security cooperation, particularly in areas such as people and drug smuggling, terrorism, illegal fishing, search and rescue and disaster relief. However, as noted, there is currently minimal bilateral cooperation in maritime security.

Scope for Indo-Australian cooperation in multilateral regional fora also seems limited, if nothing else due to the weak or non-existent regional identity in the Indian Ocean. The only regional forum of a political or economic nature is the Indian Ocean Rim-Association for Regional Cooperation (IOR-ARC), which was formed in the 1990s with the aim of reducing trade barriers and increasing cooperation and interaction among regional states. However, the grouping quickly became moribund. Although India and Australia may seek to breathe some life into it in coming years, this would require a major commitment of resources for little immediate return. As will be discussed in Chapter 9, the Indian Navy has also recently sponsored the establishment of the Indian Ocean Naval Symposium, although this seems unlikely to become a forum for real cooperation between regional navies. India's National Maritime Foundation has suggested that India and Australia could jointly sponsor a Regional Maritime Domain Partnership under the aegis of IONS. This would involve collaboration with Southeast Asian states in intelligence sharing, maritime domain awareness and coordinated patrolling, somewhat along the lines of the Saudi-sponsored Arab Naval Task Force in the Gulf of Aden. This could be a helpful mechanism and would satisfy Indian needs to organise regional partnerships not involving the United States.

The Indian Ocean is also an area where Australia and India's interests have the potential for some divergence. For several decades from the early 1970s

India unsuccessfully sought to exclude extra-regional powers (in particular, the United States) from having a military presence in the Indian Ocean. In contrast, Australia has generally sought to maintain or enhance the US security presence, including through the provision of communications and port facilities and support for the US presence at Diego Garcia. Through the 1970s and 1980s it successfully worked against attempts to limit the US military presence in the region. While these divergent perspectives on the US role in the Indian Ocean caused only occasional friction between India and Australia, it was clear that they were on opposite sides of the argument. The US–Indian strategic rapprochement has largely removed this as an explicit source of disagreement between Australia and India. However, the underlying issue remains: India aspires, at least in the long term, to secure a dominant role in the Indian Ocean, while Australia would wish to see the maintenance of a dominant role for the United States for as long as possible. Australia may, for example, be concerned if it perceived that the strategic rapprochement between India and the United States may result in India taking primary responsibility over significant parts of in the Indian Ocean (such as the northeast quadrant) without the close involvement of Australia. Australia would also be worried about the possibility of the current positive trajectory of the US–Indian relationship not being sustained. Australia will therefore likely be sensitive to any suggestions that India take a greater role in Indian Ocean security if that is seen to be facilitating a reduction in the US military presence.

A related issue is different perspectives on the legitimacy of a Chinese security role in the Indian Ocean. Indian concerns about the String of Pearls are not widely shared in Australia, where analysts have tended to treat Indian claims about the extent and nature of Chinese interests in the Indian Ocean with a degree of scepticism.[41] Australian analysts tend to see any Chinese presence in the Indian Ocean less in terms of an encirclement of India and more as an expression of China's legitimate interests in protecting its SLOCs to the Middle East and Europe. Australia might well be inclined to see the potential for Sino-Indian naval rivalry as constituting a greater threat to the *Pax Americana* than a modest Chinese presence in the region. It is not clear what role Australia may play in this. It has been suggested that rather than tilting toward one side or another, Australia's interests lie in working with both India and China to shape Asia's future security order to accommodate the demands of both and the legitimate interests of other regional powers.[42] Australia might conclude, for example, that its interests are to facilitate China's role as a responsible stakeholder in the Indian Ocean (e.g. by allowing China a voice on issues relating to the Indian Ocean in regional fora).

In general, Australia would look positively on India taking greater responsibility for maritime security in the Indian Ocean region, taking a constabulary role in consultation or cooperation with other interested states. However, Australia will be sensitive to any assertion by India that it is the leading maritime power of the Indian Ocean with a sphere of influence or sphere of unilateral intervention that extends much past South Asia.

Prospects for cooperation in the Asia Pacific

Australia regards the Asia Pacific, and particularly Southeast Asia, as its primary strategic focus. It has played a significant security role in Southeast Asia since the 1950s and has actively pursued closer political and economic relations with East Asia since the 1970s. Australia has a formal security role in the region through the Five Power Defence Arrangements with Malaysia and Singapore, bilateral security arrangements with Indonesia and its peacekeeping presence in Timor Leste. In many ways, India, which has been pursuing strategic links in Southeast Asia only since the 1990s, has much less developed relationships in the region.

The convergence in the security dynamics of South and Southeast Asia, have highlighted the many common strategic interests that Australia and India share in Southeast Asia, and this may drive a degree of cooperation between them in coming years. These include interests in maritime security (such as in the Malacca Strait) and terrorism. They both have significant stakes in the maintenance of the political stability of more or less secular Muslim majority states such as Indonesia and Malaysia. The installation of an Islamist regime in Indonesia, for example, would be a matter of serious concern for both India and Australia (although, perhaps, for somewhat different reasons). There is therefore much scope for cooperation between Australia and India in taking actions to assist in maintaining the political stability and territorial integrity of Southeast Asian states.

There are also many shared diplomatic interests between India, Australia and ASEAN, particularly to ensure that middle or emerging powers are not marginalised in the regional decision-making by the major powers. This was demonstrated by ASEAN support for membership of India and Australia in the East Asia Summit. While neither Australia nor India readily admit it, they are both geographical and cultural outsiders to East Asia and neither are automatically accorded a place in regional fora. Australia and India may find each other useful in advocating that regional fora adopt a broad and inclusive definition of 'East Asia'.

However, one should not necessarily assume consensus on ASEAN-centred institutions as the basis for regional security architecture. There is a growing school of thought in Australia in favour of a 'Concert of Powers' approach to Asia Pacific security in which the locus of much decision-making would move from the current ASEAN-centred institutions to an informal understanding among the major powers (which, according to Australian thinking generally includes the United States, China, Japan and India).[43] This contrasts somewhat with the Indian approach which, as discussed in Chapter 7, has strongly supported the extension of ASEAN-centred regional arrangements.

India and Australia also have a strong interest in seeing a balanced role for China in the Asia Pacific, particularly in Southeast Asia. However, as noted above, India and Australia currently see China in very different terms. India regards China as a strategic competitor, and one which has claims over significant portions of Indian territory. While Australia has growing concerns over China's military capabilities, Australia still generally sees the rise of China not in terms of a direct military threat, but as part of a long-term strategic shift in Asia, to which Australia will need to adapt in one way or another.[44]

Further, there is potential for the interests of Australia and India in Southeast Asia to diverge, particularly if India is perceived as being too assertive in the region. However, the days when Australia was ringing alarm bells about India's naval expansion plans in Southeast Asia are long past and Australia now sees India as having a valuable and legitimate role in the region, provided that it does not try to displace the role of the United States as an offshore security provider in Southeast Asia.

An uncertain partnership?

The strategic relationship between India and Australia is interesting in a number of respects. There are many obvious areas of common interest between Australia and India in Indian Ocean and Asia Pacific security. It is for this reason that Australia has been making significant efforts to gain New Delhi's attention. However, in contrast with some of its relationships elsewhere in the Asia Pacific, India has been cautious in giving practical effect to the relationship. To some extent this simply reflects a matter of priorities: from India's perspective Australia is a middle power that lies beyond the immediate arc of East Asia. Australia is neither a potentially important peer state like Japan nor a small and useful 'gateway' state like Singapore. As an emerging power, India is also particularly demanding of recognition of its major power status, an issue which underlies India's strong reactions on the question of uranium sales. As discussed above, there are also underlying tensions relating to geopolitical perspective, identity and race.

There are several reasons for uncertainty as to how the relationship may develop. First, Australia is unlikely to allow itself to be placed in a position where it will choose 'between' China and India. Although Australia will want to develop India as a hedge to China it will not allow its relationship with India to be framed by any China threat theory. While India sees benefit in having the ability to control China's sea lanes of communication in the Indian Ocean, Australia arguably has a greater interest in ensuring that China's security dilemma in the Indian Ocean is not worsened.

Nor will Australia easily accede to India's aspirations to be recognised as the leading naval power in the Indian Ocean. Australia sees India as playing a potentially important constabulary role in the Indian Ocean region in cooperation with other interested states, but is unlikely to recognise any regional order in which India has special rights. Rather, Australia will seek to extend the predominance of US naval power throughout the Indian Ocean region for as long as possible, while maintaining its own position as one of the major naval powers on the Indian Ocean littoral.

Finally, while there is some recognition of the potential for cooperation, there is no mutual understanding that each is a crucial element in the other's security. Australia first and foremost relies on the United States as its security guarantor. While New Delhi sees the United States as its key strategic relationship, it sees little need to invest much in a relationship with Canberra. Although Australia is, along with Indonesia, one of the major states sitting between the Indian and Pacific Oceans, India does not yet see Australia as an 'indispensible partner' in the Asia Pacific.

9 India's maritime security ambitions in Southeast Asia and the western Pacific

India's ambitions to play a direct security role in the Asia Pacific are focused on the maritime dimension. Over the last two decades, the Indian Navy has led the way in expanding India's role in the region. In coming years, India is likely to increasingly assert a direct maritime security role in Southeast Asia and further into the western Pacific.

India's emphasis on naval power as the primary means of projecting power into the Asia Pacific is a result of several factors. At one level it merely reflects the inherent capabilities of the navy as a force capable of projecting power beyond India's borders. Its focus on maritime power is also a consequence of the opening of India's economy and expansion of its maritime trading relationships, which includes a growing dependence on imported energy. It also reflects India's geographic constraints. India's ability to project economic, political or military power on the Asian continent is severely constrained by the geographic barrier of the Himalayas and its difficult relationships with Pakistan to the northwest, China to the north and Burma to the west. To some extent India can only expand its area of influence in the maritime dimension. Finally, an emphasis on naval power is also a question of status. In the late nineteenth century the United States and Japan saw maritime power as a requisite of great power status, as did the Soviet Union in the latter part of the twentieth century, and arguably China in recent years. Some in New Delhi now see maritime power as an essential element in India's 'destiny' as a great power. The Indian Navy's apparent focus on the acquisition of prestige assets such as aircraft carriers and nuclear submarines seems driven at least in part by India's search for status.

India's primary maritime security objectives in the Asia Pacific region involve the consolidation of India's role as the leading naval power in the northeast Indian Ocean and, in the longer term, gaining a direct security role in the Malacca Strait. India has a secondary objective of gaining a significant role in the South China Sea and the western Pacific generally.

India's leading role in the northeast Indian Ocean

Since the 1990s India has placed considerable emphasis on achieving a predominant position in the northeast Indian Ocean generally and specifically in the western approaches to the Malacca Strait. This is part of a broader strategy of developing the capability to project power into the main entry/exit choke points in the Indian Ocean. The Indian Navy has given particular focus to the choke points at entrances to the ocean around southern Africa (including the Mozambique Channel), the Arabian peninsula (including the Strait of Hormuz and Bab-el-Mandeb) and the straits connecting the Indian and Pacific Oceans through the Indonesian archipelago (the Malacca, Sunda and Lombok straits). These choke points were recognised by the Portuguese explorer and imperialist Alfonso de Albuquerque in the sixteenth century as being the key to domination of the Indian Ocean. In the following centuries this understanding guided the Portuguese, Dutch and British naval strategies in the Indian Ocean and it now guides India's regional strategy.[1] According to the Indian Navy's 2004 Maritime Doctrine:

> By virtue of geography, we are ... in a position to greatly influence the movement/security of shipping along the [sea lines of communication] in the [Indian Ocean region] provided we have the maritime power to do so. Control of the choke points could be useful as a bargaining chip in the international power game, where the currency of military power remains a stark reality.[2]

The northeast Indian Ocean, as the principal connection between the Indian and Pacific Oceans, is a primary area of maritime interest for India, and it is an area in which India can credibly aspire to become the predominant naval power.

The construction of the Eastern Fleet's new base south of Visakhapatnam on India's east coast and major naval and air force facilities in the Andaman and Nicobar Islands over the last two decades are clear statements of India's intention to be the predominant naval power in the Bay of Bengal and the Andaman Sea. India's Andaman and Nicobar islands, which run north–south through the Andaman Sea, form a natural base to project power into the Malacca Strait and beyond into the South China Sea. From the mid-1990s, India developed military facilities in the Andaman Islands as a base for a new tri-service Andaman and Nicobar Command. This chain of bases now includes extensive port facilities to service elements of the Indian Eastern Fleet and several air bases for surveillance and strike aircraft. The operational radius of aircraft based in, or staging through, the Andamans encompasses the Malacca Strait and large portions of the South China Sea.[3] The Andaman Islands have particular significance for the security of the Malacca Strait and have been described by a Chinese naval writer as constituting a 'metal chain' that could lock the western end of the Strait tight.[4]

While developing its capabilities in the northeast Indian Ocean, the Indian Navy has made considerable efforts to prove itself a useful partner to Southeast Asian states and as a leading provider of 'public goods' in dealing with many security issues such as piracy, smuggling, refugees, terrorism and separatism, and disaster relief. Since 1995 the Indian Navy has hosted the MILAN biennial naval meetings at Port Blair in the Andaman Islands. This is not primarily intended as a naval exercise, but rather is an opportunity to increase military-to-military relationships with Southeast Asian navies as well as other regional navies from Japan, Australia and New Zealand. The absence of the United States and China from the MILAN meetings is a none too subtle reminder of India's assertion of regional leadership. Beginning in 2008, the Indian Navy has also sponsored the biennial Indian Ocean Naval Symposium (IONS) in which the heads of navies of all littoral states can discuss matters of mutual concern.[5] IONS is modelled after the US-sponsored Western Pacific Naval Symposium (WPNS) which has become a useful forum for navy-to-navy interaction in the Pacific. It follows the success of India's MILAN naval gathering in fostering greater interaction between navies in Southeast Asia. The establishment of IONS by India was intended to emphasise India's leading role throughout the Indian Ocean region, particularly in organising a regional response to maritime policing and humanitarian issues. However, the extreme diversity of Indian Ocean states in terms of strategic perspectives and naval capabilities has made effective cooperation very difficult to achieve, and India's enthusiasm for the initiative may be waning.

Nevertheless, India will continue to emphasise naval diplomacy and regional cooperation in which it can play a leading role. Since 2001, India has emphasised its strengths in maritime policing and anti-terrorism, including the interdiction of supply routes across the Andaman Sea used by Indonesian and Thai separatists. The Indian Navy made a prominent contribution to relief efforts in Aceh following the December 2004 tsunami and has since enhanced its capabilities to provide humanitarian assistance and disaster relief (HADR). The joint India–Indonesia naval patrols off the northern tip of Sumatra (and less publicised joint training and patrols between India and Thailand)[6] arguably involve a tacit acceptance of India's role in the northeast Indian Ocean.

India's ambitions in the northeastern Indian Ocean have been given greater force by a perceived imperative to respond to China's so-called 'String of Pearls' strategy. However, there is little evidence that concerns about a Chinese naval presence in the Indian Ocean are high on the agenda of ASEAN states. Instead, most ASEAN states are focused on China's disputed territorial claims in the South China Sea. These include Vietnam and China's competing claims over large parts of the South China Sea, Indonesia's dispute with China over the oil-rich waters adjacent to its Natuna Islands and Malaysia's disputed claims over the Spratly Islands. There are also intra-ASEAN maritime territorial disputes such as the Indonesia–Malaysia dispute in the Ambalat area in the Celebes Sea. It is apparent that regional concerns about China have not yet coalesced into a shared perspective on a China threat to maritime security in the Indian Ocean. Nevertheless, the 'String of Pearls' continues to be a significant issue in Indian strategic thinking about its security relationships with ASEAN states.

India's maritime security ambitions in the Malacca Strait

A focal point of India's maritime security ambitions in Southeast Asia is its ambition to take a direct security role in the Malacca Strait, which has been identified by the Indian Navy as part of its 'primary area of interest'.[7] As noted above, the Malacca Strait is the primary choke point for sea traffic between the Indian and Pacific Oceans and Indian control over the Strait is important for effective control of the northeastern Indian Ocean. Some have claimed that the Malacca Strait represents a rough counterpart to the importance of the Panama Canal to the United States.[8] Others place it as the significant mid-point in an 'arc of rivalry' between India and China stretching from the Persian Gulf to the Sea of Japan.[9] Robert Kaplan has rather colourfully described the strait as being as strategically significant in coming decades as was the Fulda Gap during the Cold War.[10] At the very least, for India, a degree of control over the Malacca Strait would provide an implicit check on Chinese actions in the Indian Ocean region.

The Malacca Strait is one of the world's busiest waterways, with more than 71,000 ship movements in 2009. It is the key trade route between East Asia and Europe, carrying an estimated one-third of global trade and the bulk of energy supplies from the Middle East to East Asia (including an estimated 70–80 per cent of China's energy imports and 90 per cent of Japan's).[11] The Strait, which is some 550 nautical miles long and whose navigable routes narrow to less than one nautical mile, is considered to be particularly prone to commercial piracy and terrorist attacks. In the early years of last decade there were widely held concerns about piracy and sea-robbery of ships transiting the Strait, concerns which India has used to justify a security role for itself. However, reported cases of sea robbery in the Malacca Strait and surrounding areas have fallen significantly in recent years, principally due to improved land policing in Indonesia, improved economic conditions and the end of the insurgency in Indonesia's Aceh province. Since 2001 politically motivated piracy or terrorism has also been of concern, including attacks believed to have been planned by jihadist organisations on merchant and naval vessels in the Strait and surrounding areas, although no such attacks have eventuated.

After September 2001, India stepped up interest in the Strait itself. In 2002, following an unsolicited request from the United States, India provided naval escorts for high-value commercial traffic through the Strait as part of the US-led Operation *Enduring Freedom*. India's participation in the operation was supported by Singapore (which hosted Indian naval vessels), while India is believed to have consulted Malaysia and Indonesia as well as the Philippines and Australia on the initiative. The United States appears to support a direct security role for India in the Strait. According to the Chairman of the US Joint Chiefs of Staff, General Pace, the United States was 'very comfortable with the fact that India has offered its assistance' in providing security in the Strait.[12] India is now seeking a more permanent security role inside the Strait, which is an important factor in India's strategic relationships with both Singapore and Indonesia.

Security in the Strait is complicated by legal and political issues surrounding its status. The Strait (as traditionally defined) is largely within the territorial waters of Indonesia, Malaysia and Singapore and under international law foreign naval vessels have a right of transit only. Foreign naval vessels may 'escort' other transiting vessels while transiting themselves, but, at least according to the littoral states, may not conduct armed 'patrols'. Indonesia and Malaysia are particularly jealous in safeguarding their sovereignty over the Strait and are highly sensitive to the presence of any 'external' maritime security providers in it. In light of sensitivities about any perceived internationalisation of the Strait, some have argued for an extended definition of the 'Malacca Strait' from the Singapore Strait in the south to the Six Degree Channel in the north that would include Thailand and India as 'littoral' states and allow the creation of a composite security system of joint patrols throughout the relevant waters.[13] India has also sought to categorise itself and Thailand as 'funnel states' to the Strait of Malacca, thereby justifying a greater status than mere 'user' states such as the United States, Japan and China.

There has been controversy in the last decade over moves by the United States and other major users to take a role in providing maritime security in the Strait. In April 2004, the United States announced its Regional Maritime Security Initiative under which it proposed to provide security in the Malacca Strait in partnership with littoral states. The initiative was strongly opposed by Indonesia and Malaysia, which construed it as proposing the deployment of US special forces in the Strait. Indonesia and Malaysia also refused to participate in the Japanese-sponsored multilateral ReCAAP initiative involving the voluntary exchange of information on piracy and other security threats in the Strait. In July 2004, at the initiative of Indonesia, the three littoral states commenced the so-called MALSINDO 'co-ordinated' naval patrols in the Strait. Although seen as a step in addressing international security concerns, the effectiveness of this programme is hampered by significant limitations in their maritime security capabilities. In June 2005, with continued piracy incidents, the Lloyds insurance association declared the Strait as a war-risk zone and shipping companies began regularly employing armed private security operators.[14] Indonesia is particularly sensitive to claims that it is the 'weakest link' among littoral states in terms of maritime security and air surveillance capabilities.[15] Although there has been some success in recent years in reducing incidents of piracy, observers are concerned about Indonesia's acute lack of resources and the likelihood that it will succumb to 'patrol fatigue'.[16]

Since 2001 India has been careful to position itself as a potential benign security provider in the Strait and to ensure that any naval presence was seen as 'non-intrusive, cooperative and benign' by the littoral states.[17] According to one Indian naval officer: 'Our role [in the Malacca Strait] is being perceived as that of a responsible nation, which can create a balance in the region. Also, everyone realises that India has no ambitions of hegemony.'[18] In the wake of the controversy over the Regional Maritime Security Initiative, India publicly distanced itself from the United States. In February 2006, the United States convened a 'user-state' conference in California to discuss security of the Strait. The Indians were vocal in opposing what was claimed to be a US unilateralist approach, insisting that any proposal from the meeting must be subject to the unanimous consent of littoral states.[19] At the same time, India has consistently lobbied littoral states for an active role in the Strait both at the political and military level.[20] Over the last five years, India has periodically reaffirmed offers to provide assistance, but only subject to the desire of the littoral states. It supported an Indonesian proposal for a compulsory pilotage programme and other cooperative proposals relating to safety and environmental protection.

While Singapore has generally encouraged India's offers to contribute to the security of the Malacca Strait, Indonesia has been more ambivalent. In July 2005, an Indonesian Foreign Ministry spokesman publicly rebuffed Indian requests for a security role, telling the Indian Chief of Naval Staff, Admiral Arun Prakash, that responsibility for safety in the Malacca Strait lay with 'Indonesia, Malaysia and Singapore only', leading Prakash to deny that India had any intention of patrolling the Malacca Strait.[21] In June 2007 Indonesian Defence Minister, Juwono Sudarsono, deflected renewed requests from the Indian Defence Minister for a role in patrolling the Strait, claiming that Jakarta was keen that India, South Korea, China and Japan 'pitch in to provide infrastructure' in the Strait.[22] Nevertheless, the Indonesian military appears to take a generally benign view of an Indian maritime security role in and around the Strait. In March 2009, a meeting of the ASEAN Regional Forum in Jakarta produced an invitation to Thailand to join with Indonesia, Malaysia and Singapore in coordinated patrols of the Strait,[23] and an Indonesian military spokesman reportedly requested India to take part in maintaining security in the Malacca Strait, on the basis that 'all approaches to the strait will be more secure for international shipping.'[24] Similarly, the Indonesian Defence Minister Purnomo Yusgiantoro was reported in June 2010 as commenting that Indonesia had 'no reservations at all' about India maintaining security in the Malacca Strait.[25]

Although Malaysia has previously firmly opposed any Indian role in the Strait, this may have softened somewhat in recent years. In 2005, the Malaysian Prime Minister Abdullah Badawi is reported to have told Indian Prime Minister Manmohan Singh that Malaysia holds the key to India's ambitions in the Malacca Strait and the South China Sea, and that his country is ready for a strategic partnership with India, *provided* that India's security ties with Thailand are scaled down.[26] In 2008, Malaysia consented to an Indian role in the 'Eye in the Sky' project to provide air surveillance over the Strait.[27] Malaysia's views may have been helped by Indian offers of training and technical support for Malaysia's MiG-29 aircraft and Scorpène submarines. Malaysia may now be somewhat less inclined to veto Indian security initiatives in the region, although it may not publicly support them.

There can be little doubt that India's interest in the Strait is largely motivated by strategic considerations. The official justifications for India's security interest in the Strait – that is, securing the Strait from threats of piracy and terrorism – hold little water. Not only are these primarily policing rather than military issues, the reported statistics in recent years clearly demonstrate that there is no crisis that requires external intervention.[28] It is evident that India's interest in the Strait is primarily motivated by a desire to enhance its role as the leading maritime security provider in the Indian Ocean and to control access to the Indian Ocean in case of potential threats from extra-regional powers, particularly China. For its part, China regards risks from the intervention in the Malacca Strait by an external power as far outweighing any risk of piracy.[29] However, it is possible that China may be prepared to tolerate a limited role for India as an alternative to a US presence. As the Chinese ambassador to India reportedly commented in 2005, 'Now, geographically, you [India] have access to that area. As far as India is concerned, we don't have any problem. ... But if Americans come and put their battleships there, we might worry about it.'[30] Nevertheless, China may well be encouraging some Southeast Asian states to resist any Indian presence.

Any invitation to India to take a direct security role would represent an important departure from the Indonesian and Malaysian positions on sovereignty of the Strait. However, in certain circumstances India might be able to present itself as a convenient 'compromise candidate' for an external security provider in the Strait. If the littoral states come under increased pressure to take action on Strait security they may find it politically more acceptable for India to take a role compared with the United States, Japan or certainly China. In the event of increased international pressure to take action on Strait security, Indonesia and perhaps even Malaysia may allow India to participate in it on their terms.[31] Any security role for India in the Malacca Strait would be a significant step for India. Beyond the immediate security implications in the Strait, it would help legitimise India's claims as a major power and a benign security provider to the region as a whole. However, without agreement on any role in the Strait, India will need to content itself with assisting littoral states to build maritime surveillance capacities and rely on its relationships with the United States and Singapore to gain a Recognised Maritime Picture of shipping in the Strait and surrounding areas.

India's naval ambitions in the South China Sea and western Pacific

India also has ambitions to take a significant role in western Pacific maritime security. This is primarily focused on projecting power into the South China Sea, although India aspires to project naval power into Northeast Asia and the South Pacific, if perhaps only symbolically. Some claim that India is a potential factor in the naval balance of power as far north as the Taiwan

Strait.[32] Mohan believes that India, simply by virtue of its growing economic and military power, will become a significant naval power in the western Pacific, with Singapore acting as the 'fulcrum' of India's extended reach into the Pacific.[33] As discussed previously, the United States has been encouraging greater Indian naval activity in the western Pacific, from Alaska to Okinawa and Guam.

The South China Sea is likely to be the major focus of India's maritime security ambitions in the Pacific. The Indian Navy currently identifies the South China Sea as a 'secondary area' of interest after key parts of the Indian Ocean region.[34] India's interest in the South China Sea appears to be primarily motivated by the expansion of China's interests in the Indian Ocean. Indian strategists dating back to K.M. Panikkar have long recognised the potential role of Vietnam in controlling the South China Sea and blocking Chinese naval penetration of the Indian Ocean.[35] This has been a significant factor in India's attempts to deepen its security relationship with Vietnam and, to a lesser extent, Singapore.

Since the turn of this century, India has been quietly extending its naval power into the South China Sea through regular visits, unilateral exercises and bilateral exercises with Singapore and Vietnam in what has been called 'deliberate, significant and maintained long-range Indian naval appearances'.[36] The Indians began implementing a 'detailed plan' to expand the horizons of Indian naval diplomacy in late 2000, when Indian warships made an extended visit to the South China Sea, including port visits to Vietnam, China and the Philippines, and as far north as South Korea and Japan.[37] During 2004, the Indian Navy made three separate deployments into the South China Sea as part of 'Presence-cum-Surveillance Missions' in the Malacca Strait, and in 2005 the Indian aircraft carrier INS *Vikraat* and task force made a first ever visit to Singapore, Malaysia and Indonesia. However, to date, Indian naval activity north of Singapore appears to have been more in the nature of demonstrations towards China than any credible attempt to project significant naval power into the western Pacific.

Much of India's naval activity in the South China Sea has been conducted in conjunction with Singapore and Vietnam. As has been discussed previously, in the early 1990s and at the turn of the century, India sought access to Vietnam's Cam Ranh Bay naval and air base for use by Indian naval vessels and aircraft. In doing so, the Indian Defence Minister Georges Fernandes proffered India's capabilities in policing sea lanes of communication in the South China Sea and 'containing' local conflicts. Hanoi declined the Indian request, emphasising the potential to convert the facilities for commercial uses.[38] In 2010, in the wake of heightened tensions in the South China Sea, Vietnam announced that facilities at Cam Ranh Bay would be available for use by all navies on a commercial basis. However there was no suggestion that Vietnam would allow any onshore physical presence so that it could be used as a maintenance or forward-operating base. While the Vietnamese might welcome an increased Indian naval presence (for example, through regular visits to Nha Trang), China's reaction to any permanent Indian naval presence at Cam Ranh Bay would hardly seem worth the relatively minor strategic benefit it would bring to Vietnam. India has been more successful in developing a security relationship with Singapore that extends into the South China Sea. Since 2005, India has conducted biennial naval exercises with Singapore in the South China Sea (which have been expanded to joint naval and air exercises) and some suggest that India may obtain non-exclusive arrangements for the use of Singapore's Changi Naval Base, just as it is currently used by the United States navy.[39]

While a cooperative role for the Indian Navy in the region west of the Malacca Strait is now more or less accepted within Southeast Asia, the extension of Indian naval power north into the South China Sea on anything other than a periodic basis remains controversial. To some extent this reflects India's lack of economic leverage in the region. Though its economic influence is growing, India has significantly less economic leverage in dealing with the relatively wealthy states in Southeast Asia, compared to China's ability to use economic leverage with the poorer states of the Indian Ocean region. There is also a sense that any Indian naval presence would be primarily motivated by Sino-Indian rivalry in the Indian Ocean rather than reflecting India's legitimate regional interests. It is not at all clear what security role India might have in the South China Sea. Would the primary purpose of any Indian presence be to support ASEAN littoral states against Chinese territorial claims, to protect India's SLOCs to Northeast Asia or to project power against China?[40] Although a significant proportion of Indian trade passes through the South China Sea, it currently includes only a small proportion of energy imports (although this will likely grow over time as Sakhalin island oil and gas production increases). ASEAN states may be happy to have India's political support over the South China Sea dispute,[41] but at least for the moment, an Indian naval presence would not be seen as having any clear rationale.

Further, the projection of Indian naval power north of Singapore will be of limited credibility without logistical support in Southeast Asia, something which is unlikely to be forthcoming at least in the current security environment. There are significant regional concerns about China's growing military capacity in Southeast Asia (including the new Chinese Sanya Naval Base on Hainan Island) and China's increasing assertiveness over its maritime territorial claims in the South China Sea. However, ASEAN states have made great efforts in recent years to reduce tensions and engage China in dialogue over the South China Sea territorial disputes. Any naval rivalry between India and China in the South China Sea would likely be seen as further complicating the regional security environment and adversely affecting ASEAN's ability to build regional security institutions that include China.

Although India wants the capability to project credible naval power into the South China Sea, it is primarily in response to perceived incursions by China into India's space. New Delhi understands that China would regard the presence of any Indian surface warships based in Southeast Asia as a major strategic challenge that could affect the whole framework of India–China relations. Provided that China develops no more than a 'recessed' naval presence in the Indian Ocean, there seems little need for India to push too hard for a direct security role in the Malacca Strait, to establish anything more than a discreet naval presence in Singapore or to venture into the South China Sea more than on an occasional basis. For the present, in building its relationships in Southeast Asia, India will focus on its capabilities in maritime policing and disaster relief functions.

10 Understanding India's engagement with the Asia Pacific

There is no single template for understanding India's strategic engagement with the Asia Pacific. Since the end of the Cold War, India has been feeling its way forward in developing a role in the region through strategic relationships with key partners. India has not articulated any 'grand strategy' in the Asia Pacific and seems unlikely to do so in the near future. Nevertheless it is possible to identify key themes underlying India's engagement with the region. These include:

- the economic integration of India with the Asia Pacific;
- balancing China;
- achieving strategic autonomy and a multipolar regional order;
- the recognition of India's proper status in the region; and
- expanding India's strategic space into Southeast Asia.

The economic integration of India with the Asia Pacific

It is difficult to overemphasise the importance of economics in India's strategic engagement with the Asia Pacific. India's Look East policy was initially focused on India's economic engagement with the region and trade and investment continues to be a driving force in most of India's relationships. India's economic and strategic relationships are also mutually reinforcing. India's comprehensive strategic partnership with Singapore is an excellent model for combining the economic, political and security spheres in a relationship. In contrast, its relatively weak economic relationship with Japan creates the risk of misalignment of economic, political and strategic objectives.

Economic development is an overriding national objective for India. The integration of India's economy with the dynamic Asia Pacific economies is now critical to India's economic development and remains India's most immediate regional goal. Access to East Asia's capital, technology and markets will be a key factor in driving India's future economic growth and in transforming India's economy into an outward-looking trade-orientated economy comparable with other major powers. India's other neighbouring regions present much fewer opportunities than the Asia Pacific. India's economic integration into South Asia is likely to be constrained in the foreseeable future by political factors and regional fears of Indian economic domination. Although India has a growing economic role in West Asia, its opportunities there are also constrained by political and other factors.

Despite the region's importance to India, its economic relationships in the Asia Pacific are patchy. India has had the most success in Southeast Asia, where ASEAN states have been particularly keen to encourage India's economic integration with the region. They are attracted to the huge Indian market and, for relatively less developed ASEAN states, the prospect of investment from India. Closer economic relations with India are also seen as potentially 'balancing' China's growing economic power and concomitant political influence. Wealthier ASEAN states such as Singapore (and, to a lesser extent, Malaysia) see significant economic benefit in positioning themselves as trading, services and financial intermediaries between the huge economies of India and China. As Prime Minister Goh Chok Tong explained in 2004:

> We see Singapore as being lifted by two economies. I visualize ASEAN as a fuselage of a jumbo plane with China as one wing, and India the other wing. If both wings take off, ASEAN as the fuselage will also be lifted.[1]

India's comprehensive economic cooperation agreement with Singapore has also allowed it to successfully position itself as India's economic gateway into Southeast Asia and as the gateway for Southeast Asian investment into India. As Singaporean Minister of Trade and Industry (now Foreign Minister), George Yeo, commented, Singapore could be to India what Hong Kong is to China.[2]

India has been much slower to develop its economic relationships with the larger and relatively poorer ASEAN states such as Indonesia and Vietnam. These countries look to India as a major market for agricultural commodities such as palm oil and as a source of investment. However India has failed to finalise comprehensive bilateral free trade arrangements with any ASEAN states other than Singapore (and, more recently, Malaysia). In considering trade arrangements, New Delhi has often focused on the immediate costs/benefits of opening its agricultural and manufacturing sectors to competition, allowing domestic political considerations to trump longer-term strategic and economic considerations. India's non-strategic approach in this respect contrasts sharply with the more generous approach shown by China in negotiating trade agreements which has facilitated the growth of China's political-economic influence in Southeast Asia.

India's economic relationship with Japan is also relatively weak and seems likely to develop slowly. This could raise questions about the alignment of their interests vis-à-vis China and could restrict the effectiveness of the political and security relationship. Japan's anaemic economic relationship with India compares poorly to its strong relationship with China and the fast-growing trade links between India and China. This could allow China to create a wedge between Japan and India on a broad range of issues in the same way that asymmetrical economic relationships inhibited Japan–India strategic cooperation during the Cold War. As Japanese Prime Minister Sato put it in the 1960s, China may seek to 'isolate India and tempt Japan with trade'.[3] Japan appears to have a growing recognition of the strategic importance of expanding its economic relationship with India and reducing its reliance on China, which has led to a free trade agreement and plans for the Delhi–Mumbai Industrial Corridor. However it may be difficult to overcome the longstanding cultural and other factors that have restricted expansion of business relationships between Japan and India for many decades.

On the other hand, over the last few years India's trading relationship with China has exploded, making China India's largest trading partner. Increased economic interdependence could significantly alter the dynamics of the relationship by creating greater strategic alignment. However, the overall economic relationship remains shallow and very lopsided in China's favour. Trade largely involves the exports of manufactured goods from China while India exports largely low-value-added commodities. Bilateral investment is virtually non-existent, meaning that there is little economic stake in the other. While the economic relationship may mature and broaden in coming years, the expansion of trade between China and India is currently as much a potential source of friction as a driver for strategic cooperation.

India's essential role in the Asia Pacific balance of power

It is often claimed that India's engagement with the Asia Pacific is necessary to ensure a 'balance of power' in the region. How likely is it that India will come to play an essential role in such a balance? According to the so-called 'balance of threats' theory, states that perceive a potential threat from a rising China (greater than any threat presented by, say, the more powerful but distant United States) might be expected to establish balancing coalitions against China. If this is true, would such a coalition necessarily involve India? There is no simple answer to this. In fact, there are several different perspectives on India's potential role in the regional balance of power.

Balancing against China's growing power in the Asia Pacific is a major imperative for India. From New Delhi's perspective, an imbalance of power in China's favour raises the prospect of a bipolar regional order in which power is shared between the United States and China, or even the prospect of Chinese predominance in the event of US withdrawal from the region. Either result would be seen as inimical to India's interests. While many in New Delhi celebrated India being described as the major 'swing state' in the international system, in fact India's strategic aspirations compel it to work with the United States and balance against China in the Asia Pacific. However, there are unresolved tensions between imperatives to balance China and India's goal of strategic autonomy. India needs to develop good working relationships with the United States and its allies. But India's need to demonstrate strategic autonomy could limit its commitment to such arrangements. New Delhi is also very much aware that any coalition involving India, the United States and its allies would carry a significant risk of provoking increased assertiveness by China in South Asia and/or the Indian Ocean region.

The United States envisages India as playing an important role in the Asia Pacific balance of power in the context of the rise of China. Over the last two decades the United States has actively sought to engage with India in South Asia, the Indian Ocean region and in the Asia Pacific. The United States has encouraged India to play a greater direct security role in the Asia Pacific and has also encouraged India to improve its security relationships with its allies and friends such as Japan, Australia and Singapore. The United States is generally sensitive both to Indian requirements that it not be seen as a junior partner in any US-led coalition against China and to Chinese perceptions of any such coalition. Although elements in the United States have supported moves towards bringing India into a soft coalition against China, the United States currently prefers to see India improving its bilateral security relationships in the Asia Pacific as an implicit message to China.

In contrast, China, as the putative object of any balancing coalition, does not recognise India as playing a legitimate role in the Asia Pacific balance of power. It regards India as strictly a South Asian power with only limited interests in East Asia or elsewhere in the Asia Pacific. It also publicly regards India's strategic ambitions as far exceeding its capabilities. Nevertheless, China was highly sensitive to suggestions in 2007 that the major Asia Pacific maritime powers, the United States, Japan and Australia might enter into a strategic dialogue with India. This suggests that China sees India as more than an irrelevance in the Asia Pacific.

A balancing relationship against China (at least in a 'soft' sense) is a major factor in the India–Japan relationship. New Delhi hopes that a political partnership with Tokyo with a significant security dimension will limit China's assertiveness and help ensure India's inclusion at the top table of the region. Japan is motivated to develop the India relationship by heightened threat perceptions of China and increased anxieties over its alliance with the United States. The relationship provides a clear message of the potential for India and Japan to join a 'hard' balancing coalition if China's strategic behaviour goes beyond certain bounds. However, Japan has not yet articulated how a political-security relationship with India might fit with its alliance with the United States or its other regional relationships, and seems unlikely to do so in the immediate future. While the relationship between India and Japan could become more intense in coming years it is unlikely to evolve into a 'hard' balancing coalition for some time. Japan's self-imposed limitations severely restrict its ability to be an active security partner. In any event, New Delhi may find Japan's strategic limitations convenient, given Japan's apparent willingness to recognise India's role as a leading maritime security provider in the Indian Ocean. India and Japan also have few direct security interests in each other's 'home turf'. This will limit the degree of support that each will give to the other in dealing with local security concerns (e.g. Pakistan for India and North Korea for Japan). However, a lack of strategic competition between them also arguably strengthens a balancing relationship vis-à-vis China.

The relationships between India and the middle and lesser states in the Asia Pacific are somewhat different to its relationships with the major powers. The imperatives central to neorealist balance of power theory operate very differently with smaller or less powerful states that have relatively low stakes in the international system. They are much less likely than powerful states to be prepared to take risky and costly action against a perceived threat and are therefore unlikely to join in any balancing coalition if they can avoid it. Indeed, in the current security environment there seems little likelihood that any of the lesser Asia Pacific powers would join a balancing coalition with India against China, however informal.

Rather than joining any coalition with India against China, many Southeast Asian states want to create a balanced *distribution* of power through developing a balanced role for extra-regional powers with interests in the region. This would involve encouraging the United States to continue its stabilising role in the region, while accommodating or facilitating the regional roles of China, Japan and India. While Indonesia sees India as potentially playing an important balancing role with China, consistent with its long-standing views on extra-regional powers, it would also see any direct role for India in the region in quite limited terms. Singapore has been the most enthusiastic and articulate sponsor of an increased security role for India in the region. Singapore has consistently welcomed and encouraged a balanced role for external security providers on the basis that competition between major regional powers 'must be squarely confronted and cannot be wished away'.[4] Singapore's conception of a 'balance of power' involves a multipolar balance that provides freedom to smaller states. As Singapore's first and long-serving Foreign Minister, S. Rajaratnam, explained: 'Where there is a multiplicity of suns, the gravitational pull of each is not only weakened but also by a judicious use of the pulls and counter-pulls of gravitational forces, the minor planets have a greater freedom of navigation.'[5] Similarly, as the current Prime Minister Lee Hsien Loong has argued, Singapore's concept of a balance of power:

> depends on the competing interests of several big powers in the region, rather than on linking the nation's fortunes to one overbearing power. The big powers can keep one another in check, and will prevent any one of them from dominating the entire region, and so allow small states to survive in the interstices between them.[6]

Michael Leifer, the noted observer of Southeast Asian strategic affairs, characterised this policy as a paradoxical combination of nonalignment and balance of power, with an emphasis on the latter.[7]

Vietnam has a slightly different perspective due to its history and proximity to China. Concerned about China's increasing assertiveness over territorial claims in the South China Sea, since the turn of this century Vietnam has been engaging with the United States as well as Japan, Russia and India in an effort to draw them into the region, while also periodically showing a calculated level of deference towards China. Some in New Delhi hope that India can cultivate a *de facto* alliance with Vietnam aimed at China in the nature of China's relationships with Pakistan or Burma in southern Asia, which are seen as being aimed at India. However, it seems unlikely that Vietnam would risk entering into any alliance with India which would provoke China and add little to Vietnam's capabilities. If Vietnam requires a balancing partner against China it would almost certainly turn to the United States, not India.

Australia too seems an unlikely coalition partner for India against China. Although Australia is keen to develop its strategic relationship with India, it is very cautious about placing the relationship in the context of balancing China. Australia would like to see India develop as a friendly power to balance China's rise. However, Australia would not wish to position itself as trying to contain China and would also see Sino-Indian strategic rivalry either in Southeast Asia or the Indian Ocean – potentially caused by an overly assertive India – as detrimental to its interests.

Southeast Asian and Australian perspectives on a regional balance of power suggest that while India may be encouraged to enhance its political and security presence in Southeast Asia, there will be some important limitations. India might be seen as a useful partner, but it does not have the capabilities or credibility to play the role of a primary security provider much beyond South Asia. Further, an Indian security presence that was seen as unduly provocative to China would not be encouraged. Nor would ASEAN states or Australia wish to become involved in Sino-Indian strategic rivalry. Singapore was thus reportedly uneasy about the way in which the Bush administration cultivated the India–US relationship in the context of its China policy, which was thought to add to regional uncertainties.[8] While the growing power of China is a source of concern, Singapore's desire to encourage India to act as a security provider is intended create an overall balance of power in the region among all the extra-regional powers, not only China but also the United States and Japan.

Another factor in the Southeast Asian strategic calculus, and one that is rarely discussed, is India's potential impact on the *intra-regional* balance of power in Southeast Asia. Although India largely eschewed any security role in Southeast Asia during the Cold War, it still played an important role in the intraregional balance. This included India's diplomatic support for Malaya/Malaysia against Indonesia during the *Konfrontasi* period; India's failure to support the newly independent Singapore against a potentially *revanchist* Malaysia in the late 1960s and early 1970s; and India's perceived support for Vietnam's bid to dominate Indochina during the 1980s. With India's increased engagement with Southeast Asia, its potential role in the intra-regional balance of power will increase even as India tries to avoid intra-regional disputes. Singapore's 'special relationship' with India improves its power and political bargaining position vis-à-vis its large Muslim neighbours, Malaysia and Indonesia. The extent to which Singapore is able to make itself *indispensible* to India's regional ambitions will help leverage Singapore's bargaining position throughout the region. The relatively warm state of India's relations with Indonesia also contrasts with India's cooler relations with Indonesia's rival, Malaysia. Malaysia has also shown itself to be sensitive about enhanced security cooperation between India and Thailand. While largely inchoate, this dimension could become more prominent if ASEAN is unable to mitigate longstanding rivalries or if regional rivalries (e.g. in Indochina) otherwise become enmeshed in broader Sino-Indian rivalry.

In short, although India is generally regarded as a potentially important element in an Asia Pacific balance of power it is not widely regarded as playing an essential role. Despite claims about India being the 'swing state' of the international system, India's economic and military capabilities are still limited, as are its strategic options. In coming years imperatives to form an Asia Pacific balancing coalition involving India will be driven by the evolution of China threat perceptions. But without a major change in the strategic environment the prospects of India forming part of a balancing coalition in anything other than very vague terms seem low. India's objectives may be better achieved by a series of bilateral relationships that allow India to exert greater influence and carry an implicit message that such a coalition could be established.

A multipolar regional order

Hopes to build a multipolar regional order also have a significant impact on the nature of India's relationships in the Asia Pacific.

For India, a multipolar regional order is often seen as an essential corollary to its 'Holy Grail' of strategic autonomy. As noted above, the development of a US–Chinese bipolar regional order would be seen as inimical to India's interests. Instead, New Delhi aspires to see a multipolar regional order involving the United States, China, Japan, India and perhaps Russia, as the major powers. Japan is seen by New Delhi as crucial to these aspirations. As Asia's other major indigenous power with major concerns about China's growing power, India sees an important opportunity to make common cause with Japan. During the Cold War, Japan and India had very different perspectives on strategic autonomy. Japan demonstrated a willingness to cede its strategic autonomy in favour of economic goals. In contrast, India looked down upon Japan's strategic choices, while allowing its own aspirations towards strategic and economic autonomy to impede its economic development. India is now more accepting of Japan's alliance with the United States and aspires to develop the Japan relationship in the hope that it will increasingly play an independent strategic role in Asia. Some in New Delhi hope that India may eventually be able to loosen Japan's position in the US orbit, although it chances of doing so seem questionable. To some extent this reflects wishful thinking by those in the Indian security community who continue to be influenced by Nehruvian ideas and assume that strategic autonomy not only should be a key objective for India, but for other states as well. They may not fully appreciate the extent to which, despite its ups and downs, the US alliance forms the bedrock of Japan's security and is likely to continue to do so for the foreseeable future. Japan is a long way from wishing to play an autonomous role in a multipolar regional order.

Nevertheless, India and Japan have flagged their intention to engage in closer political coordination in the region, which will help India gain a much greater voice in various regional fora. This is not just aimed at containing or limiting China. Several proposals in recent years for regional cooperation arrangements (e.g. Australian proposals for an Asia Pacific Community in 2008) have foundered on fears held by smaller Asia Pacific states about the potential economic or political domination of such arrangements by China and/or the United States. Arguably, a political coalition between India and Japan could play a positive role in helping to develop regional institutions in which both China and the United States play 'balanced' roles together with other major powers.

To some extent, Indonesia shares India's dreams of a multipolar regional order – provided that it is recognised as one of the major powers of the region. As Indonesia's strategic posture evolves and it looks beyond ASEAN for a role in the broader region, it is increasingly likely to see India as a partner. India and Indonesia have long shared concerns about China and improvements in the India–US security relationship have brought India's strategic posture much closer to Indonesia's. While both India and Indonesia see the United States as providing regional stability, they also want to see the creation of regional institutions in which the United States and China play balanced roles.

The recognition of India's major power status

India's desire for recognition of its 'rightful' international status has been an important factor in its regional engagement. Its acceptance into several ASEAN-centred institutions was seen by India as an important recognition of its international status, as was the willingness of ASEAN states to accept India's status as a *de facto* nuclear power following its 1998 nuclear tests. In contrast, the failure of both Japan and Australia to formally accept India as a legitimate nuclear weapons state is a significant factor in India's relations with them both. Their acceptance of India's nuclear legitimacy will be a key test of those relationships in coming years.

Despite its attempts to join regional fora over the last two decades, India remains somewhat of an outsider in Asia Pacific multilateral institutions. While India has been admitted to membership of some fora, it continues to be excluded from membership of others such as APEC and ASEAN + 3. In some institutions to which India has been admitted, such as the East Asia Summit, there is a perception that India has not even been granted full membership, let alone recognition as a principal power. China has not welcomed India's presence in East Asian institutions and there may be lingering questions among some other East Asian states (such as Malaysia and even South Korea) as to how the presence of India might affect the 'East Asian' identity of such institutions. Despite India's claims to the contrary, gaining a major role in these institutions is an important objective for New Delhi. India will therefore be expected to leverage its relationships throughout the Asia Pacific to ensure it has a key role in new multilateral institutions. India's reliance on ASEAN in extending its influence into the region also means that it is an important supporter of ASEAN's continued role as the organisational focus of Asia Pacific political, economic and security arrangements.[9] However, it has been argued that a reduction of the relevance of ASEAN-centred institutions due to the rise of China may lead India to opt to transcend existing regional organisations and deal directly with other major powers of the Asia Pacific in a Concert of Powers-type arrangement.[10]

The expansion of India's strategic space into Southeast Asia

The other important factor underlying India's strategic engagement with the Asia Pacific is the gradual expansion of its strategic influence in Southeast Asia and the potential for India to see Southeast Asia, or at least parts of it, as forming part of its strategic space. The expansion of strategic space is a common – if not universal – feature of aspiring great powers, and one would expect India to have similar ambitions as its economic and military power grows.[11]

India does not have an expansionist military tradition beyond South Asia and, as Stephen Cohen has observed, the culture of 'strategic restraint' runs deeply through Indian thinking. Nevertheless, since the end of the Cold War there has been an increasing view of a 'natural' sphere of Indian influence extending well beyond the subcontinent. This has frequently found practical expression through India's naval ambitions in the Indian Ocean region and Southeast Asia. India's 'strategic footprint', at least in maritime terms, is seen as extending from Southern Africa to the Persian Gulf and the Malacca Strait, and beyond into the South China Sea. Its anxieties over China's increased influence in the Indian Ocean undoubtedly serve to heighten New Delhi's defensive imperatives to secure the Malacca Strait and expand its strategic space into the South China Sea. The security dilemma created by India and China's conflicting perspectives suggests that Sino-Indian naval rivalry in the Indian Ocean is likely to continue and perhaps increase as a source of regional tension.

However, India's aspirations are driven not only by a wish to counter China but also by its ambitions to develop its own regional order. Some draw an analogy between India's position and the choices faced by the United States and Japan when they aspired to leading naval roles in their respective regions in the nineteenth and twentieth centuries. Just as the United States and Japan cooperated with Britain, India too finds it both necessary and useful to cooperate with the United States, the leading naval power of the day, in order to enhance its regional naval role. An enhanced naval role can then be used to expand its strategic space, just as the United States did through its Monroe Doctrine and Japan through its short-lived East Asian Co-Prosperity Sphere. India would ideally like to assert its own Monroe Doctrine in the Indian Ocean region, potentially including parts of Southeast Asia. Although Lee Kuan Yew invited India to be Singapore's 'protecting power' and impose a Monroe Doctrine on Southeast Asia in the 1960s, it does not seem likely that India would be able to assume such a role today. While the United States is encouraging India to take a leading security role in the northeast Indian Ocean and to play an increased role in the western Pacific, it is not clear how the United States would react to attempts by India to convert a greater role into what could be loosely called a 'sphere of influence' in Southeast Asia. A more likely outcome – at least in the medium term – may be the recognition of India as a leading naval power in the northeast Indian Ocean region, within limits imposed by the United States and others.

Although India sees a number of imperatives to play a greater role in the Asia Pacific, India's lack of economic and military strength compared with other major powers, particularly China, means it must remain flexible and discreet in its engagement with the region with the expectation that its relative power will grow in coming decades. Some have argued that India's approach in the Asia Pacific can be compared with Deng Xiaoping's advice about China 'keeping a low profile and never taking the lead'.[12] This is only partly true: while India has shown a degree of political sensitivity in its dealings in the Asia Pacific, it has been far from passive in pursuing a security role in Southeast Asia and has been much more active than, say, China in developing security relationships in the region.

India has been somewhat successful in recent years in expanding its strategic influence in Southeast Asia in a cooperative and relatively benign manner. It will continue trying to prove itself as a dependable security partner and as a net provider of security to the region. India has little choice but to proceed in that way. As Mohan points out, no great power has built a blue water navy capable of projecting force without physical access and political arrangements for 'forward presence'.[13] India's bases in the Andaman Islands are useful in projecting power into the Malacca Strait and even the South China Sea. However, India has no forward bases in the Pacific Ocean and certainly no territories in the Pacific (such as the United States has in Hawaii and Guam) on which a base could be sited (although it could conceivably 'piggy back' off existing US bases). India has naval access to the Pacific region only via the straits through archipelagic Southeast Asia or around Australia and can therefore only project significant and sustained naval power in the Pacific in cooperation with local states.

India is very much aware of this constraint. While Southeast Asian states have largely accepted India's predominant position in the northeast Indian Ocean, they have avoided taking any public position on India's claims about China's String of Pearls and would likely see heightened naval rivalry between India and China in the Indian Ocean as an unwelcome source of instability.

India's initial focus in expanding its influence into archipelagic Southeast Asia has been on Singapore which historically recognised India as having a *natural* strategic role in Southeast Asia. This view was expressed most strongly by Lee Kuan Yew who, as has been seen, saw India as the natural 'protecting power' for Singapore. As K. Kesavapany, a former senior Singaporean diplomat, put it: 'India has *de facto* inherited the British security role' stretching from Aden to Singapore.[14] However, this view is given less emphasis by Singapore's current leaders who see India's role more in terms of regional balance. Nevertheless, Singapore's support for India – including an apparent recognition of a direct security role – has been a major factor in helping India expand its influence in the region.

Other states are generally more hesitant in recognising India as having a natural direct security role in Southeast Asia. India's most important potential partner in Southeast Asia is Indonesia. There is an opportunity for a broad-based strategic partnership between India and Indonesia that could transform India's role in Southeast Asia. This could include a security relationship with a focus on maritime security and potentially even some type of role for India in the Malacca Strait. However, as has been discussed, while Indonesia has for many decades encouraged India to take a greater strategic role in Southeast Asia, it has also been careful to ensure that it maintains its own leading role in the region. There are also questions about what could be called India's 'strategic cultural' ability to form a close working partnership with Indonesia that would allow it to significantly expand its influence in Southeast Asia. The Indonesian relationship would involve a much different level of commitment by India compared to its commitment to Singapore. The extreme asymmetry in size between India and Singapore has made their relationship relatively easy from New Delhi's standpoint, as do the economic complementarities and Singapore's clear-sighted and proactive approach to foreign policy. The development of a broad-based relationship with Indonesia would require a major political, economic and security commitment by New Delhi that has so far not been forthcoming and could even be beyond its current economic and military capabilities.

Australia is another potentially important partner that could facilitate the expansion of India's security role in Southeast Asia. Australia's longstanding activist security role is largely accepted in the region and there are many opportunities for India and Australia to cooperate in such areas as maritime security, peacekeeping and in the stabilisation of weak or failing states in the Indian Ocean, Southeast Asia and even the South Pacific. However, India has not identified Australia as an important partner in its broader ambitions and has not been willing to overcome various cultural or political constraints to engage with it in a substantive way.

The prospects for significant developments in India's other relationships in Southeast Asia also seem limited for the moment. Malaysia is likely to be important to India's long-term strategic aspirations in Southeast Asia. However, it has shown considerable sensitivity about India's ambitions to expand its strategic space into the Malacca Strait and there are a number of political irritations in the relationship, although these concerns may be gradually easing. Political instability in Thailand may also limit decision-making abilities in Bangkok for some time. While India has long regarded Indochina as somehow forming part of its strategic space, India's relationship with Vietnam seems unlikely to develop into a security alliance. Although India believes it can help Vietnam in 'containing' the South China Sea dispute, it is difficult to imagine India being prepared to play anything other than a rhetorical role in support of Vietnam. Although the Indian Navy may make greater use of Cam Ranh Bay, its presence in the South China Sea is likely to remain 'recessed' for the foreseeable future. Taking a leaf out of China's strategy in the Indian Ocean, India may try to develop the necessary relationships and infrastructure to support an Indian naval presence in the Sout China Sea if one were ever required in the future.

There are several circumstances in which India could move to more assertively expand its strategic role in Southeast Asia. A major security crisis in the Malacca Strait could lead India to press its case for a security role with greater vigour. It is possible that littoral states may concede a role to India in the face of significant international pressure to accept outside assistance. A substantial expansion of China's naval presence in the Indian Ocean could also lead India to project power much more assertively into the South China Sea. However, without any direct military threat to Southeast Asia, it is not clear to what extent ASEAN states would be prepared to support a significant Indian security presence in the region.

Northeast Asia clearly lies beyond what India regards as its area of direct strategic interest. India is unlikely to involve itself in a security crisis involving Taiwan or the Koreas, even one that clearly involved Chinese aggression. However, both Japan and South Korea see India potentially as a major contributor to their maritime security needs in the Indian Ocean, complementing the US role. Japan's constitutional limitations and its apparent willingness to recognise India as a leading security provider throughout the Indian Ocean west of the Malacca Strait make it an ideal partner in this respect. This suggests that Japan will support the expansion of India's naval capabilities and India's attempt to limit China's presence in the Indian Ocean. Japan may, however, be less likely to support an Indian naval presence north of the Singapore Strait. In the longer term, if there was a perceived reduction of commitment to regional security by the United States one might even imagine a tacit division of responsibilities between Japan and India involving the mutual recognition of spheres of responsibility for maritime security in the western Pacific and Indian Oceans.

11 India as an Asia Pacific power

This book began with a discussion of some of the ways in which India might be seen as a major power. It asked whether, as India's economy develops in coming decades, it will find a place alongside states that are currently recognised as major Asia Pacific powers, such as the United States, China, Japan and, perhaps, Russia. India has many imperatives to project its power into the Asia Pacific and will undoubtedly play a growing role in regional security. But will it come to be seen as an Asia Pacific power, playing a fundamental role in the region's security system, or will it be seen as an essentially extra-regional power? What are India's strategic alternatives?

The strategic convergence of the Indian and Pacific Oceans

One way of considering India's likely future role is to ask whether the security dynamics of the Asia Pacific area and the Indian Ocean region are converging. Might the Asia Pacific strategic order grow to include India and the Indian Ocean? Might the Pacific and Indian Oceans come to be seen as a strategic whole?

As has been seen, until recent years India occupied a different strategic world to the Asia Pacific. However, the divisions between the different regions of Asia are becoming less distinct. India is emerging as a significant player in the security dynamics of Southeast Asia and to a lesser extent in Northeast Asia and the South Pacific. The separation of Asia into different regions of strategic interaction was at its clearest between South Asia and Northeast Asia. This is well illustrated by the trajectory of the India–Japan relationship. Through much of the twentieth century, Japan saw its own strategic space, even in its most extended form, as effectively ending at the Indian border where the Japanese army halted in 1942. For 50 years after independence, India was preoccupied with security threats in South Asia and its own attempts to achieve predominance within that region. It is only recently that India and Japan have made common cause. The end of the Cold War and India's reach for major power status also forced it to end its passive approach towards Southeast Asia. India now recognises the need to transcend its security concerns in South Asia and play a major role in Southeast Asia. This is well understood by some. As Singapore's Foreign Minister, George Yeo, commented, 'India's rise compels us to look at our environment in new ways. It will be increasingly less tenable to regard South Asia and East Asia as distinct strategic theatres operating only at the margins.'[1]

The extension of India's strategic reach into the Asia Pacific is in some ways mirrored by the expansion of China's interests into the Indian Ocean. China has long had close relationships with some of its southern Asian neighbours, particularly its *de facto* alliance with Pakistan and its security relationship with Burma. But it is only in recent years that China has sought to extend its influence in the broader Indian Ocean region, from the Middle East to Africa and to island states such as Mauritius, the Seychelles and Sri Lanka. While China's influence is now primarily economic, many of its relationships also have clear strategic overtones. Other Asia Pacific states, however, have been slower to extend their strategic vision to the Indian Ocean. Even the middle powers that straddle the Pacific and Indian Ocean regions – Australia, Indonesia and Malaysia – still have their geopolitical gaze firmly on the Pacific and show only a limited strategic interest in the Indian Ocean. Only with the rise of India as a major power and the expansion of its influence across the Indian Ocean region are these states paying more attention to their western seas.

Should the increased strategic interaction between India and the Asia Pacific, and China and the Indian Ocean be seen as part of a long run strategic convergence between the Asia Pacific and Indian Ocean regions? Should the Pacific and Indian Ocean regions be seen as a strategic whole? This view is gaining adherents among strategic analysts. Commentators with a geopolitical perspective see common strategic outlooks of an arc of maritime or 'rimland' states around the periphery of the Asian continent, particularly in their interaction with the 'continental' state of China. Robert Kaplan claims that the maritime world from Africa eastward to Indonesia and north to Korea and Japan will become one sweeping continuum – a process that will be hastened by the various canal and land-bridge projects that will provide links between the two oceans in addition to the existing straits.[2] Certainly the economic rise of China and India has considerably increased the importance of trading routes from Northeast Asia to the Middle East and beyond (with the Malacca Strait in the middle). At the very least, the Pacific and Indian Oceans should now be regarded as 'linked' security systems.

Some Indian thinkers have used the idea of strategic convergence between the Indian and Pacific Oceans to reframe their country's security concerns in the Indian Ocean and its ambitions in the Pacific. Shiv Shankar Menon, former Indian Foreign Secretary and current National Security Advisor, has proposed that the major powers concerned in the Indian Ocean should consider collective security arrangements not only to address threats from piracy and terrorism but also interstate conflicts. He argues that Indian Ocean security concerns cannot be considered in isolation from the Pacific. Menon proposes that there should be a discussion of what he calls:

a real concert of Asian powers, including the USA which has a major maritime presence and interests in Asia, to deal with issues of maritime security in all of Asia's oceans. As Asia becomes more integrated from Suez to the Pacific, none of Asia's seas or oceans can be considered in isolation.[3]

The idea of a 'Concert of Powers' spanning the Pacific and Indian Oceans is interesting. In recent years, there has been increased discussion about a Concert of Powers in the Asia Pacific as a way of engaging with China as a responsible member of a new strategic order.[4] The idea harks back to the first half of the nineteenth century when a 'concert' of four or five European powers explicitly took collective managerial responsibility for the security of Europe. This was seen as a way of mitigating competition between them and reducing the risk of unintended conflicts. It required major powers to assume a leadership role in maintaining security and for the lesser powers to accept that role. A rising India would seem to be an essential member of any such concert in Asia, although as Menon implicitly acknowledges, India may only have the necessary credibility if the managerial scope of such a concert extends to the Indian Ocean.

Are proposals of this nature likely to be attractive to major Asia Pacific powers? Arrangements in which India gains a greater voice in Asia Pacific security are consistent with US policies, although it is not clear to what extent the United States is prepared to cede a major role to China in Indian Ocean security. It is certainly not an idea that China (or for that, matter, Japan) has agreed with. Despite claiming its own role in South Asia and to some extent in the Indian Ocean, China argues that India is an 'outsider' to East Asia. Given the broader context of Sino-Indian strategic rivalry it is difficult to conceive of China relying on India for its maritime security needs in the Indian Ocean. While Japan sees India as a balancing partner and a useful provider of maritime security in the Indian Ocean, it too sees it as an essentially Indian Ocean power with a limited role in the Asia Pacific.

The conceptualisation of the Asia Pacific and Indian Ocean regions as a strategic whole could also be a two-edged sword for India. Such an approach would certainly legitimise a much greater role for India in the Asia Pacific. The development of a working concert of major powers with a focus on maritime security would also involve a much more multipolar Asian security order than is currently the case. However, such an approach would require India to concede a role to China in the Indian Ocean region that it has never before conceded. India might be forced to give up any dream of the Indian Ocean being 'India's Ocean'.

One point must be emphasised. If the security dynamics of South Asia and the Asia Pacific (or, more broadly, the Indian Ocean region and the Asia Pacific) are converging, they are only doing so *gradually and partially*. While India's economic influence in the Asia Pacific will almost certainly grow in coming years, it should not be assumed that greater economic influence will automatically translate into the strategic dimension. There are still significant limitations on strategic interaction between different parts of Asia and these limitations will continue for some time. While there has been increased security interaction between India and Japan – due to their broader regional interests as major regional powers – India's primary area of interest remains South Asia while Japan's is overwhelmingly Northeast Asia. There is little suggestion, for example, that Japan would be interested in taking a substantive security role in South Asia. Similarly, notwithstanding its great power aspirations, India has avoided any involvement in North Korea or Taiwan and is generally seen as having little natural role in the South Pacific. While there is greater security interaction between South and Southeast Asia, most Southeast Asian states still regard India as essentially an extra-regional power. Southeast Asian states have a northwards strategic orientation and have a relatively low level of interest in the Indian Ocean. They certainly have little inclination to become involved in the problems of South Asia.

Furthermore, the political, economic and security dynamics in the Indian Ocean region are quite different from the Asia Pacific. The Asia Pacific has an economic coherence and an established and relatively well-developed pattern of strategic interaction between major powers (the United States, China, Japan and to a lesser degree, Russia) and middle powers (ASEAN, South Korea, Australia). In contrast, the Indian Ocean has little economic coherence and there is little history of interaction between even the major Indian Ocean littoral states (South Africa, Iran, India, Pakistan, Indonesia, Australia) on Indian Ocean security issues. Few of these states have found reason to organise any regional security order and attempts to do so have been largely unsuccessful. It is not at all clear what security issues littoral states could coalesce around. Somalian pirates are unlikely to be sufficient. The ambitions of India, the largest Indian Ocean state, are viewed by many states – and not just those in South Asia – with a degree of suspicion.

It seems that India may have more compelling reasons to see the Pacific and Indian Ocean areas as a strategic whole than do most Asia Pacific states.

India's strategic options in the Asia Pacific

India may choose to play several different strategic roles in the Asia Pacific. Before discussing India's options, there is value in reviewing India's strategic constraints.

Despite its broader aspirations, India's strategic perspectives are primarily focused on the Indian Ocean region. India wants to be recognised as the predominant South Asian power and more broadly as the leading Indian Ocean power. It will take a long time for India to consolidate its position in South Asia and the broader Indian Ocean region, especially in the face of resistance from Pakistan, China and potentially others in the region. While India is seeking a strategic role in the Asia Pacific it has not been able to clearly articulate the extent of its ambitions.

Most obviously, India is not geographically contiguous with the Asia Pacific (as that region is currently understood), nor is it traditionally part of the East Asian 'mental map' as to what constitutes Asia. It is not just Chinese rhetoric that labels India as an 'outsider' to East Asia. The history of India's relationship with Japan demonstrates that these mental maps can be a powerful determinant of perceived strategic interests.

As a corollary to its geographic limitations, to a significant extent India will need to rely on local partners to project power into and beyond Southeast Asia. The fact that archipelagic Southeast Asia sits between the Indian and Pacific Oceans means that India faces its own 'Malacca Dilemma' in projecting naval power into the western Pacific in any sustained manner. India will therefore be highly dependent upon the goodwill of Indonesia, Singapore, Malaysia and, to a lesser extent, Australia, in building a security presence in the Asia Pacific. While many of these states see India's strategic engagement with the Asia Pacific in positive terms, they are yet to clearly support a direct security role for India in the western Pacific basin. A desire by Southeast Asian states to avoid unnecessary provocation of China means that they are likely to seek to limit India's security role north of Singapore.

There are also considerable limitations on India's ability to project power beyond South Asia and these are likely to continue for some years. In practice, India is much more cautious than some of the rhetoric coming from New Delhi implies. India has a long history of strategic restraint which inhibited the projection of power much beyond South Asia. Although Indian strategic thinking has developed markedly since the days of the Cold War, aspects of India's strategic doctrine (in particular, a need to continually demonstrate its strategic autonomy) are likely to constrain its ability to project power into the Asia Pacific. In addition, India has a track record of poor defence planning and coordination and there is a real possibility that its naval modernisation plans will not be fully realised in the expected timeframe, or at all. India's history is replete with examples of lack of follow-through in developing capabilities to meet strategic ambitions.

While the United States is facilitating the development of India's relationships in the Asia Pacific, it could also act as an implicit inhibitor of India's role in the region. The United States may see some benefit in Sino-Indian strategic rivalry, and may even at times encourage that rivalry, at least in the Indian Ocean. However, there may be circumstances in which the United States may come to regard India as a destabilising factor in regional security (for example, in case of conflict in the South China Sea). It is difficult to imagine India being able to take a substantial direct security role in the Asia Pacific in the face of strong opposition from the United States.

Having regard to these limitations, one could imagine four basic scenarios of India's future as a power in the Asia Pacific. Given India's failure to articulate its desired role in the Asia Pacific, these scenarios may be useful in understanding India's basic strategic choices over the coming decades.

An Indian Ocean first strategy

One scenario is for India to primarily focus on building or consolidating a sphere of influence in South Asia and the Indian Ocean region while developing a secondary role in the Asia Pacific. One could call this the 'Indian Ocean first' scenario. This would involve India consolidating its naval predominance in the northeast Indian Ocean up to the Malacca Strait and aspiring (probably unsuccessfully) for a direct security role in the Strait. India, along with the United States, would be recognised as a leading naval power in the western Indian Ocean. India would expend much of its energy in extending its influence throughout the Indian Ocean and countering China's influence in the region. A major naval focus would be to strengthen its domination of China's SLOCs across the northern Indian Ocean.

India's strategic role in the Asia Pacific would be an important, but secondary, priority. India would continue to build its economic influence in the Asia Pacific, but this may not be matched fully by an expansion of its strategic influence. In building a role in the Asia Pacific, India would rely primarily on its strategic relationship with the United States and to a lesser extent, Japan. It would continue to build its relationship with Singapore, perhaps even establishing a logistical presence there. While India would hope to build closer security relationships with states such as Indonesia, Vietnam and Australia it would only make a limited commitment to those relationships and they would therefore only develop slowly. Under this scenario, India would develop the role as an important, but definitely *extra-regional* power in the Asia Pacific.

A focus on extending its influence in the Indian Ocean region would be comparatively low risk for India, although as noted above it does have competitors in that region. However, a relatively narrow scope of regional influence could also make it more difficult for India to be recognised as a power of global significance. Despite some of the rhetoric, India may now be drifting towards this approach.

An active engagement strategy

Another scenario may be for India to expand its influence in the Indian Ocean region while also actively seeking to become a major power in the Asia Pacific through building an informal coalition with the United States and its Asia Pacific allies to balance against China. One could call this an 'active engagement' strategy. Such a coalition would help to expand India's economic and political role in the Asia Pacific, while gradually building India's security presence in the western Pacific. India would work with Japan to increase its political role in the region. India would also need to make a psychological and material commitment to building much closer and more productive economic and security partnerships with middle powers such as Indonesia, Australia, Vietnam and even South Korea. Such a coalition could be organised around a multilateral 'security dialogue' or take the form of a series of parallel bilateral relationships in which the United States and India would play leading coordinating roles.

In this scenario, the Indian Navy would become increasingly active in the western Pacific, primarily in cooperation with the United States and its allies. India would participate (if sometimes reluctantly) in various US-sponsored multilateral maritime security initiatives and would commit to enhancing the interoperability of India's armed forces with the United States and its allies. While India's primary focus would be on extending its role in Southeast Asia, its many relationships in the region would also provide opportunities to increase its role throughout the Asia Pacific, including in Northeast Asia and the South Pacific. India would over time become partly 'enmeshed' in a web of US-centred relationships while retaining sufficient strategic autonomy to pursue its long-term objectives. Paradoxically this would be a price India pays for faster recognition of its status as a major power by most Asia Pacific states.

Such a strategy of actively balancing China in the Asia Pacific would carry a not-insignificant risk of reaction from China. China could, for example, become more assertive in South Asia or the Indian Ocean. However the development by India of a series of relatively informal security relationships would also allow it to move incrementally and calibrate its moves in line with China's actions.

A 'go it alone' strategy

A further alternative may be for India to become a disruptive force in the Asia Pacific strategic order, just as China is now widely seen as a disruptive force to the strategic order. This could be called a 'go it alone' strategy. This change in India's strategic posture could be triggered by a number of developments, including significant and sustained economic growth at or above the level of China's current growth; an enhanced Chinese military presence in the Indian Ocean region leading to heightened rivalry; and/or a deterioration of the India–US strategic partnership. These or other developments could potentially propel India out of its defensive tradition of strategic restraint into a much more assertive strategic posture and to seek its 'place in the sun' in the Asia Pacific while simultaneously emphasising a need for strategic autonomy.

Such an approach would require a major commitment of India's political, economic and military resources to the region. It could involve limited cooperation with the United States and its partners in the Asia Pacific on an issue-by-issue basis. India might also seek to develop a series of strategic relationships – and even an informal coalition – outside the US sphere, including, for example, with Vietnam and/or Russia. This may lead to significantly greater instability in the region as major powers compete to influence the smaller states. At its most extreme, it could even involve a jostle for position among three power blocs in the Asia Pacific led by the United States, China and India.

This scenario would carry numerous risks for India. There is a greater likelihood that China could respond in South Asia and the Indian Ocean to India's detriment. India could lose many of the benefits it may otherwise gain from close cooperation with the United States. In addition, Southeast Asian states, and even Australia, could seek to limit India's role in the region in order to mitigate the potentially destabilising effects of India's actions.

A convergence strategy

A further possibility may be for India to decide that its optimal path to power and influence in the Asia Pacific lies through seeking to build some type of concert of powers among the major powers of the Asia Pacific and the Indian Ocean. This would be likely initially to focus on maritime security issues, but would gradually expand its scope. This could be called a 'convergence' strategy. It would to some extent involve a recognition by China and Japan of a major role for India in the Asia Pacific, although at the price of India ceding a role to China in the Indian Ocean region. India would also need to be prepared to take managerial responsibility in areas that lie beyond its immediate area of strategic interest (e.g. Northeast Asia or the South Pacific).

It is far from certain that such an arrangement would be acceptable to the major and lesser powers of the Asia Pacific. It would also require a major shift in Indian strategic thinking. It would effectively require India to transcend its reflexive defensiveness about the Indian Ocean and decide that the path to greater security in the Indian Ocean and greater influence in the Asia Pacific could be best achieved through cooperation rather than competition with China. Whether such an approach could be achieved is doubtful.

Will India become an Asia Pacific power?

India is without a doubt becoming an ever more important factor in the Asia Pacific strategic order and the world. But while India's economic power and influence in the Asia Pacific is likely to grow considerably in coming years, it is by no means certain that India will be recognised as a major power of the Asia Pacific any time soon.

India's future strategic role in the Asia Pacific will largely be determined by its ability and willingness to overcome a number of geographic, material and psychological limitations. In order to substantially extend its strategic power in the Asia Pacific, it will need to commit the resources to develop comprehensive economic and security relationships with several key Asia Pacific states. India would need to make a major commitment to building closer relationships with important potential partners such as Indonesia, Vietnam and Australia to facilitate the expansion of its role in the region. In building relationships throughout the Asia Pacific, particularly with the United States and its allies, India would also need to overcome the limitations of its traditionally defensive strategic thinking, which still work against its ability to project power and influence in the region.

India has the potential to become a positive force in the Asia Pacific strategic order. But a major strategic role in the Asia Pacific will not come automatically with its growing economic power. To fulfil its self-described 'destiny', including aspirations to become an Asia Pacific power, India will need to go beyond its rhetoric and demonstrate a significant commitment to provide security to the region.

Notes

1 India as a great power

1 Vernon Marston Hewitt, *The International Politics of South Asia*, Manchester: Manchester University Press, 1992, p.195.
2 See for example, comments by Prime Minister Manmohan Singh in Indo-Asian News Service, 'Want dialogue? Then contain terror, PM tells Gilani', *Thaindian News*, 16 July 2009.
3 Stephen Cohen, *India: emerging power*, Washington: Brookings Institute, 2001, p.51.
4 Henry Kissinger, *Diplomacy*, New York: Touchstone, 1994, p.26.
5 See, for example, Ross Babbage and Sandy Gordon (eds), *India's Strategic Future: regional state or global power?*, London: Macmillan, 1992; Cohen, *India: emerging power*; C. Raja Mohan, *Crossing the Rubicon: the shaping of India's new foreign policy*, New York: Palgrave Macmillan, 2003; Ashok Kapur, *India, from Regional to World Power*, New York: Routledge, 2006; and Robert D. Kaplan, *Monsoon: the Indian Ocean and the future of American power*, New York: Random House, 2010.
6 Office of Spokesman, US Department of State, 'Background briefing by administration officials on U.S.–South Asia relations', Washington DC, 25 March 2005.
7 George Tanham, *Indian Strategic Thought: an interpretative essay*, Santa Monica, CA: Rand, 1992.
8 Baldev Raj Nayar and T.V. Paul, *India in the World Order: searching for major power status*, Cambridge: Cambridge University Press, 2003, p.252.
9 Kanti Bajpai, 'Indian conceptions of order/justice in international relations: Nehruvian, Gandhian, Hindutva and Neo-Liberal', in V.R. Mehta and Thomas Pantham (eds), *Political Ideas in Modern India: thematic explorations*, New Delhi: Sage, 2006, pp.367–92.
10 Yashwant Sinha, 'Geopolitics: what it takes to be a world power', speech in New Delhi, 12 March 2004.
11 See, for example, Sandy Gordon, *Widening Horizons: Australia's new relationship with India*, Canberra: Australian Strategic Policy Institute, 2007.
12 George Perkovich, 'Is India a major power?', *The Washington Quarterly*, Vol.27, No.1, Winter 2003–4, pp.129–44.
13 Nitin Pai and Aruna Urs 'Look before you hop: a discussion on strategic affairs with Stephen Cohen', *Pragati: the Indian national interest review*, No.15, June 2008, p.9.
14 Andrew Scobell, '"Cult of defense" and "Big power dreams": the influence of strategic culture on China's relationship with India', in Malcolm R.Chambers (ed.), *South Asia in 2020: future strategic balances and alliances*, Carlisle: US Army War College, Strategic Studies Institute, 2002, pp.329–59.

15 Nayar and Paul, *India in the World Order*, pp.1, 25.
16 Paul Kennedy, *The Rise and Fall of the Great Powers: economic change and military conflict from 1500 to 2000*, New York: Random House, 1987, p.xxiii.
17 Selig Harrison, 'A nuclear bargain with India', paper presented at the conference India at the Crossroads, Southern Methodist University, Dallas, Texas, 27 March 1998, quoted in Nayar and Paul, *India in the World Order*, p.77.
18 See, for example, P.R. Kumaraswamy, 'National security: a critique', in P.R. Kumaraswamy (ed.), *Security Beyond Survival: essays for K. Subrahmanyam*, New Delhi: Sage Publications, 2004, pp.11–32.
19 Kenneth Waltz, *Theory of International Politics*, New York: McGraw Hill, 1979, p.131.
20 See, for example, John J. Mearsheimer, *The Tragedy of Great Power Politics*, New York: W.W. Norton & Co, 2001, p.5.
21 Waltz, *Theory of International Politics*, p.131.
22 Kennedy, *The Rise and Fall of the Great Powers*, pp.xxii–xxiv.
23 See, for example, Saul Bernard Cohen, *Geography and Politics in a World Divided* (2nd edn), New York: Oxford University Press, 1973.
24 Hedley Bull, *The Anarchical Society: a study of order in world politics*, London: Macmillan, 1977, p.200.
25 Nayar and Paul, *India in the World Order*, pp.57–63. However, Nye, the leading exponent of soft power, believes that while India's soft power is expanding, India does not rank high on the indices of soft power possessed by other major powers. Joseph S. Nye, *Soft Power: the means to success in world politics*, New York: Public Affairs, 2004, pp.88–89.
26 Stockholm International Peace Research Institute. http://milexdata.sipri.org/result.php4 (accessed 28 February 2011).
27 'India's nuclear forces, 2007', *Bulletin of Atomic Scientists*, Vol.63, No.4, July/August 2007, pp.74–78.
28 See James R. Holmes, Andrew C. Winner and Toshi Yoshihara, *Indian Naval Strategy in the Twenty-First Century*, London: Routledge, 2009, ch.6.
29 Excluding expenditure on nuclear weapons. US dollar figures are at constant 2008 exchange rates. Stockholm International Peace Research Institute. http://milexdata.sipri.org/result.php4 (accessed 28 February 2011).
30 Harsh V. Pant, 'India in the Indian Ocean: growing mismatch between ambitions and capabilities', *Pacific Affairs*, Vol.82, No.2, Summer 2009, pp.279–97.
31 From which must be deducted population growth of around 2 per cent per annum for real GDP growth per capita.
32 Ross H. Munro, 'The loser: India in the nineties', *The National Interest*, No.33, Summer 1993, pp.62–63.
33 Baldev Raj Nayar, 'Political structure and India's economic reforms of the 1990s', *Pacific Affairs*, Vol.71, No.3, Autumn 1998, pp.335–58 at p.345.
34 Munro, 'The loser', p.62.
35 CIA World Factbook. www.cia.gov/library/publications/the-world-factbook/geos/in.html (accessed 28 February 2011).
36 John Hawksworth, 'The world in 2050: how big will the major emerging market economies get and how can the OECD compete?' PricewaterhouseCoopers, March 2006. www.pwc.com/en_GX/gx/world-2050/pdf/world2050emergingeconomies.pdf (accessed 28 February 2011).
37 Dominic Wilson and Anna Stupnytska, 'The N11: more than an acronym', Goldman Sachs Global Economics Paper No.153, 28 March 2007. www.chicagobooth.edu/alumni/clubs/pakistan/docs/next11dream-march%20'07-goldmansachs.pdf (accessed 28 February 2011).
38 To name a few, see Gurcharan Das, *India Unbound: the social and economic revolution from independence to the global information age*, New Delhi: Viking,

2000; Brahma Chellaney, *Asian Juggernaut: the rise of China, India and Japan*, New Delhi: HarperCollins, 2006; and Edward Luce, *In Spite of the Gods: the strange rise of modern India*, New York: Doubleday, 2007.
39 CIA World Factbook.
40 2009 estimates, each at purchasing power parity. CIA World Factbook.
41 CIA World Factbook.
42 2009 estimates.
43 2009 estimates at international exchange rates.
44 For a general discussion of India's 'Monroe Doctrine', see Holmes *et al.*, *Indian Naval Strategy in the Twenty-First Century*, ch.3.
45 See generally, Krishan Gopal and Sarbjit Sharma, *India and Israel: towards strategic partnership*, New Delhi: Authorspress, 2007.
46 See generally, Christine Fair, 'India and Iran: New Delhi's balancing act', *The Washington Quarterly*, Vol.30, No.3, Summer 2007, pp.145–59.
47 C. Raja Mohan, 'Is India an East Asian power? Explaining New Delhi's security politics in the Western Pacific', ISAS Working Paper No.81, 11 August 2009, p.5.
48 P. Stobdan, 'Central Asia and India's security', *Strategic Analysis*, Vol.28, No.1, 2004, pp.54–83.
49 For general discussions of India's maritime strategy and capabilities, see Holmes *et al.*, *Indian Naval Strategy in the Twenty-First Century*; David Scott, 'India's "Grand Strategy" for the Indian Ocean: Mahanian visions', *Asia-Pacific Review*, Vol.13, No.2, 2006, pp.97–129; and Leszek Buszynski, 'Emerging naval rivalry in East Asia and the Indian Ocean: implications for Australia', *Security Challenges*, Vol.5, No.3, 2009, pp.73–93.
50 Arun Prakash, 'A vision of India's maritime power in the 21st century', *USI Journal*, July–September 2006, pp. 454–63.
51 See generally, David Brewster, 'An Indian sphere of influence in the Indian Ocean?', *Security Challenges*, Vol.6, No.3, Spring 2010, pp.1–20.
52 See generally, Gurpreet S. Khurana, 'Indian Ocean Naval Symposium (IONS): where from. ... whither-bound?', *IDSA Comment*, 22 February 2008.
53 Holmes *et al.*, *Indian Naval Strategy in the Twenty-first Century*, pp.50–52.
54 See generally, Joseph A. Camilleri, *Regionalism in the New Asia-Pacific Order*, Cheltenham: Edward Elgar, 2003.
55 Christophe Jaffrelot, 'India's Look East policy: an Asianist strategy in perspective', *India Review*, Vol.2, No.2, April 2003, pp.35–68, p.55.
56 When the Japanese government organised a rollover of short-term Indian government debt to Japanese banks to avert an almost certain default on India's sovereign debt.
57 The Bay of Bengal Initiative for MultiSectoral Technical and Economic Cooperation organisation.
58 Jaswant Singh, 'Statement by Deputy Chairman Planning Commission of India Jaswant Singh on the occasion of the ASEAN 31st Post Ministerial Conference (ASEAN+9) Plenary Session', 28 July 1998.
59 C. Raja Mohan, 'Look East policy: phase two', *The Hindu*, 9 October 2003.
60 E. Ahamed, press release of Minister of State for External Affairs, 'Reinforcing "Look East" policy', 16 January 2006. http://pib.nic.in/release/rel_print_page1.asp?relid=14984 (accessed 28 February 2011).
61 Mohan Malik, 'China's strategy of containing India', *Power and Interest News Report*, 6 February 2006. www.pinr.com/report.php?ac=view_report&report_id=434 (accessed 28 February 2011).
62 Atal Vajpayee, 'India's perspective on ASEAN and the Asia-Pacific region', speech to Institute of Southeast Asian Studies, Singapore, 9 April 2002.
63 Frederick Grare, 'In search of a role: India and the ASEAN regional forum', in Frederick Grare and Amitabh Mattoo (eds), *India and ASEAN: the politics of*

India's Look East policy, New Delhi: Centre de Sciences Humaines, 2001, pp.119–45 at p.136.

2 Developments in Indian strategic thinking about the Asia Pacific

1 For studies on Nehruvian strategic doctrine, see Mannaraswamighala Sreeranga Rajan, *Studies on Nonalignment and the Nonaligned Movement: theory and practice*, New Delhi: ABC Publishing House, 1986; and K. Subrahmanyam, *Indian Security Perspectives*, New Delhi: ABC Publishing House, 1982.
2 For discussions of India's political relations in Southeast Asia during the Cold War see Mohammed Ayoob, *India and Southeast Asia: Indian perceptions and policies*, New York: Routledge, 1990; and Kripa Sridharan, *The ASEAN Region in India's Foreign Policy*, Aldershot: Dartmouth Publishing, 1996.
3 C. Raja Mohan, *Crossing the Rubicon: the shaping of India's new foreign policy*, New York: Palgrave Macmillan, 2003, p.27.
4 See generally, Stephen P. Cohen and Sunil Dasgupta, *Arming without Aiming: India's military modernisation*, Washington DC: Brookings Institution Press, 2010.
5 Rahul Sagar, 'State of mind: what kind of power will India become', *International Affairs*, Vol.85, No.4, 2009, pp.801–16.
6 Kanti Bajpai, 'Indian strategic culture', in Michael R. Chambers (ed.), *South Asia in 2020: future strategic balances and alliances*, Carlisle, PA: Strategic Studies Institute, 2002, pp.245–305.
7 C. Raja Mohan, 'India's changing strategic profile in East and Southeast Asia', paper presented at the Regional Outlook Forum, Singapore, 8 January 2008, p.12. www.iseas.edu.sg/rof08/s1_raja.pdf (accessed 28 February 2011).
8 Ashley J. Tellis, 'India in Asian geopolitics', in Prakash Nanda (ed.), *Rising India: friends and foes*, New Delhi: Lancer, 2007, pp. 118–30 at 129.
9 Varun Sahni, 'India and the Asian security architecture', *Current History*, Vol.105, No.690, April 2006, pp.163–67.
10 Guillem Monsonis, 'India's strategic autonomy and rapprochement with the US', *Strategic Analysis*, Vol.34, No.4, July 2010, pp.611–24 at p.624.
11 C. Raja Mohan, 'India and the changing geopolitics of the Indian Ocean', speech at the National Maritime Foundation, New Delhi, 19 July 2010.
12 C. Raja Mohan, 'The evolution of Sino-Indian relations: implications for the United States', in Alyssa Ayres and C. Raja Mohan, *Power Realignments in Asia: China, India and the United States*, New Delhi: Sage Publications, 2009, pp.270–90 at p.288.
13 Rajesh Rajagopalan and Varun Sahni, 'India and the great powers: strategic imperatives, normative necessities', *South Asian Survey*, Vol.15, No.5, 2008, pp.5–32.
14 C. Raja Mohan, 'The Asian balance of power', *Seminar*, No.487, 2000.
15 See, for example, Anindya Batabyal, 'Balancing China in Asia: a realist assessment of India's Look East strategy', *China Report* (New Delhi), Vol.42, No.2, 2006, pp.79–197; and Bharat Karnad, 'India's future plans and defence requirements', in N. Sisodia and C. Udaya Bhaskar (eds), *Emerging India: security and foreign policy perspectives*, New Delhi: Institute for Defence Studies and Analysis, 2005, pp.61–76.
16 Pranab Mukherjee, address to the 5th IISS Asian Security Summit, 3 June 2006.
17 Pranab Mukherjee, address to the 7th Asian Security Conference, 29 January 2005.
18 Sudhir Devare, *India and Southeast Asia: towards security convergence*, Singapore: Institute of Southeast Asian Studies, 2006, p.211.
19 C. Raja Mohan, 'India's geopolitics and Southeast Asian security', in Daljit Singh and Tin Maung Maung (eds), *Southeast Asian Affairs 2008*, Singapore: Institute of Southeast Asian Studies, 2008, pp.43–60 at p.53.

20 Purnendra Jain, 'From condemnation to strategic partnership: Japan's changing view of India (1998–2007)', Institute of South Asian Studies Working Paper No.41, 10 March 2008; and Brahma Chellaney and Horimoto Takenori, 'Indo kara mita Nihon, Ajia' [Japan–India links critical for Asia-Pacific security], *Gaiko Forum*, Vol.7, No.2, Fall 2007.
21 Ashley J. Tellis, 'The changing political-military environment: South Asia', in Zalmay Khalilzad *et al.*, *The United States and Asia: towards a new US strategy and force posture*, Santa Monica, CA: Rand Corporation, 2001, pp.203–40 at p.214.
22 For example in Ashley Tellis, *India as a New Global Power: an action agenda for the United States*, Washington DC: Carnegie Endowment for World Peace, 2005.
23 Robert D. Kaplan, 'Power plays in the Indian Ocean: the maritime commons in the 21st century', in Abraham M. Denmark, Dr James Mulvenon, Frank G. Hoffman, Lt Col Kelly M. Martin, Oliver Fritz, Eric Sterner, Dr Greg Rattray, Chris Evans, Jason Healey and Robert Kaplan, *Contested Commons: the future of American power in a multipolar world*, Washington DC: Center for a New American Security, 2010, p.188.
24 See, for example, Siddharth Varadarajan, 'Bush, India and two degrees of separation', *The Hindu*, 3 March 2006; Amit Gupta, 'US-India-China: assessing tripolarity', *China Report* (New Delhi), Vol.42, No.1, 2006, pp.69–83; Mohan, 'The Asian balance of power', p.17; and Rajiv Sikri, *Challenge and Strategy: rethinking India's foreign policy*, New Delhi: Sage, 2009.
25 C. Raja Mohan, 'India, China and Asian security,' *The Hindu*, January 27, 2003.
26 Kanti Bajpai, 'India: modified structuralism', in Muthiah Alagappa (ed.), *Asian Security Practice: material and ideational influences*, Stanford, CT: Stanford University Press, 1998, pp.157–97.
27 S.D. Muni argues that Nehru gave significant emphasis to democracy in India's policies towards its South Asian neighbours, but this commitment was diluted considerably after his death. S.D. Muni, *India's Foreign Policy: the democracy dimension*, Foundation Books: New Delhi, 2010.
28 Manmohan Singh, 'PM's speech at India Today conclave', New Delhi, 25 February 2005. www.pmindia.nic.in/speech/content.asp?id=510 (accessed 28 February 2011).
29 Joint Statement of Prime Minister Singh and Prime Minister Abe, 16 December 2006.
30 B. Raman, 'India & Japan: democracy as a strategic weapon', South Asia Analysis Group, Paper No.206, 17 December 2006.
31 Brahma Chellaney, 'Towards Asian power equilibrium', *The Hindu*, 1 November 2008.
32 Stephen M. Walt, *The Origins of Alliances*, Ithaca, NY: Cornell University Press, 1987), p.266.
33 Victor D. Cha, 'The ideational dimension of America's alliances in Asia', in Amitav Acharya and Evelyn Goh (eds), *Reassessing Security Cooperation in the Asia Pacific: competition, congruence and transformation*, Cambridge, MA: The MIT Press, 2007, pp.41–70.
34 G. John Ikenberry, *Liberal Order and Imperial Ambition: essays on American power and world politics*, Malden, MA : Polity, 2006.
35 C. Raja Mohan, 'Balancing interests and values: India's struggle with democracy promotion', *The Washington Quarterly*, Vol.30, No.3, Summer 2007, pp.99–115.
36 Lee Kuan Yew, 'India's peaceful rise', *Forbes*, 24 December 2007.
37 Shyam Saran, 'India and its neighbours', address in New Delhi, 14 February 2005.
38 James R. Holmes, Andrew C. Winner and Toshi Yoshihara, *Indian Naval Strategy in the Twenty-First Century*, London: Routledge, 2009, p.33.

39 Quoted in David Scott, 'India's "Grand Strategy" for the Indian Ocean: Mahanian visions', *Asia-Pacific Review*, Vol.13, No.2, 2006, pp.97–129 at p.109.
40 Pranab Mukherjee, speech for the Admiral A.K. Chatterjee Memorial Lecture, Kolkata, 30 June 2007.
41 Sikri, *Challenge and Strategy*, p.250.
42 Scott, 'India's "Grand Strategy" for the Indian Ocean', p.99.
43 Brewster, 'An Indian sphere of influence in the Indian Ocean?', *Security Challenges*, Vol.6, No.3, Spring 2010, pp.1–20.
44 Atul Aneja 'India, Vietnam partners in safeguarding sea lanes', *The Hindu*, 15 April 2000.
45 India, Ministry of Defence, *Annual Report 2000–2001*.
46 Chidanand Rajghatta, 'Singhing Bush's praise', *Times of India*, 13 April 2001.
47 Singh, 'PM's address at the Combined Commander's Conference', 24 October 2004.
48 Scott, 'India's "Grand Strategy" for the Indian Ocean'.
49 See generally, Rahul Roy-Chaudhury, *Sea Power and India's Security*, London: Brassey's, 1995, p.199.
50 George Tanham, 'Indian strategic thought: an interpretive essay', in George Tanham, Kanti P. Bajpai and Amitabh Mattoo (eds), *Securing India: strategic thought and practice in an emerging power*, New Delhi: Manhora, 1996, p.73.
51 S. Bilveer, 'Operation Cactus: India's "prompt action" in Maldives', *Asian Defense Journal*, February 1989, p.33.
52 J. Mohan Malik, 'India and China: bound to collide', in P.R. Kumaraswamy (ed.), *Security Beyond Survival: essays for K. Subrahmanyam*, New Delhi: Sage Publications, 2004, pp.127–65.
53 James R. Holmes and Toshi Yoshihara, 'India's "Monroe Doctrine" and Asia's maritime future', *Strategic Analysis*, Vol.32, No.6, November 2008, pp.997–1011.
54 According to Indira Gandhi. See John W. Garver, 'Chinese-Indian rivalry in Indochina', *Asian Survey*, Vol.27, No.11, November 1987, pp.1205–19 at pp.1207–8.
55 Mohan, *Crossing the Rubicon*, p.205.
56 Quoted in Holmes *et al.*, *Indian Naval Strategy in the 21st Century*, p.38.
57 Mohan, *Crossing the Rubicon*, p.209.
58 Amit Baruah, 'Not seeking exclusive sphere of influence', *The Hindu*, 11 February 2007.
59 Mohan, *Crossing the Rubicon*, ch.8.
60 Holmes *et al.*, *Indian Naval Strategy in the 21st Century*, p.155.
61 For a discussion of these different ways of exerting hegemony, see Rajagopalan and Sahni, 'India and the great powers'.
62 Tanham, 'Indian strategic thought', p.69.
63 C. Raja Mohan, 'Is India an East Asian power? Explaining New Delhi's security politics in the Western Pacific', ISAS Working Paper No.81, 11 August 2009.
64 Which contrasts with the United States' effective refusal to recognise any regional security role for China in the Pacific Ocean.
65 Dean G. Acheson, *A Democrat Looks at his Party*, New York: Harper, 1955, p.64.
66 M. Pardesi, *Deducing India's Grand Strategy of Regional Hegemony from Historical and Conceptual Perspectives*, Singapore: Institute of Defence and Strategic Studies, 2005, p.53.
67 John Mearsheimer, *The Tragedy of Great Power Politics*, New York: W.W. Norton & Co, 2001, p.232.
68 Pardesi, *Deducing India's Grand Strategy*, p.55.
69 Saul Bernard Cohen, *Geography and Politics in a World Divided* (2nd edn), New York: Oxford University Press, 1973, p.viii.
70 Admiral Arun Prakash, 'China and the Indian Ocean region', *Indian Defence Review*, Vol.21, No.4, October–December 2006, pp.7–12 at p.11.

71 See, for example, Colonel Gurmeet Kanwal, 'Countering China's strategic encirclement of India', *Indian Defence Review*, Vol.15, No.3, July–September 2000, p.17; Bharat Karnad, *Nuclear Weapons and Indian Security: the realist foundations of strategy*, Delhi: Macmillan India, 2005; Mohan Malik, 'Sino-Indian relations in the 21st century: the continuing rivalry', in Brahma Chellaney (ed.), *Securing India's Future in the New Millenium*, New Delhi: Centre for Policy Research, 1999; and Iskander Rehman, 'Keeping the Dragon at bay: India's counter-containment of China in Asia', *Asian Security*, Vol.5, No.2, May 2009, pp.114–43.
72 Karnad, *Nuclear Weapons and Indian Security*, p.541 and Malik, 'China's strategy of containing India'.
73 See, for example, Mohan, 'Is India an East Asian power?', p.17.

3 Sino-Indian strategic competition and the Asia Pacific

1 Austin Coates, *China, India and the Ruins of Washington*, New York: The John Day Company, 1972.
2 For detailed studies of the history of the India–China strategic relationship in modern times, see John W. Garver, *Protracted Contest: Sino-Indian rivalry in the twentieth century*, Seattle: University of Washington Press, 2001; and Francine R. Frankel and Harry Harding (eds), *The India–China Relationship: what the United States needs to know*, New York: Columbia University Press, 2004.
3 D.R. Makekar, *The Guilty Men of 1962*, Bombay: Tulsi Shah Enterprises, 1968, p.110.
4 'Nuclear anxiety; Indian's letter to Clinton on the nuclear testing', *The New York Times*, 13 May 1998.
5 C. Raja Mohan, *Crossing the Rubicon: the shaping of India's new foreign policy*, New York: Palgrave Macmillan, 2003, p.149.
6 Tushar Poddar and Eva Yi, 'India's rising growth potential', Goldman Sachs Global Economics Paper No.152, January 2007. www.usindiafriendship.net/viewpoints1/Indias_Rising_Growth_Potential.pdf (accessed 28 February 2011).
7 See, for example, B. Raman, 'China & India: reality behind statistics', South Asia Analysis Group Paper No.2567, 28 January 2008.
8 India, Department of Commerce and Industry. http://commerce.nic.in/eidb (accessed 28 February 2011).
9 Amardeep Athwal, *China–India relations: contemporary dynamics*, New York: Routledge, 2007, p.88.
10 India, Ministry of Commerce and Industry. http://commerce.nic.in/eidb (accessed 28 February 2011).
11 Athwal, *China–India relations*, pp.91–92.
12 See generally, Bimal Kumar Sikdar and Amitabh Sikdar, *India & China: strategic energy management and security*, New Delhi: Manas Publications, 2009; and Hongyi Lai (ed.), *Asian Energy Security: the maritime dimension*, London: Palgrave MacMillan, 2009.
13 Jeffrey G. Brown, Vijay Mukherji and Kang Wu, 'The energy race between China and India: motivations and potential opportunities for cooperation', in *China, India and the United States: competition for energy resources*, Abu Dhabi: The Emirates Centre for Strategic Studies and Research, 2008, pp.223–54.
14 Athwal, *China–India relations*, p.105; and Sudha Mahalingam, 'India–China energy cooperation: commonalities, synergies and complementarities', in Ligia Noronha and Anant Sudarshan (eds), *India's Energy Security,* London: Routledge, 2009, pp.97–107.
15 William T. Tow, 'Strategic dimensions of energy competition in Asia', in Michael Wesley (ed.), *Energy Security in Asia*, London: Routledge, 2008, pp.161–73.

16 Toshi Yoshihara and James R. Holmes, *Red Star over the Pacific: China's rise and the challenge to U.S. maritime strategy*, Annapolis, MD: Naval Institute Press, 2010, p.88.
17 For lengthy discussions of China's naval capabilities and doctrine, see United States, Department of Defense, *Annual Report to Congress: military and security developments involving the People's Republic of China 2010*. www.defense.gov/pubs/pdfs/2010_CMPR_Final.pdf (accessed 28 February 2011); and Yoshihara and Holmes, *Red Star over the Pacific*.
18 The term was first used in a 2005 report titled 'Energy futures in Asia' prepared for the US Secretary of Defense by the private consultants, Booz-Allen-Hamilton, and was quickly adopted by Indian strategists.
19 Brahma Chellaney, 'Assessing India's reactions to China's "Peaceful Development" doctrine,' *NBR Analysis*, Vol.18, No.5, April 2008, pp.23–36.
20 Ramtanu Maitra, 'India bids to rule the waves', *Asia Times*, 19 October 2005; and Sudha Ramachandran, 'China moves into India's back yard', *Asia Times*, 13 March 2007.
21 The Port of Gwadar is currently operated by the Singapore port authority and Hambantota by Sri Lankan authorities.
22 Although there is only a low level of coordination.
23 'China mulling naval base in Gulf of Aden: admiral', *Agence-France Presse*, 29 December 2009.
24 Yoshihara and Holmes, *Red Star over the Pacific*, p.173.
25 Arun Prakash, 'India's maritime strategy', *Indian Defence Review*, Vol.137, No.568 (April–June 2007), pp.157–76.
26 'India not competing with China: navy chief', *NDTV India*, 26 December 2007.
27 Gurpreet Khurana, 'China–India maritime rivalry', *Indian Defence Review*, Vol.23, No.4, July–September 2009, pp.139–53.
28 See for example, Andrew Selth, 'Chinese military bases in Burma: the explosion of a myth', Regional Outlook Paper No.10, Brisbane: Griffith University, 2007; and You Ji, 'Dealing with the Malacca Dilemma: China's effort to protect its energy supply', *Strategic Analysis*, Vol.31, No.3, May 2007, pp.467–89.
29 Robert D. Kaplan, *Monsoon: the Indian Ocean and the future of American power*, New York: Random House, 2010, p.194.
30 Kaplan, *Monsoon*, p.289.
31 A term coined by Indian strategist, Jasit Singh, to describe nuclear capabilities that would require lengthy preparation time before they could be used.
32 Ye Hailin, 'Securing SLOCs by cooperation – Chinese perspectives of maritime security in the Indian Ocean', paper presented at Karichi, Pakistan, 2009.
33 Mohan, *Crossing the Rubicon*, p.143.
34 Steven A. Hoffman, 'Perception and China policy in India', in Frankel and Harding, *The India–China Relationship*, pp.33–74.
35 C. Raja Mohan, 'The evolution of Sino-Indian relations: implications for the United States', in Alyssa Ayres and C. Raja Mohan, *Power Realignments in Asia: China, India and the United States*, New Delhi: Sage Publications, 2009, pp.270–90 at p.288.
36 Mohan Malik, 'Eyeing the Dragon: India's China debate', Asia-Pacific Center for Security Studies, Special Assessment, December 2003. www.apcss.org/Publications/SAS/ChinaDebate/ChinaDebate_Malik.pdf (accessed 28 February 2011).
37 Mark W. Frazier, 'Quiet competition and the future of Sino-Indian relations', in Frankel and Harding, *The India–China Relationship*, pp.294–318.
38 Garver, *Protracted Contest*, p.6.
39 John W. Garver, 'Asymmetrical Indian and Chinese threat perceptions', in Sumit Ganguly, *India as an Emerging Power*, London: Frank Cass, 2003, pp.109–134;

and Susan L. Shirk, 'One-sided rivalry: China's perceptions and policies toward India', in Frankel and Harding, *The India–China Relationship*, pp.75–100.
40 Andrew Scobell, '"Cult of Defense" and "Big Power Dreams": the influence of strategic culture on China's relationship with India', in Malcolm R. Chambers (ed.), *South Asia in 2020: future strategic balances and alliances*, Carlisle: US Army War College, Strategic Studies Institute, pp.329–59.
41 Gary Klintworth, 'Chinese perspectives on India as a great power', in Ross Babbage and Sandy Gordon (eds), *India's Strategic Future: regional state or global power?*, London: Macmillan, 1992, pp.94–106 at p.96.
42 Ashley J. Tellis, 'China and India in Asia', in Frankel and Harding, *The India–China Relationship*, pp.134–77 at p.143; and Garver, 'Asymmetrical Indian and Chinese threat perceptions', p.131.
43 Dipankar Banerjee, 'India and China – what next? Discussion led by Major General (Retd.)', Centre for Strategic and International Studies, 5 June 2008. http://csis.org/files/media/csis/events/080701_summary_india-china_talk.pdf (accessed 28 February 2011).
44 Mohan Malik, 'The Proliferation Axis: Beijing-Islamabad-Pyongyang', *Korean Journal of Defense Analysis*, Vol.15, No.1, Spring 2003, pp.57–100 at p.80.
45 Barry Buzan, Ole Waever and Jaap de Wilde, *Security: a new framework for analysis*, Boulder, CO: Lynne Rienner Publishers, 1998; and Barry Buzan and Gowher Rizvi, *South Asian Insecurity and the Great Powers*, New York: St Martin's Press, 1986.
46 Mohan Malik, 'Sino-Indian relations and India's Eastern strategy', in Gordon and Henningham, *India Looks East*, pp.119–63.
47 J. Mohan Malik, 'China and the East Asian Summit: more discord than accord', Asia-Pacific Center for Security Studies, February 2006. www.apcss.org/Publications/APSSS/ChinaandEastAsiaSummit.pdf (accessed 28 February 2011).
48 Shirk, 'One-sided rivalry'.
49 Li Hongmei, 'India's "Look East policy" means "look to encircle China"?', *People's Daily Online*, 27 October 2010. http://english.peopledaily.com.cn/90002/96417/7179404.html (accessed 28 February 2011).
50 Sankar Ghose, *Jawaharlal Nehru, a Biography*, New Delhi: Allied Publishers, 1993, p.298.
51 Tellis, 'China and India in Asia'.
52 However, it is argued that China–ASEAN trade figures are exaggerated because much of China's exports are 'processing' trades involving the re-export of goods to which Chinese companies have added little value.
53 India, Ministry of Commerce and Industry. http://commerce.nic.in/eidb (accessed 28 February 2011).
54 ASEAN Secretariat. www.aseansec.org/22122.htm (accessed 28 February 2011).
55 'China attracts $52 bln investment from ASEAN', *Xinhua*, 21 October 2008.
56 India, Ministry of Commerce and Industry.
57 Jürgen Haacke, 'Seeking influence: China's diplomacy towards ASEAN after the Asian Crisis', *Asian Perspective*, Vol.26, No.4, 2002, pp.13–52.
58 Bronson Percival, *The Dragon Looks South: China and Southeast Asia in the new century*, Westport, CT: Praeger Security International, 2007, p.79.
59 Vincent Wei-cheng Wang, 'The logic of China-ASEAN free trade agreement: economic statecraft of "Peaceful Rise"', paper presented at Institute of China Studies University of Malaya Conference, 5–6 August 2007.
60 'China–ASEAN FTA to accelerate RMB regionalization', *Peoples Online Daily*, 23 October 2009.
61 Debashis Chakraborty, 'China factor in India-ASEAN relations', IPCS China Seminar Report # 273, 15 December 2008.

62 Zhang Guihong, 'US–India strategic cooperation: implications for China', paper submitted to The Asia Fellow China Alumni Conference, 13–14 November 2005, Beijing University, China; and Zhao Hong, 'India's changing relations with ASEAN in China's Perspective', East Asia Institute Background Paper No.313, 7 December 2006.
63 Sudhir Devare, *India and Southeast Asia: towards security convergence*, Singapore: Institute of Southeast Asian Studies, 2006, p.211.
64 C. Raja Mohan, 'India's geopolitics and Southeast Asian security', in Daljit Singh and Tin Maung Maung (eds), *Southeast Asian Affairs 2008*, Singapore: Institute of Southeast Asian Studies, 2008, pp.43–60 at p.53.
65 C. Raja Mohan, 'Is India an East Asian power? Explaining New Delhi's security politics in the Western Pacific', ISAS Working Paper No.81, 11 August 2009.
66 Jane Perlez, 'Faster ASEAN integration urged', *International Herald Tribune*, 29 November 2004.
67 Sinderpal Singh and Syeda Sana Rahman, 'The next stage of Singapore–India relations: possibilities and prospects', ISAS Working Paper No.91, 24 September 2009, pp.12–13.

4 The United States and India's strategic role in the Asia Pacific

1 For an account of the India–US relationship during the Cold War, see Dennis Klux, *India and the United States: estranged democracies, 1941–1991*, Washington DC: National Defense University Press, 1992.
2 See generally, Strobe Talbott, *Engaging India: diplomacy, democracy and the bomb*, Washington DC, Brookings Institution, 2004.
3 K.P. Nayar, 'Vajpayee describes India and US as natural allies', the *Telegraph*, 29 September 1998.
4 C. Raja Mohan, *Crossing the Rubicon: the shaping of India's new foreign policy*, New York: Palgrave Macmillan, 2003, p.100.
5 Rajiv Chandrasekaran, 'India offers bases to U.S. for retaliatory attacks', *Washington Post*, 17 September 2001.
6 Described by a Secretary of the Indian Foreign Ministry as a 'free ego massage'. See Rajiv Sikri, *Challenge and Strategy: rethinking India's foreign policy*, New Delhi: Sage, 2009, p.187.
7 Ashley Tellis, 'Assessing America's War on Terror: confronting insurgency, cementing primacy', *NBR Analysis*, Vol.15, No.4, 2004.
8 Office of Spokesman, US Department of State, 'Background briefing by administration officials on U.S.–South Asia relations', Washington DC, 25 March 2005.
9 Condoleezza Rice, 'US–India civil nuclear cooperation agreement: opening remarks before house International Relations Committee', 5 April 2006.
10 Quoted in Daniel Twining, 'America's grand design in Asia', *The Washington Quarterly*, Vol.30, No.3, 2007, pp.79–94 at p.82.
11 Condoleezza Rice, speech at Sophia University, Tokyo, 19 March 2005.
12 Bronson Percival, 'Regional security environment in the Indian Ocean: threats on the margins; partnership with India,' in C. Uday Bhaskar and Kamlesh K. Agnihotri (eds), *Security Challenges along the Indian Ocean Littoral: Indian and US perspectives*, Delhi: National Maritime Foundation, 2010, pp.21–32.
13 For a discussion of the 123 agreement, see Teresita C. Schaffer, *India and the United States in the 21st Century: reinventing partnership*, Washington DC: The CSIS Press, 2009.
14 Stephen P. Cohen and Sunil Dasgupta, *Arming without Aiming: India's military modernisation*, Washington DC: Brookings Institution Press, 2010, p.167.

15 Merle David Kellerhals Jr, 'India an indispensable partner, U.S. officials say', 1 June 2010. www.america.gov/st/peacesec-english/2010/June/20100601090431 dmslahrellek0.7037622.html (accessed 28 February 2011).
16 T.P. Sreenivasan, 'Obama has gone further than Bush on India', *Rediff.com*, 9 June 2010. http://news.rediff.com/column/2010/jun/09/tps-sreenivasan-on-the-obama-platter-for-india.htm (accessed 28 February 2011).
17 B. Raman, 'Obama ducks Dalai Lama issue', *South Asia Analysis Group*, Paper No.3418, 16 September 2009.
18 'A third country role cannot be envisaged nor is it necessary', *Outlook India*, 18 November 2009.
19 Michele Flournoy, 'Investing in the future of U.S.–India defense relations', speech to the Asia Society, Washington DC, 1 July 2010.
20 William J. Burns, speech to Council on Foreign Relations, Washington DC, 1 June 2010.
21 Schaffer, *India and the United States in the 21st century*, p.213.
22 Schaffer, *India and the United States in the 21st century*, p.216.
23 Amandeep Gill and Rory Medcalf, *Unconventional Partners: Australia–India cooperation in reducing nuclear dangers*, Lowy Institute Policy Brief, October 2009.
24 United States Department of Defense, *Quadrennial Defense Review Report*, February 2010, p.60.
25 Jim Garamone, 'Officials praise growth of U.S.–India military partnership', *American Armed Services Press*, 23 July 2010.
26 Juli A. Macdonald, 'Indo–U.S. military relationship: expectations and perceptions', Booz Allen Hamilton, Report for the Director, Net Assessment, Office of the Secretary of Defense, October 2002, p.xxviii.
27 Schaffer, *India and the United States in the 21st century*, p.86.
28 For details of exercises up to 2006, see V.P. Malik, 'Indo-US defense and military relations: from "estrangement" to "strategic partnership"', in Sumit Ganguly, Brian Shoup and Andrew Scobell (eds), *US–Indian Strategic Cooperation into the 21st Century*, London: Routledge, 2006, pp.82–112.
29 Paul Noronha, 'China woos Mauritius and eyes the Indian Ocean', *The Hindu*, 1 July 2009.
30 Which for political reasons has been rebadged as a Logistics Support Agreement.
31 There were also reportedly serious discussions over the transfer of the *USS Kitty Hawk*, an 80,000 tonne aircraft carrier. M.D. Nalapat, 'Will the USS Kitty Hawk cement U.S.-India military ties?', *UPI Asia.com*, 28 November 2007. www.upiasia.com/Security/2007/11/28/commentary_will_the_uss_kitty_hawk_cement_usindia_military_ties/7273/ (accessed 28 February 2011).
32 'US offers F-35 for Indian Navy', *Indian Military*, 13 January 2010.
33 Sheela Bhatt, 'As Obama arrives, US bids for heavy arms business', *Rediff News*, 5 November 2010. www.rediff.com/news/special/obama-visit-special-as-arrives-us-bids-for-heavy-arms-business/20101105.htm (accessed 28 February 2010).
34 See generally, A.Vinod Kumar, 'Indo-US missile defence cooperation: hype or happening?', *ISDA Strategic Comments*, 30 January 2009.
35 Brian Shoup and Sumit Ganguly, 'Introduction', in Sumit Ganguly, Brian Shoup and Andrew Scobell (eds), *US–Indian Strategic Cooperation into the 21st Century*, London: Routledge, 2006.
36 Schaffer, *India and the United States in the 21st century*, p.79.
37 Bronson Percival, 'Growing Chinese and Indian naval power: U.S. recalibration and coalition building', in Sam Bateman and Joshua Ho (eds), *Southeast Asia and the Rise of Chinese and Indian Naval Power: between rising naval powers*, London: Routledge, 2010, pp.36–47 at p.38.
38 Sandeep Dikshit, 'No strings attached to sale of ships', *The Hindu*, 29 March 2008.

39 Rahul Bedi, 'Strategic partners in defence', *SPAN Magazine*, New Delhi, March–April, 2005, pp.20–24 at p.24.
40 Robert D.Kaplan, 'Center stage for the twenty-first century', *Foreign Affairs*, Vol.88, 2009, pp.16–32 at p.24. The United States has officially welcomed the increased participation of the Chinese navy in anti-piracy operations in the Gulf of Aden.
41 Kaplan, 'Center stage for the twenty-first century'.
42 Mike Mullen, speech in New Delhi, 23 July 2010.
43 Manu Pubby, 'China proposed division of Pacific, Indian Ocean regions, we declined: US Admiral', *Indian Express*, 15 May 2009.
44 James R. Holmes, Andrew C. Winner and Toshi Yoshihara, *Indian Naval Strategy in the Twenty-First Century*, London: Routledge, 2009, ch.3.
45 Percival, 'Growing Chinese and Indian naval power', p.37.
46 US Navy, US Marine Corps and US Coast Guard, *Cooperative Strategy for 21st Century Seapower*, October 2007.
47 Holmes *et al.*, *Indian Naval Strategy in the Twenty-first Century*, p.122.
48 'Global maritime partnerships', US Department of State Unclassified Telegram, 13 May 2008.
49 Rajat Pandit, 'US eyes naval ties with India', *Times of India*, 19 April 2007.
50 Macdonald, 'Indo–U.S. military relationship'.
51 Macdonald, 'Indo–U.S. military relationship', p.51.
52 CTF 151 was established as a counter-piracy task force under a 2008 UN Security Council Resolution.
53 As of late 2010, Pakistan has led the associated CTF 150 on four occasions.
54 Sandeep Unnithan, 'The hijack dilemma', *India Today*, 17 October 2008; and 'Lack of consensus holding back anti-piracy policy', *Thaindian News*, 20 November 2008.
55 James R. Holmes, 'India and the Proliferation Security Initiative: a US perspective', *Strategic Analysis*, Vol.31, No.2, 2007, pp.315–37.
56 For a good example of this perspective, see the views of a former Secretary of the Ministry of External Affairs in Sikri, *Challenge and Strategy*.
57 C. Raja Mohan, 'Rising India: partner in shaping the global commons?', *The Washington Quarterly*, July 2010, pp.133–48.
58 See for example, US Undersecretary for Defense Policy, Michele Flournoy, 'Investing in the future of U.S.–India defense relations', speech to the Asia Society, Washington DC, 1 July 2010; and G. Parthasarathy, 'New US thinking on India: coming Obama visit offers an opportunity', *The Tribune*, 22 July 2010.
59 With the exception of APEC where the US has been cool towards India's membership, fearing that India's restrictive trade regime may act as a potential drag on further trade liberalisation. Schaffer, *India and the United States in the 21st Century*, p.150.
60 William J. Burns, 'India's rise and the promise of U.S.–Indian partnership', address in Washington DC, 1 June 2010.
61 Hillary Rodham Clinton, 'America's engagement in the Asia-Pacific', address at Honululu, 28 October 2010.
62 Josh Rogin, 'U.S. and India take their relationship beyond South Asia', *The Cable*, 15 November 2010. http://thecable.foreignpolicy.com/posts/2010/11/15/the_us_and_india_take_their_relationship_beyond_south_asia (accessed 28 February 2011).
63 Percival, 'Regional security environment in the Indian Ocean', p.25.
64 Macdonald, 'Indo-U.S. military relationship', p.xx.
65 According to a senior Indian naval officer, its application was opposed by China. Others believe that India's application was not supported by the United States.

66 Ashley Tellis, 'South Asia', in Richard J. Ellings and Aaron L. Friedberg (eds), *Strategic Asia 2001–02 Power and Purpose*, Seattle: National Bureau of Asian Research, 2002, pp.223–26.

5 Northeast Asia: India's peer relationship with Japan

1 Durga Das, 'Japan's role in Asia', *Indian and Foreign Review*, Vol.7, No.18, 1 July 1970, pp.11–17 at p.11.
2 J.D.B. Miller (ed.), *India, Japan, Australia, partners in Asia?*, Canberra: Australian National University Press, 1968, pp.86–7.
3 See generally, T.A. Keenleyside, 'Nationalist Indian attitudes towards Asia: a troublesome legacy for post-independence Indian foreign policy', *Pacific Affairs*, Vol.55, No.2, Summer 1982, pp.210–30 at p.213.
4 Nakane Chie, 'Logic and the smile: when Japanese meet Indians', *Japan Quarterly*, Vol.11, No.4, October/December 1964, pp.434–38.
5 K. Venugopal, 'Japan's guarded, positive response on nuclear issue', *The Hindu*, 16 December 2006.
6 Yasukuni Enoki, 'The Japan–India new partnership', speech to the United Services Institute, New Delhi, 28 May 2004.
7 Purnendra Jain, 'India's calculus of Japan's foreign policy in Pacific Asia', in Takashi Inoguchi (ed.), *Japan's Asian Policy: revival and response*, New York: Palgrave, 2002, pp.211–36 at p.232.
8 Milan Hauner, *India in Axis Strategy: Germany, Japan, and Indian nationalists in the Second World War*, Stuttgart: Klett-Cotta, 1981, p.107. A perspective which had echoes in Japan's relative indifference towards the expansion of Soviet influence in India in the 1970s.
9 The INA was led by Subhash Chandra Bose, who had been a leader of the mainstream Indian National Congress but resigned in 1939 due to his opposition to its policies of non-violence. Bose fled to Germany in 1941 where he tried to organise Indian prisoners of war to fight with the Nazis and was then transported by submarine to Singapore in 1943. After the war, the INA remained somewhat controversial in newly independent India and its members were not welcomed into the Indian nationalist establishment, although Bose, who died in 1945, is now officially lauded.
10 Joyce C. Lebra (ed.), *Japan's Greater East Asia Co-Prosperity Sphere in World War II: selected readings and documents*, London: Oxford University Press, 1975, p.64; and Hauner, *India in Axis Strategy*, p.407.
11 Willard H. Elsbree, *Japan's Role in Southeast Asian Nationalist Movements 1940 to 1945*, New York: Russell & Russell, 1970.
12 P.A. Narasimha Murthy, *India and Japan: dimensions of their relations: historical political*, New Delhi: ABC Publishing House, 1986, p.162.
13 Reported in *The Hindu*, 1 December 1961.
14 Statement by Prime Minister Ikeda to the Japanese Diet on 10 December 1962 as reported in *The Hindustan Times*, 13 December 1962.
15 Memorandum of Harriman–Shiga Conversation, 14 November, 1962, US Department of State, as quoted in Michael Schaller, *Altered States: the United States and Japan since the occupation*, New York: Oxford University Press, 1997, p.174.
16 US Department of State Memorandum of Conversation by Swayne, Department of State, Secretary's Memoranda of Conversation: Lot 65 D330, as quoted in US Department of State Memorandum of Conversation, Washington December 3, 1962, 5.30pm, FRUS 1961–63, Vol.XXII Doc # 362.
17 Durga Das, *India: from Curzon to Nehru and after*, London: Collins, 1969, p.415.

18 Vincent Smith, 'Australia urged to seek own defence', *The Australian*, 1 October 1968.
19 According to junior Indian Foreign Minister, B.R. Bhagat. Justus M. van der Kroef, 'The Gorton Manner: Australia, Southeast Asia and the U.S.', *Pacific Affairs*, Vol.42, No.3, 1969 pp.311–33 at p.328.
20 Hedley Bull, 'The new balance of power in Asia and the Pacific', *Foreign Affairs*, Vol.49, 1971, pp.669–81 at p.680.
21 Marian P. Kirsch, 'Soviet security objectives in Asia', *International Organization*, Vol.24, No.3, Summer 1970, pp.451–78 at p.471. See also *Far Eastern Economic Review*, 24 July 1969, p.249.
22 Malnotra, 'Japanese not interested in Indian pact', *The Australian*, 26 June 1969.
23 John Welfield, *An Empire in Eclipse: Japan in the postwar American alliance system: a study of the interaction of domestic politics and foreign policy*, London: The Athlone Press, 1988, p.196.
24 *Kyokuto no Anzen Hosho*, p.14, cited in Lawrence Olson, *Japan in Postwar Asia*, London: Council on Foreign Relations, 1970, p.135.
25 Takashi Terada, 'The origins of Japan's APEC policy: Foreign Minister Takeo Miki's Asia-Pacific policy and current implications', *The Pacific Review*, Vol.11, No.3, 1988, pp.337–63.
26 Takako Hirose, 'Japan's role in South Asia in the post-Cold War period', in K.V. Kesavan and Lalima Varma (eds), *Japan–South Asia: Security and Economic Perspectives*, New Delhi: Lancer's Books, 2000, ch.6 at p.105.
27 See, for example, Baldev Raj Nayar, *India and the Major Powers after Pokhran II*, New Delhi: Har-Anand Publications, 2001.
28 National Institute of Defense Studies, *East Asian Strategic Review, 1998–99*.
29 Satu P. Limaye, 'Tokyo's dynamic diplomacy: Japan and the subcontinent's nuclear tests', *Contemporary Southeast Asia*, Vol.22, No.2, August 2000, pp.322–39 at p.329.
30 S. Jaishankar, 'India–Japan relations after Pokharan II', *Seminar* (New Delhi), No.487, March 2000, p.42.
31 See Limaye, 'Tokyo's dynamic diplomacy'.
32 'India, Japan will have close defence ties, says Fernandes', *Times of India*, 16 January 2000.
33 Venugopal, 'Japan's guarded, positive response on nuclear issue'. Abe, in his 2006 political manifesto 'Utsukushii kuni e: jishin to hokori no moteru Nihon e [Towards a beautiful country: A confident and proud Japan]', includes a lengthy discussion of how Japan should strengthen ties with India, stating: 'It will not be a surprise if in another decade, Japan–India relations overtake Japan–US and Japan–China ties.'
34 Sudha Ramachandran, 'What are friends for ... ?', *AsiaTimes Online*, 25 August 2007. www.atimes.com/atimes/Japan/IH25Dh03.html (accessed 28 February 2011).
35 For a detailed account of these developments, see Purnendra Jain, 'Westward ho! Japan eyes India strategically', *Japanese Studies*, Vol.28, Issue 1, May 2008, pp.15–30.
36 Sun Cheng, 'A comparative analysis of Abe's and Fukada's Asia diplomacy', *China International Studies*, No.10, Spring 2008, pp.58–72.
37 D.S. Rajan, 'China: media fears over India becoming part of Western Alliance', Chennai Centre for China Studies Paper No.46, 29 August 2007.
38 'Joint statement on the advancement of the strategic and global partnership between Japan and India', 22 October 2008.
39 Siddhart Varadarajan, 'India, Japan say new security ties not directed against China', *The Hindu*, 23 October 2008.
40 D.S. Rajan, 'Beijing: suspicions on Japan–India Security Declaration targeting China', Chennai Centre for China Studies Paper No.221, 2 November 2008.

41 For a detailed examination of the terms of the Security Declaration, see David Brewster, 'The India–Japan Security Declaration: an enduring security partnership?', *Asian Security*, Vol.6, No.2, 2010, pp.95–120.
42 See generally, David Brewster, 'Developments in India's strategic relations with South Korea: a useful friend in East Asia?', *Asian Survey*, Vol. 50, No.2, 2010, pp.407–25.
43 Mohan Malik, 'The Proliferation Axis: Beijing-Islamabad-Pyongyang', *Korean Journal of Defense Analysis*, Vol.15, No.1, Spring 2003, pp.57–100 at p.80.
44 Kim Il-young and Lakhvinder Singh, 'The North Korean nuclear program and external connections', *The Korean Journal of Defense Analysis*, Vol.16, No.1, Spring 2004, pp.73–98.
45 India withheld criticism of North Korea over its April 2009 ballistic missile test and gave only muted criticism of its May 2009 nuclear test. Although India condemned the sinking of the South Korea frigate, *Cheonan*, in May 2010, it avoided expressly naming North Korea as the perpetrator.
46 Which have included, since 2005, an annual Track II trilateral security dialogue between India, Taiwan and Japan.
47 Ting-I Tsai, 'For Taiwan, India's in the slightly-less-hard basket', *AsiaTimes Online*, 15 February 2006. www.atimes.com/atimes/China_Business/HB15Cb02.html (accessed 28 February 2011).
48 John Daly, 'Can the Dragon swim? The naval balance in the Taiwan Strait', *China Brief*, Vol.4, No.2, 20 January 2004. www.jamestown.org/programs/chinabrief/single/?tx_ttnews[tt_news]=3621&tx_ttnews[backPid]=194&no_cache=1 (accessed 15 July 2011).
49 *China Defence Daily*, 20 August 2007, quoted in D.S. Rajan, 'Is China wary of India's "Look East policy"?', Chennai Centre for China Studies, C3S Paper No.97, 13 January 2008.
50 Ting-I Tsai, 'For Taiwan, India's in the slightly-less-hard basket'.
51 Ibid.
52 Japan's views on the Chinese threat has been described as 'something approaching panic'. Aurelia George Mulgan, 'Breaking the mould: Japan's subtle shift from exclusive bilateralism to modest minilateralism', *Contemporary Southeast Asia*, Vol.30, No.1, 2008, pp.52–72 at p.60.
53 'A glance at features of Hillary Clinton's Asian tour', *Xinhua (English edition)*, 22 February 2009.
54 Richard J. Samuels, *Securing Japan: Tokyo's Grand Strategy and the future of East Asia*, Ithaca, NY: Cornell University Press, 2007.
55 Peter J. Katzenstein, *Rethinking Japanese Security: internal and external dimensions*, London: Routledge, 2008, pp.3–4.
56 Peter J. Katzenstein and Nobuo Okawara, 'Japan's security policy: political, economic and military dimensions', in Katzenstein, *Rethinking Japanese Security*, pp.59–75.
57 Heigo Sato, 'Arc of freedom and prosperity', in Centre for Strategic and International Studies, *Bridging Strategic Asia: the rise of India in East Asia and implications for the US-Japan alliance*, Winter 2008. http://csis.org/programs/international-security-program/asia-division/bridging-strategic-asia-rise-india-east-asia-a (accessed 28 February 2011).
58 See, Centre for Strategic and International Studies, 'The United States, Japan and India: toward new trilateral cooperation', 16 August 2007. http://csis.org/files/media/csis/pubs/070816_us_j_ireport.pdf (accessed 28 February 2011).
59 *The US–Japan Alliance: getting Asia right through 2020*, co-authored by former US Deputy Secretary of State Richard Armitage, which asserted the importance of cooperation by Japan with Australia and India founded on 'common values'.

Despite its unofficial status, the report was considered in Japan as intended as a policy guide for the then current and next US administrations.
60 Denis Shanahan, 'Pacific allies enlist India', *The Australian*, 15 March 2007.
61 See Centre for Strategic and International Studies, 'US-Japan-India strategic dialogue October 17–19 in Delhi, India – key recommendations', 6 November 2008. http://csis.org/files/media/csis/pubs/081105_india-japan-us_trilateral_delhi_statement.pdf (accessed 28 February 2011).
62 Comments at Symposium on 'Japan and India: challenges and prospects in Asia and Pacific in the 21st century', Tokyo, 10 March 2006.
63 See generally, Sven Saaler and J. Victor Koschmann (eds), *Pan Asianism in Modern Japanese History: colonialism, regionalism and borders*, New York: Routledge, 2007.
64 See, for example, S. Javed Maswood, 'Japanese foreign policy and regionalism', in S. Javed Maswood, *Japan and East Asian Regionalism*, London: Routledge, 2001, pp.6–25.
65 The Japanese defendants in the Tokyo trials almost included Abe's grandfather, Nobusuke Kishi. He had been armaments minister in Japan's wartime cabinet, but was released from prison by the Americans in 1948 in somewhat obscure circumstances.
66 Kenneth B. Pyle, 'Abe Shinzo and Japan's change of course', *NBR Analysis*, Vol.17, No.4, October 2006, pp.5–9; and Kenneth B. Pyle, *Japan Rising: the resurgence of Japanese power and purpose*, New York: Public Affairs, 2007.
67 The Japanese and Indian Coastguards have held annual joint search and rescue and anti-piracy exercises since 2000 and signed a Memorandum on Cooperation in 2007. The Japanese Coastguard is administered separately from the Japanese Self Defence Forces and is not subject to the same constitutional or political limitations as the Self Defence Forces.
68 In October 2010, India and Japan agreed to facilitate the escort of Japanese vessels by Indian warships in the Gulf of Aden and *vice versa*.
69 Such as the cooperation demonstrated between India and Japan during the December 2004 Indian Ocean tsunami.
70 Former Foreign Minister, Kakizawa Koji, quoted in Paul R. Daniels, 'Beyond "Better than Ever": Japanese independence and the future of US-Japan relations', Institute for International Policy Studies, IIPS Policy Paper 308E, July 2004, p.10.
71 National Institute of Defense Studies, *East Asian Strategic Review 2005*, p.36. See also Samuels, *Securing Japan*, p.201.
72 See, for example, Takenori Horimoto, 'The world as India sees it', *Gaiko Forum*, Vol.6, No.3, Fall 2006, pp.4–5.
73 Daniels, 'Beyond "Better than Ever"', p.10.
74 Kazuya Natsukawa, 'Opening address, Indo-Japan dialogue on ocean security', Tokyo, 12 October 2006.
75 Sandeep Dikshit, 'Japanese energy security is dependent on the Indian Navy', *The Hindu*, 1 October 2007.
76 National Institute of Defense Studies, *East Asian Strategic Review 2008*, p.219.
77 Author interviews with Japanese security analysts, June 2009.
78 For example, Horimoto, 'The world as India sees it'.
79 See generally, Leif-Eric Easley, Tetsuo Kotani and Aki Mori, 'Electing a new Japanese security policy? Examining foreign policy visions within the Democratic Party of Japan', *Asia Policy*, No.9, January 2010, pp.x–xx.
80 'India, Japan ink action plan on security cooperation', *NetIndian News Network*, 29 December 2009. http://netindian.in/news/2009/12/29/0004571/india-japan-ink-action-plan-security-cooperation (accessed 28 February 2011).

81 The Security Declaration was pressed on Aso by LDP's Kishi faction (on which Aso depended) and seen as a 'low cost' diplomatic achievement.
82 Varadarajan, 'India, Japan say new security ties not directed against China'.
83 Purnendra Jain, 'From condemnation to strategic partnership: Japan's changing view of India 1998–2007', Institute of South Asian Studies Working Paper No.41, 10 March 2008'; and Brahma Chellaney and Horimoto Takenori, 'Indo kara mita Nihon, Ajia' [Japan–India links critical for Asia-Pacific security], *Gaiko Forum*, Vol.7, No.2, Fall 2007.
84 G.V.C. Naidu, 'Indo-Japan relations: emerging contours of strategic partnership', paper presented at the 10th IDSA-JIIA Bilateral Seminar, New Delhi, 15–16 December 2008.
85 Ibid.
86 Chellaney and Takenori, 'Indo kara mita Nihon, Ajia'. As unlikely as such a vision may seem, it is not necessarily new – Indian commentators speculated about the development of an India–Soviet–Japan axis against China in the early 1970s. Press Trust of India, 'Reaction to Indo-Soviet treaty – Japan's isolation heightened', *The Patriot*, 19 August 1971.
87 Dr Subhash Kapila, 'Japan-India "strategic dialogue" (March 2007) a misnomer', *South Asia Analysis Group*, Paper No. 2187, 29 March 2007.
88 Li Hongmei, 'India's "Look East policy" means "look to encircle China"?' *People's Daily Online*, 27 October 2010. http://english.peopledaily.com.cn/90002/96417/7179404.html (accessed 28 February 2011).
89 See, for example, Rajesh Rajagopalan and Varun Sahni, 'India and the great powers: strategic imperatives, normative necessities', *South Asian Survey*, Vol.15, No.5, 2008, pp.5–32.
90 S.D. Muni and C. Raja Mohan, 'Emerging Asia: India's options', *International Studies*, Vol. 41, No. 3, 2004, pp.313–33.
91 C. Raja Mohan, 'Japan and India: the making of a new alliance?', *RSIS Commentaries*, 27 August 2007.
92 K.V. Kesavan, 'The Indo-Japanese partnership: the security factor', Observer Research Foundation, ORF Issue Brief No.19, May 2009.
93 Gurpreet S. Khurana, 'Security of sea lines: prospects for India–Japan cooperation', *Strategic Analysis*, Vol.31, No.1, January–February 2007, pp.139–53.
94 Evan S. Medeiros *et al.*, *Pacific Currents: the responses of US allies and security partners in East Asia to China's rise*, Santa Monica, CA: Rand Corporation, 2008.
95 Among the extensive literature on the relationship between trade and alliances, see Edward D. Mansfield, *Power, Trade & War*, Princeton, NJ: Princeton University Press, 1994; Joanne Gowa, *Allies, Adversaries and International Trade*, Princeton, NJ: Princeton University Press, 1994; and Michael P. Gerace, *Military Power, Conflict and Trade*, London: Frank Cass, 2004.
96 See generally, Brewster, 'Developments in India's strategic relations with South Korea'.
97 India Brand Equity Foundation 'India and Japan'. www.ibef.org/india/indiajapan. aspx (accessed 28 February 2011).
98 Hitachi Research Institute, 'Manmohan Singh's visit to Japan: recent trends, historical perspectives', 7 February 2007.
99 Sourabh Gupta, 'Japan–India joint declaration on security cooperation: groping towards an Asia-wide security architecture', *Nautilus Institute Policy Forum Online* 08–085A, 4 November 2008.
100 Varadarajan, 'India, Japan say new security ties not directed against China'.
101 'Manmohan Singh leaves Japan, heads to Malaysia', *The Times of India*, 26 October 2010.

102 Sourabh Gupta, 'Japan–India economic ties and the promise of the Delhi–Mumbai industrial corridor', *East Asia Forum*, 4 November 2010. www.eastasiaforum. org/2010/11/04/japan-india-economic-ties-and-the-promise-of-the-delhi-mumbai-industrial-corridor/ (accessed 28 February 2011).

6 Indochina: India's political partnership with Vietnam

1 According to Defence Minister, George Fernandes. See, 'India must not ignore S. E. Asia: Fernandes', *The Hindu*, 28 March 2000.
2 See generally, David Brewster, 'The strategic relationship between India and Vietnam: the search for a diamond on the South China Sea?', *Asian Security*, Vol.5, Issue 1, January 2009, pp.24–44.
3 In November 1946, while praising the Vietnamese nationalists, Nehru blocked an attempt to organise an Indian volunteer brigade to fight against the French colonial forces in Vietnam. See D.R. SarDesai, *Indian Foreign Policy in Cambodia, Laos and Vietnam 1947–1964*, Berkeley: University of California Press, 1968, p.12.
4 Ibid., p.76.
5 One journalist at the Geneva talks commented, 'there is no antechamber where one does not find oneself face to face with Mr. Krishna Menon.' Quoted in Frank N. Trager, *Why Vietnam?*, London: Pall Mall Press, 1966, p.88.
6 Hubert H. Humphrey, *The Education of a Public Man: my life and politics*, New York: Doubleday, 1976, p.248.
7 Ramesh Thakur and Carlyle A. Thayer, *Soviet Relations with India and Vietnam*, New York: St. Martin's Press, 1992, p.234.
8 Ibid., pp.231–32.
9 John W. Garver, 'Chinese–Indian rivalry in Indochina', *Asian Survey*, Vol.27, No.11, November 1987, pp.1205–19, at pp.1207–8.
10 See T.N. Kaul, *India, China and Indochina*, New Delhi: Lancer Press, 1987, p.150.
11 Nayan Chanda, *Brother Enemy: the war after the war*, New York: Harcourt Brace Jovanovich, 1986, p.257.
12 Including studies of the effectiveness of Vietnamese tactics against the Chinese in 1979 and a limited three-way information sharing arrangement with the Soviet-backed Afghani government in the 1980s. Dr Subhash Kapila, 'India-Vietnam strategic partnership: the convergence of interests', South Asia Analysis Group, Paper No.177, 2 January 2001.
13 Sunanda K. Datta-Ray, 'Invasion of Vietnam brings an end to the thaw between India and China', *Canberra Times*, 21 March 1979.
14 It has been argued that Vietnam would not have expected a Chinese attack to occur during the Indian visit. Harlan W. Jencks, 'China's "Punitive" war on Vietnam: a military assessment', *Asian Survey*, Vol.19, No.8, 1979, pp.801–15 at p.805.
15 Garver, 'Chinese–Indian Rivalry in Indochina', p.1209.
16 For detailed discussions of India's recognition of the Heng Samrin regime and its impact on relations with ASEAN, see Mohammed Ayoob, *India and Southeast Asia: Indian perceptions and policies*, New York: Routledge, 1990; and Thakur and Thayer, *Soviet Relations with India and Vietnam*.
17 See generally, Henry J. Kenny, *Shadow of the Dragon: Vietnam's continuing struggle with China and its implications for U.S. foreign policy*, Washington DC: Brassey's, 2002; and Stephanie Balme and Mark Sidel, *Vietnam's New Order: international perspectives on the State and reform in Vietnam*, New York: Palgrave Macmillan, 2006.
18 Quoted in Kenny, *Shadow of the Dragon*, p.100.
19 Brantly Womack, *China And Vietnam: the politics of asymmetry*, Cambridge: Cambridge University Press, 2006, p.229.

20 Pham Cao Phong, 'Vietnam's new security perception: the role of economic security', paper prepared for the 43rd annual ISA convention, New Orleans, 24–27 March 2002.
21 According to the Thai Foreign Minister, Surin Pitsuwan. See Micool Brooke, 'India courts Vietnam with arms and nuclear technology', *Asia-Pacific Defence Reporter*, Vol. 25, August/September 2000, pp.20–21.
22 Carlyle A. Thayer, 'Vietnam's defence policy and its impact on foreign relations', paper delivered to EuroViet 6, Asien-Afrika Institüt, Universität Hamburg, Hamburg, Germany, 6–8 June 2008, p.29.
23 In 1994, India and Vietnam entered into a low-key protocol providing for limited training of Vietnamese officers at India's defence academy and provision of some maintenance services. A broader defence cooperation agreement was also negotiated but not signed.
24 'India must not ignore S.E. Asia: Fernandes', *The Hindu*, 28 March 2000.
25 Brooke, 'India courts Vietnam with arms and nuclear technology'.
26 Ian Storey and Carlyle A.Thayer, 'Cam Ranh Bay: past imperfect, future conditional', *Contemporary Southeast Asia*, Vol.23, No.3, December 2001, pp.452–73 at p.468.
27 Alexander L.Vuving, 'Strategy and evolution of Vietnam's China policy: a changing mixture of pathways', *Asian Survey*, Vol.XLVI, No.6, November/December 2006, pp.805–24 at pp.816–18.
28 Rahul Bedi, 'Despite India's protests, Vietnam buys arms from Pakistan', *India News*, 17 August 2007.
29 India Defence Consultants, 'What's hot? – analysis of recent happenings – Indian Navy update', *IDC Analysis*, 20 November 2005. www.indiadefence.com/navyupdate.htm (accessed 28 February 2011).
30 Rahul Bedi, 'Strategic realignments', *Frontline*, Vol.20, Issue 13, 21 June–4 July 2003.
31 Kripa Sridharan, 'Regional perceptions of India', in Frederick Grare and Amitabh Mattoo (eds), *India and ASEAN: the politics of India's Look East policy*, New Delhi: Centre de Sciences Humaines, 2001, pp.67–89.
32 An Indian army training team has been stationed in Laos since 1995. In 2008 India agreed to establish a Laos Air Force Academy.
33 In 2007, India and Cambodia signed a defence agreement providing for the exchange of intelligence and cooperation in military research, and counter-insurgency training of Cambodian personnel by India.
34 Amit Baruah, 'Looking East', *Frontline*, 8 December 2000, p.50.
35 E. Ahamed, Press Release of Minister of State for External Affairs, 'Reinforcing "Look East" policy', 16 January 2006. pib.nic.in/release/rel_print_ page1.asp?relid = 14984 (accessed 28 February 2011).
36 For example, in April 2000 it signed an agreement with Burma, Thailand and Laos (but not Vietnam or Cambodia) relating to Mekong River navigation.
37 K.M. Panikkar, *India and the Indian Ocean: an essay on the influence of sea power on Indian history*, London: George Allen and Unwin, 1945, p.85.
38 Annuar Kassim, 'New Delhi want use of Hanoi naval facilities', *Asian Defense Journal*, Vol.9, 1990, p.108.
39 H. Jenkins, 'Dwindling support throws *Status Quo* into Sea of Change', *Insight*, 14 January 1991, p.29.
40 Nayan Chanda, 'After the bomb', *Far Eastern Economic Review*, 13 April 2000, p.20.
41 In November 1988, Vietnamese Deputy Foreign Minister Tran Quant Co stated that 'Cam Ranh Bay will be offered to others in the future'. *Bangkok Post*, 28 November 1988.

42 Vietnamese General Secretary Nguyen Van Linh is reported to have stated in June 1990 that Japan and the United States would be allowed to use Cam Ranh Bay if they agreed to normalise relations with Vietnam. *IDSA News Review on Southeast Asia and Australia*, June 1990.
43 'Vietnam's risky game in the South China Sea', *Stratfor*, 20 May 2004. www.stratfor.com/vietnams_risky_game_south_china_sea (accessed 28 February 2011).
44 Press Trust of India, 'Vietnam for greater economic engagement with India', *The Times of India*, 20 June 2007.
45 The Hanoist, 'Vietnam hedges China risk', 30 July 2010, *Asia Times Online*. www.atimes.com/atimes/Southeast_Asia/LG30Ae01.html (accessed 28 February 2011).
46 Some see India's assistance in Vietnam's nuclear programme as being pregnant with the potential to provide a strategic parallel to the assistance given by China to Pakistan in the development of nuclear weapons aimed at India. See Bharat Karnad, *Nuclear weapons and Indian Security: the realist foundations of strategy*, Delhi: Macmillan India, 2005. However, there is no indication that India has been involved in nuclear weapons technology proliferation with Vietnam.
47 In May 2008, a Japanese company was awarded a contract to develop the Vietnamese nuclear generation industry.
48 Vuving, 'Strategy and evolution of Vietnam's China policy', p.819.
49 Bharat Karnad, 'China uses Pak, Vietnam opens to India', *Express India*, 3 October 2005.
50 C. Raja Mohan, 'The importance of being Vietnam', *indiaexpress.com*, 9 July 2007. www.indianexpress.com/story_print.php?storyid=204292 (accessed 28 February 2011).

7 Archipelagic Southeast Asia: India's strategic relationships with Singapore, Malaysia and Indonesia

1 K.M. Panikkar, *The Future of Southeast Asia: an Indian view*, New York: The Macmillan Company, 1943, pp.100–101.
2 J.N. Dixit, *Makers of India's Foreign Policy: Raja Ram Mohun Roy to Yashwant Sinha*, New Delhi: HarperCollins, 2004, p.12.
3 Michael Brecher, *India and World Politics: Krishna Menon's view of the world*, London: Oxford University Press, 1968, p.315.
4 The Malaysian Foreign Secretary, Muhammed Ghazali Bin Shafie, argued that India and Japan should 'associate' themselves for the defence and security of Southeast Asia. Muhammed Ghazali Bin Shafie, 'Defence pattern for South East Asia', in K.K. Sinha (ed.), *Problems of Defence of South and East Asia*, New Delhi: Rawat Publications, 1978, pp.241–46 at p.243.
5 V.P. Dutt, *India's Foreign Policy*, New Delhi: Vikas 1984, p.256. Lee later denied making this statement although he admitted that at the time he 'was quite confident that India would have the bomb'. Sunanda K. Datta-Ray, *Looking East to Look West: Lee Kuan Yew's mission India*, Singapore: ISEAS Publishing, 2009, p.98.
6 'Lee to urge guardian role for India', *Straits Times*, 3 September 1966.
7 Kripa Sridharan, 'Regional perceptions of India', in Frederick Grare and Amitabh Mattoo (eds), *India and ASEAN: the politics of India's Look East policy*, New Delhi: Centre de Sciences Humaines, 2001, pp.67–89 at p.74.
8 Quoted in Kripa Sridharan, *The ASEAN Region in India's Foreign Policy*, Aldershot: Dartmouth Publishing, 1996, p.40.
9 Indian Parliament, Lok Sabha debates, 1968.
10 Sridharan, *The ASEAN Region in India's Foreign Policy*, p.49.

11 Yang Razali Kassim, 'India angered by claim over Soviet subs', *Straits Times*, 13 October 1986. Although it should be noted that the Ambassador did not directly answer the allegations.
12 Michael Richardson, 'East Asia and Western Pacific brace for Indian ascendency', *The International Herald Tribune*, 4 October 1989.
13 G.V.C. Naidu, 'The Indian navy and Southeast Asia', *Contemporary Southeast Asia*, Vol.13, No.1, June 1991, p.81.
14 S.K. Bhutani, 'India–Australia bilateral relations', in Dipkar Banerjee (ed.), *Towards an Era of Cooperation: an Indo-Australian dialogue*, New Delhi: Institute for Defence Studies and Analyses, 1995, p.376.
15 Sridharan, *The ASEAN Region in India's Foreign Policy*, p.178.
16 ASEAN Secretary General, Yong Ong, 'Advancing the ASEAN–India partnership in the new millenium', addess in New Delhi, 18 October 2004.
17 See generally, David Brewster, 'India's security partnership with Singapore', *The Pacific Review*, Vol.22, No.5, December 2009, pp.597–618.
18 It has also been suggested that India, then seeking to consolidate its position in Bhutan, believed that military support for Singapore would unduly antagonise China. Lee Kuan Yew, *From Third World to First: the Singapore story: 1965–2000*, New York: HarperCollins, 2000, pp.30–31.
19 Datta-Ray, *Looking East to Look West*, p.87.
20 Dr V. Suryanarayan, 'India–Singapore relations: an overview', Chennai Centre for China Studies, C3S Paper No.140, 2 April 2008.
21 Lee, *From Third World to First*, p.452.
22 As stated by the current Foreign Minister, George Yeo, while on a visit to India in 1993. See Kripa Sridharan, 'Transcending the region: Singapore's India policy', in N.N. Vohra (ed.), *Emerging Asia: challenges for India and Singapore*, New Delhi: Manohar, 2003, pp.15–32 at p.21.
23 Escalating tensions between Singapore and Malaysia over security-related issues from the late 1980s included a large-scale military exercise by Malaysia and Indonesia in the adjacent Malaysian state of Johor in August 1991, culminating on Singapore's National Independence day. Singapore responded with a large-scale military mobilisation. Serious political tensions with Malaysia continued through the 1990s. See Timothy Huxley, *Defending the Lion City: the armed forces of Singapore*, St Leonards: Allen & Unwin, 2000, p.46.
24 Arun Mahizhnan, 'Developing Singapore's external economy', *Southeast Asian Affairs*, Vol.21, 1994, pp.285–301.
25 Kripa Sridharan, 'Regional perceptions of India', p.76.
26 Malaysia, Thailand and Philippines reportedly opposed it despite Singapore's energetic advocacy. Sridharan, 'Transcending the region: Singapore's India policy', pp.28–29.
27 Simon Elegant and Michael Elliot, 'Lee Kuan Yew Reflects', *Time Asia*, 5 December 2005.
28 Interestingly, Lee went further than the Indian proposal and suggested the inclusion also of Sri Lanka and Pakistan in such a grouping. P.S. Suryanarayana, 'A vision for Asia', *Frontline*, Vol.22, Issue 1, 1–14 January 2005. www.flonnet.com/fl2201/stories/20050114000406000.htm (accessed 23 June 2011).
29 Nirmal Gosh, 'India govt "should try to change its mindset"', *Straits Times*, 20 January 2000.
30 Pranab Mukherjee, address to the 5th IISS Asian Security Summit, 3 June 2006.
31 George Yeo, address to the Global Leadership Forum in Kuala Lumpur, 6 September, 2005.
32 Pranav Kumar, 'Singapore as a gateway for Indian companies', Institute of Peace and Conflict Studies, Paper No.2593, 10 June 2008.

33 Nagesh Kumar, 'Regionalism with an "Asian Face": an agenda for the East Asia Summit', *RSIS Policy Briefs* No.28, October 2006.
34 Something originally suggested by the Indian Air Force to Singapore in November 1995.
35 Including the opportunity for the Indian Air Force to train with US equipment such as F-16s, which are operated by the Pakistani Air Force.
36 Singapore has or has had arrangements for the training of its armed forces in Australia, Brunei, France, Indonesia, New Zealand, South Africa, Thailand, Taiwan and the United States. The Singaporean Air Force operates permanent flight training establishments in the United States, Australia, Brunei and France.
37 Bilveer Singh, *The Vulnerability of Small States Revisited: a study of Singapore's post-Cold War foreign policy*, Yogyakarta: Gadjah Mada University Press, 1999, p.301.
38 Ho Weizan, *Examining Singapore–India Security Relations after the Cold War: motivating factors, trends and implications for Singapore*, unpublished thesis, National University of Singapore, 2008.
39 Jane's Information Group, *Jane's Sentinel Southeast Asia*, 2008, Issue No.22, p.585.
40 P.S. Suryanarayana, 'India, Singapore hold "maritime exercise"', *The Hindu*, 6 March 2005.
41 C. Raja Mohan, 'India's geopolitics and Southeast Asian security', in Daljit Singh and Tin Maung Maung (eds), *Southeast Asian Affairs 2008*, Singapore: Institute of Southeast Asian Studies, 2008, pp.43–60.
42 Faizal Yahya, 'Challenges of globalisation: Malaysia and India engagement', *Contemporary Southeast Asia*, Vol.27, No.3, 2005, pp.472–98.
43 Dr V. Suryanarayan, 'Malaysian Indian society in ferment', *South Asia Analysis Group*, Paper No.2880, 14 October 2008.
44 P.S. Suryanarayana, 'India, Malaysia to step up defence ties', *The Hindu*, 8 January 2008.
45 Bertil Lintner, 'Enter the Dragon', *Far Eastern Economic Review*, 22 December 1994, p.24.
46 Mohammed Ayoob, *India and Southeast Asia: Indian perceptions and policies*, New York: Routledge, 1990, p.36.
47 See David Brewster, 'The evolving security relationship between India and Indonesia', *Asian Survey* (forthcoming).
48 'Indonesia for security cooperation with India', *The Hindu*, 30 July 1999.
49 Ralf Emmers, 'Regional hegemonies and the exercise of power in Southeast Asia: a study of Indonesia and Vietnam', *Asian Survey*, Vol.45, No.4, July–August 2005, pp.645–65 at p.664.
50 Terry Lacey, 'Indonesia looks to play on the world stage', *Asia Sentinel*, 1 February 2010.
51 Jusuf Wanandi, 'The ASEAN Charter and remodelling regional architecture', *The Jakarta Post*, 3 November 2008.
52 Daniel Novotny, *Torn between America and China: elite perceptions and Indonesian foreign policy*, ISEAS Publishing: Singapore, 2010, pp.280–81.
53 Which was reflected in recent comments by the influential Indonesian analyst, Rizal Sukma, that ASEAN was 'outmoded', the East Asian Summit consisted of too many countries and that Indonesia should work with Australia and South Korea to form a new forum in the Asia Pacific comprising the United States, China, Japan, India, Russia, South Korea, Australia and Indonesia. Lilian Budianto, 'Indonesia told to initiate new Asia Pacific forum', *The Jakarta Post*, 6 May 2009.
54 Datta-Ray, *Looking East to Look West*, p.289.

55 Jusuf Wanandi, *Global, Regional and National: strategic issues and linkages*, Jakarta: Centre for Strategic and International Studies, 2006, p.257.
56 Abdul Khalik, 'Indonesia–India security pact comes into effect', *Jakarta Post*, 3 April 2007.
57 'Indonesia and Malaysia keen on buying BrahMos', *Frontier India Strategic and Defence*, 13 April 2007. http://frontierindia.net/indianesia-and-malasia-keen-on-buying-brahmos (accessed 28 February 2011).
58 Amitav Ranjan, 'India says not yet to Indonesian plea', *India Express*, 21 April 2004.
59 See Donald K. Emmerson, 'Indonesia's eleventh hour in Aceh', *PacNet Newsletter*, No.49, 17 December 1998; and Pankaj K. Jha, 'India–Indonesia: emerging strategic confluence in the Indian Ocean', *Strategic Analysis*, Vol.32, No.3, May 2008, pp.439–58 at p.454.
60 Other observers have been highly skeptical of any link between GAM and Pakistan.
61 M. Malik, 'Sino-Indian relations and India's eastern strategy', in Sandy Gordon and Stephen Henningham (eds), *India Looks East: an emerging power and its Asia Pacific neighbours*, Canberra: Strategic and Defence Studies Centre, 1995, pp.119–63.
62 See generally, Ian James Storey, 'Indonesia's China policy in the new order and beyond: problems and prospects', *Contemporary Southeast Asia*, Vol.22, No.1, April 2000, pp.145–74. In June 2010 there was a confrontation between an Indonesian patrol boat and an armed Chinese fishing vessel in the Indonesian EEZ near the Natuna Islands.
63 C. Raja Mohan, 'Is India an East Asian power? Explaining New Delhi's security politics in the western Pacific', ISAS Working Paper No.81, 11 August 2009. p.13.

8 India's uncertain partnership with Australia

1 For a comprehensive review of Australian–Indian political relations during the 1950s and 1960s, see Meg Gurry, *India: Australia's neglected neighbour? 1947–1996*, Griffith: Centre for the Study of Australia–Asia Relations, 1996.
2 Cited in James Eayres, *Commonwealth and Suez: a documentary survey*, London: Oxford University Press, 1964, p.15.
3 K. Subrahmanyam, 'Strategic developments in the Indian and South Pacific Ocean regions', in Robert H. Bruce, *Australia and the Indian Ocean: strategic dimensions of increasing naval involvement*, Perth: Centre of Indian Ocean Studies, 1988, pp.79–95; and Madhurendra Kumar, *Super Power India and the Indian Ocean*, Allahabad: Chugh, 1995, p.55.
4 See, for example, A.W. Grezebrook, 'The Indian naval buildup: has Defence Central got it wrong?', *Pacific Defence Reporter*, February 1990, pp.14–15.
5 S.K. Bhutani, 'India–Australia bilateral relations' in Dipkar Banerjee, *Towards an Era of Cooperation: an Indo-Australian dialogue*, New Delhi: Institute for Defence Studies and Analyses, 1995, p.376.
6 Kim C. Beazley, 'The two ocean navy', in Bruce, *Australia and the Indian Ocean*, pp.9–20 at p.11.
7 See generally, Graeme Cheeseman, *Selling Mirages: the politics of arms trading*, Canberra: Strategic and Defence Studies Centre, 1992. It has been suggested that the low cash price may have been part of a contra-deal in which Australia received US equipment at a discount.
8 It has been suggested that the INS *New Delhi* responded by switching on its fire control.
9 Hamish McDonald, 'Nuclear posturing – out on a street-cred limb', *Sydney Morning Herald*, 8 February 1999.

10 Alexander Downer, 'Australian response to India's nuclear tests', Media Release, 14 May 1998.
11 Man Mohini Kaul, 'Australia–India relations: a critical survey', in D. Gopal (ed.), *Australia in the Emerging Global Order: evolving Australia–India relations*, New Delhi: Shipra, 2002, pp.220–34.
12 It seems likely that the Howard government was seeking to outflank the Labor opposition on the anti-nuclear issue in the weeks leading up to a Federal election.
13 Kevin Rudd, 'From fitful engagement to strategic partnership', address to the Indian Council of World Affairs in New Delhi, 12 November 2009.
14 For a detailed discussion of the Australia–India Security Declaration, see David Brewster, 'The Australia–India Security Declaration: the Quadrilateral redux?', *Security Challenges*, Vol.6, No.1, Autumn 2010, pp.1–9.
15 'Joint statement on the advancement of the strategic and global partnership between Japan and India', 22 October 2008.
16 See, for example, Rory Medcalf, 'Australia–India relations: hesitating on the brink of partnership', *Asia Pacific Bulletin*, No.13, 3 April 2008. www.eastwest center. org/fileadmin/stored/pdfs/apb013.pdf (accessed 23 June 2011).
17 Australian Government, *Defending Australia in the Asia Pacific Century: Force 2030*, Canberra: Commonwealth of Australia, 2009, p.96.
18 Brahma Chellaney, 'Dragon's foothold in Gwadar' *Asian Age*, 7 April 2007.
19 C. Raja Mohan, 'India in East Asia', Australia–India Strategic Lecture, Melbourne, 21 February 2007.
20 Although Australia, along with many other regional states, participates in India's MILAN biennial naval gathering in the Andaman islands. There have also been occasional passage exercises, largely involving Australian ships on the way to the Persian Gulf.
21 Rory Medcalf, 'Squaring the triangle: an Australian perspective on Asian security minilateralism', in William Tow, Michael Auslin, Rory Medcalf, Akihiko Tanaka, Zhu Feng and Sheldon Simon, *Assessing the Trilateral Strategic Dialogue*, NBR Special Report, December 2008, pp.23–31 at p.27.
22 Greg Sheridan, 'Region notices bias for Beijing', *The Australian*, 3 May 2008.
23 All economic statistics from Australian Government, *Australia–India Joint Free Trade Agreement (FTA) Feasibility Study*, Canberra: Commonwealth of Australia, 2010.
24 OECD Nuclear Energy Agency and International Atomic Energy Agency, 'Identified resources recoverable at under US$40 kg', *Uranium 2007: production, resources and demand*, Paris: OECD, 2008.
25 See for example, reported comments of senior Indian officials in Bruce Loudon and Mark Dodd, 'Confusion over uranium sales grows as Stephen Smith reaches India', *The Australian*, 10 September 2008.
26 Quoted in Ramesh Thakur, 'India and overseas Indians: the case of Fiji', *Asian Survey*, Vol.25, No.3, 1985, pp.356–70 at p.356.
27 Mihir K. Roy, *War in the Indian Ocean*, New Delhi: Lancer, 1995, pp.271–72.
28 R.G. Crocombe, *Asia in the Pacific Islands: replacing the West*, Suva: IPS Publications, 2007.
29 No doubt aware of the number of votes Pacific Island states hold in the United Nations and other international fora.
30 C. Raja Mohan, 'Superpower in the South Pacific', *The Hindu*, 30 July 2003.
31 With the somewhat odd exception of the bankrupt state of Nauru with which India has had a close relationship for many years.
32 These include military operations in Iraq 1991 and 2003–8; East Timor 1999–; Afghanistan 2001–; and Persian Gulf/Arabian Sea 2003–.
33 Quoted in Sita Gopalan, *India and Non-Alignment*, New Delhi: Spick & Span, 1984, p.2.

34 Walter Crocker, *Australian Ambassador*, Melbourne: Melbourne University Press, 1971, p.200.
35 Alison Broinowski, *About Face: Asian accounts of Australia*, Carlton North: Scribe, 2003, p.91.
36 Gwenda Tavan, *The Long Slow Death of White Australia*, Melbourne: Scribe, 2005, p.86.
37 Quoted in N.R.H. Kuruppu, *An Indian Perspective of the Relationship between India and Australia, 1947 to 1975: personalities and policies, peaks and troughs*, unpublished doctoral thesis, Victoria University of Technology, 2000.
38 According to former Indian Chief of Naval Staff, Admiral O.S. Dawson. See Raju G.C. Thomas, 'The sources of Indian naval expansion', in Robert H. Bruce (ed.), *The Modern Indian Navy in the Indian Ocean: developments and implications*, Perth: Centre for Indian Ocean Regional Studies, 1989, pp.95–107, at p.98.
39 Kaul, 'Australia–India relations: a critical survey'.
40 The differences in Indian perspectives on Japan and Australia are also somewhat ironic in light of Japan's highly restrictive and racially based immigration policy, which served to prevent any significant legal immigration from non-Japanese ethnic groups (including Indians) until the early 1990s and beyond. See Hiroshi Komai, *Foreign Migrants in Contemporary Japan*, Melbourne: Trans Pacific Press, 1999.
41 See Sandy Gordon, *Widening Horizons: Australia's new relationship with India*, Canberra: Australian Strategic Policy Institute, 2007, p.4; Leszek Buszynski, 'Emerging naval rivalry in East Asia and the Indian Ocean: implications for Australia', *Security Challenges*, Vol.5 No.3, 2009, pp.73–93 at p.86; and Andrew Selth, 'Chinese military bases in Burma: the explosion of a myth', Griffith University Regional Outlook Paper No.10, 2007.
42 Jenelle Bonnor, 'Australia–India: an important partnership', *South Asian Survey*, Vol.15, 2008, pp.165–77 at p.168.
43 See for example, Coral Bell, 'The end of the Vasco da Gama Era: the next landscape of world politics', Lowy Institute for International Policy, Paper No.21, 2007.
44 See, for example, Hugh White, *Power Shift: Australia's future between Washington and Beijing*, Collingwood: Black Inc., 2010.

9 India's maritime security ambitions in Southeast Asia and the western Pacific

1 See generally, David Brewster, 'An Indian sphere of influence in the Indian Ocean?', *Security Challenges*, Vol.6, No.3, Spring 2010, pp.1–20.
2 India, *Indian Maritime Doctrine*, 2004, p.64. This statement was not repeated in the 2009 edition of *Indian Maritime Doctrine*.
3 A.K. Dhar, 'Indian Air Force carries out exercise from Andaman Islands Base', *Press Trust of India*, 15 April 2005.
4 Zhang Ming, 'The Malacca dilemma and the Chinese Navy's strategic choices', *Modern Ships*, No.274, October 2006, p.23.
5 China and the United States were not invited to participate as members on the basis that they are not Indian Ocean littoral states. Neither are happy with India's stance.
6 Gurpreet S. Khurana, 'China–India maritime rivalry', *Indian Defence Review*, Vol.23, No.4, 2009. www.bannedthought.net/China/Capitalism-Imperialism/China-IndiaMaritimeRivalry-090409.pdf (accessed 23 June 2011).
7 Indian Navy, 'Freedom to use the seas: India's maritime military strategy', May 2007.
8 James R. Holmes, Andrew C. Winner and Toshi Yoshihara, *Indian Naval Strategy in the Twenty-first Century*, London: Routledge, 2009, p.154.
9 Khurana, 'China–India maritime rivalry'.

10 The most likely invasion route of the Soviet Union into West Germany. Robert D. Kaplan, 'Centre stage for the twenty-first century', *Foreign Affairs*, Vol.88, 2009, pp.16–32 at p.25.
11 Ian Storey, 'Securing Southeast Asia's sea lanes: a work in progress', *Asia Policy*, No.6, July 2008, pp.95–127.
12 'Indian Navy awaits regional nod for patrolling Malacca Straits', *India Defence*, 7 June 2006.
13 Rajeev Sawhney, 'Redefining the limits of the Straits: a composite Malacca Straits security system', *RSIS Commentaries*, No.37, 18 May 2006.
14 The Strait was subsequently removed from Lloyd's war risk list in August 2006.
15 See generally, Shafiah Fifi Muhibat, 'Competing to secure the Straits of Malacca and Singapore', *The Indonesian Quarterly*, Vol.35, No.3, 2007, pp.242–53.
16 Storey, 'Securing Southeast Asia's sea lanes', p.120.
17 *Asia Times*, 19 October 2005.
18 Gurpreet S. Khurana, 'Safeguarding the Malacca Straits', *IDSA Comment*, 5 January 2005.
19 Gurpreet S. Khurana, 'The Malacca Straits "conundrum" and India', in N.S. Sisodia and Sreeradha Datta (eds), *Changing Security Dynamics in Southeast Asia*, New Delhi: Magnum Books, 2008, pp.125–42 at p.134.
20 Shiv Aroor, 'Centre approves Navy's Malacca plan', *Indian Express*, 11 January 2006.
21 Rakesh Sinha, 'Jakarta says no to Indian patrol in Malacca Straits', *Indian Express*, 13 July 2005.
22 P.S. Suryanarayana, 'Indonesia for defence tie-up with India', *The Hindu*, 5 June 2007.
23 'Thai to join RI patrolling Malacca Strait', *The Jakarta Post*, 16 March 2009. This conveniently extended the definition of the Malacca Strait north towards Indian waters.
24 'Indonesia asks India to help maintain Malacca Strait security', *Xinhua*, 5 March 2009.
25 P.S. Suryanarayana, 'Indonesia to "learn" from India's defence sector', *The Hindu*, 18 June 2010.
26 This has included India–Thai joint naval patrols in the Andaman Sea. 'Malaysia warns India against Thailand', *Newsinsight*, 3 January 2005.
27 P.S. Suryanarayana, 'India, Malaysia to step up defence ties' and 'Indian Air Force Chief to visit Malaysia; boost in military ties', *India Defence*, 17 August 2008.
28 According to official figures, cases of piracy and sea robbery within the Straits of Malacca and Singapore peaked at some 38 reported cases in 2004, falling in recent years to nine reported cases in 2009. ReCAAP Information Sharing Centre, *Annual Report 2009*, Singapore, 2009.
29 Hongyi Lai, 'Security of China's energy imports', in Hongyi Lai (ed.), *Asian Energy Security: the maritime dimension*, London: Palgrave MacMillan 2009, pp.49–77.
30 Khurana, 'The Malacca Straits "conundrum" and India', p.137.
31 See comments by former Indian Foreign Secretary Rajiv Sikri, in *Challenge and Strategy: rethinking India's foreign policy*, New Delhi: Sage, 2009.
32 John Daly, 'Can the Dragon swim? The naval balance in the Taiwan Strait', *China Brief*, Vol.4, No.2, 20 January 2004. www.jamestown.org/programs/chinabrief/single/?tx_ttnews[tt_news]=3621&tx_ttnews[backPid]=194&no_cache=1 (accessed 15 July 2011).
33 C. Raja Mohan, 'Is India an East Asian Power? Explaining New Delhi's security politics in the Western Pacific', ISAS Working Paper No.81, 11 August 2009.
34 Indian Navy, 'Freedom to use the seas'.
35 K.M. Panikkar, *India and the Indian Ocean: an essay on the influence of sea power on Indian history*, London: George Allen and Unwin, 1945, p.85.

36 David Scott, 'India's drive for a "Blue Water" navy', *Journal of Military and Strategic Studies*, Vol.10, Issue 2, Winter 2007, pp.1–42 at p.33.
37 Josy Joseph, 'Navy hails successful South China Sea visit', *Rediff on the Net*, 17 October 2000. www.rediff.com/news/2000/oct/17spec.htm (accessed 28 February 2011).
38 Ian Storey and Carlyle A. Thayer, 'Cam Ranh Bay: past imperfect, future conditional', *Contemporary Southeast Asia*, Vol.23, No.3, December 2001, pp.452–73 at p.461.
39 C. Raja Mohan, 'India's geopolitics and Southeast Asian security', in Daljit Singh and Tin Maung Maung (eds), *Southeast Asian Affairs 2008*, Singapore: Institute of Southeast Asian Studies, 2008, pp.43–60 at p.49.
40 Some believe that limitations in India's missile delivery technology will compel the deployment of Indian nuclear-powered ballistic missile submarines (when they become operational) into the South China Sea and the western Pacific in range of China's East Coast. Holmes *et al.*, *Indian Naval Strategy in the Twenty-first Century*, p.155. It is not clear how this would square with India's stated willingness to abide by the Southeast Asian Nuclear Weapons Free Zone treaty.
41 At the ASEAN Regional Forum meeting in July 2010, India joined with ASEAN states for the first time to 'openly declare that the South China Sea should remain open for international navigation'. Indrani Bagchi, 'India to discuss China with US later this month', *The Times of India*, 4 September 2010.

10 Understanding India's engagement with the Asia Pacific

1 Asad-ul Iqbal Latif, *Between Rising Powers: China, Singapore and India*, Singapore: ISEAS Publishing, 2007, p.274.
2 George Yeo, speech in New Delhi, 18 February 2004.
3 Durga Das, *India: from Curzon to Nehru and after*, London: Collins, 1969, p.415.
4 Goh Chok Tong, 'Constructing East Asia', speech to Asia Society, 15th Asian Corporate Conference, Bangkok, 9 June 2005.
5 Chong Guan Kwa (ed.), *S Rajaratnam on Singapore: from ideas to reality*, Hackensack, NJ: World Scientific, 2006, p.7.
6 *Straits Times*, 6 November 1984.
7 Michael Leifer, *Singapore's Foreign Policy: coping with vulnerability*, London: Routledge, 2000, pp.5–6.
8 Kripa Sridharan, 'Transcending the region: Singapore's India policy', in N.N. Vohra (ed.), *Emerging Asia: challenges for India and Singapore*, New Delhi: Manohar, 2003, pp.15–32 at p.30.
9 Something acknowledged by Singapore's current Prime Minister. Sunanda K. Datta-Ray, *Looking East to Look West: Lee Kuan Yew's mission India*, Singapore: ISEAS Publishing, 2009, p.328.
10 Sandy Gordon, 'India "Looks East" as history', *East Asia Forum*, 17 July 2010. www.eastasiaforum.org/2010/07/17/india-looks-east-as-history/ (accessed 28 February 2011).
11 M. Pardesi, *Deducing India's Grand Strategy of Regional Hegemony from Historical and Conceptual Perspectives*, Singapore: Institute of Defence and Strategic Studies, 2005.
12 C. Raja Mohan, 'India in the emerging Asian architecture', in William T.Tow and Chin Kin Wah, *Asean India Australia: towards closer engagement in a New Asia*, Singapore: Institute of Southeast Asian Studies, 2009, pp.40–57 at p.50.
13 C. Raja Mohan, 'India and the changing geopolitics of the Indian Ocean', address in New Delhi, 19 July 2010.

14 K. Kesavapany, *India's Tryst with Asia*, New Delhi: Asian Institute of Transport Development, 2006, p.48.

11 India as an Asia Pacific power

1 George Yeo, speech to India Economic Summit 2002, New Delhi.
2 Robert D. Kaplan, *Monsoon: the Indian Ocean and the future of American power*, New York: Random House, 2010, p.283.
3 Shiv Shankar Menon, 'Maritime imperatives of Indian foreign policy', speech to the National Maritime Foundation, New Delhi, 11 September, 2009.
4 See, for example, Coral Bell, 'The end of the Vasco da Gama Era: the next landscape of world politics', Lowy Institute for International Policy, Paper No.21, 2007.

Bibliography

Abe, Shinzo, *Utsukushii kuni e: jishin to hokori no moteru Nihon e* [Towards a beautiful country: A confident and proud Japan], Tokyo: Bungei Shunju, 2006.
Acharya, Amitav and Evelyn Goh (eds), *Reassessing Security Cooperation in the Asia Pacific: competition, congruence and transformation*, Cambridge, MA: MIT Press, 2007.
Acheson, Dean G., *A Democrat Looks at his Party*, New York: Harper, 1955.
'A glance at features of Hillary Clinton's Asian tour', *Xinhua (English edition)*, 22 February 2009.
Ahamed, E., press release of Minister of State for External Affairs, 'Reinforcing "Look East" policy', 16 January 2006. pib.nic.in/release/rel_print_ page1.asp? relid=14984 (accessed 28 February 2011).
Alagappa, Muthiah (ed.), *Asian Security Practice: material and ideational influences*, Stanford, CT: Stanford University Press, 1998.
Aneja, Atul, 'India, Vietnam partners in safeguarding sea lanes', *The Hindu*, 15 April 2000.
Aroor, Shiv, 'Centre approves Navy's Malacca Plan', *Indian Express*, 11 January 2006.
ASEAN Secretariat. www.aseansec.org/22122.htm (accessed 28 February 2011).
'A third country role cannot be envisaged nor is it necessary', *Outlook India*, 18 November 2009.
Athwal, Amardeep, *China–India Relations: contemporary dynamics*, New York: Routledge, 2007.
Australian Government, *Defending Australia in the Asia Pacific Century: Force 2030*, Canberra: Commonwealth of Australia, 2009.
——*Australia-India Joint Free Trade Agreement (FTA) Feasibility Study*, Canberra: Commonwealth of Australia, 2010.
Ayoob, Mohammed, *India and Southeast Asia: Indian perceptions and policies*, New York: Routledge, 1990.
Ayres, Alyssa and C. Raja Mohan, *Power Realignments in Asia: China, India and the United States*, New Delhi: Sage Publications, 2009.
Babbage, Ross and Sandy Gordon (eds), *India's Strategic Future: regional state or global power?*, London: Macmillan, 1992.
Bagchi, Indrani, 'India to discuss China with US later this month', *The Times of India*, 4 September 2010.
Bajpai, Kanti, 'India: modified structuralism', in Muthiah Alagappa (ed.), *Asian Security Practice: material and ideational influences*, Stanford, CT: Stanford University Press, 1998, pp.157–97.

Bibliography

——'Indian Strategic Culture', in Michael R. Chambers (ed.), *South Asia in 2020: future strategic balances and alliances*, Carlisle, PA: Strategic Studies Institute, 2002, pp.245–305.

——'Indian conceptions of order/justice in international relations: Nehruvian, Gandhian, Hindutva and Neo-Liberal', in V.R. Mehta and Thomas Pantham (eds), *Political Ideas in Modern India: thematic explorations*, New Delhi: Sage, 2006, pp.367–92.

Balme, Stephanie and Mark Sidel, *Vietnam's New Order: international perspectives on the State and reform in Vietnam*, New York: Palgrave Macmillan, 2006.

Banerjee, Major General Dipankar (ed.), *Towards an Era of Cooperation: an Indo-Australian dialogue*, New Delhi: Institute for Defence Studies and Analyses, 1995.

——'India and China – what next?', Centre for Strategic and International Studies, 5 June 2008. http://csis.org/files/media/csis/events/080701_summary_india-china_talk.pdf (accessed 28 February 2011).

Baruah, Amit, 'Looking East', *Frontline*, 8 December 2000.

——'Not seeking exclusive sphere of influence', *The Hindu*, 11 February 2007.

Batabyal, Anindya, 'Balancing China in Asia: a realist assessment of India's Look East strategy', *China Report*, Vol.42, No.2, 2006, pp.79–197.

Bateman, Sam and Joshua Ho (eds), *Southeast Asia and the Rise of Chinese and Indian Naval Power: between rising naval powers*, London: Routledge, 2010.

Beazley, Kim C., 'The two ocean navy', in Robert H. Bruce, *Australia and the Indian Ocean: strategic dimensions of increasing naval involvement*, Perth: Centre of Indian Ocean Studies, 1988, pp.9–20.

Bedi, Rahul, 'Strategic realignments', *Frontline*, Vol.20, Issue 13, 21 June–4 July 2003. www.hindu.com/fline/fl2013/stories/20030704002104700.htm (accessed 23 June 2011).

——'Strategic partners in defence', *SPAN Magazine*, New Delhi, March–April, 2005, pp.20–24.

——'Despite India's protests, Vietnam buys arms from Pakistan', *India News*, 17 August 2007.

Bell, Coral, 'The end of the Vasco da Gama Era: the next landscape of world politics', Lowy Institute for International Policy, Paper No.21, 2007.

Bhaskar, C. Uday and Kamlesh K. Agnihotri (eds), *Security Challenges along the Indian Ocean Littoral: Indian and US perspectives*, Delhi: National Maritime Foundation, 2010.

Bhatt, Sheela, 'As Obama arrives, US bids for heavy arms business', *Rediff News*, 5 November 2010. www.rediff.com/news/special/obama-visit-special-as-arrives-us-bids-for-heavy-arms-business/20101105.htm (accessed 28 February 2010).

Bhutani, S.K., 'India–Australia bilateral relations', in Dipkar Banerjee (ed.), *Towards an Era of Cooperation: an Indo-Australian dialogue*, New Delhi: Institute for Defence Studies and Analyses, 1995, p.376.

Bilveer, S., 'Operation Cactus: India's 'prompt action' in Maldives', *Asian Defense Journal*, February 1989, p.33.

Bonnor, Jenelle, 'Australia–India: an important partnership', *South Asian Survey*, Vol.15, 2008, pp.165–77.

Brecher, Michael, *India and World Politics: Krishna Menon's view of the world*, London: Oxford University Press, 1968.

Brewster, David, 'The strategic relationship between India and Vietnam: the search for a diamond on the South China Sea?', *Asian Security*, Vol.5, No.1, January 2009, pp.24–44.

—— 'India's security partnership with Singapore', *The Pacific Review*, Vol.22, No.5, December 2009, pp.597–618.

—— 'Developments in India's relations with South Korea: a useful friend in East Asia', *Asian Survey*, Vol.50 No.2, March 2010, pp.407–25.

—— 'An Indian sphere of influence in the Indian Ocean?', *Security Challenges*, Vol.6, No.3, Spring 2010, pp.1–20.

—— 'Australia and India: the Indian Ocean and the limits of strategic convergence', *Australian Journal of International Affairs*, Vol.64, No.5, 2010, pp.549–65.

—— 'The Australia–India Security Declaration: the quadrilateral redux?', *Security Challenges*, Vol.6, No.1, Autumn 2010, pp.1–9.

—— 'The India–Japan Security Declaration: an enduring security partnership?', *Asian Security*, Vol.6, No.2 2010, pp.1–27.

—— 'The evolving security relationship between India and Indonesia', *Asian Survey*, forthcoming.

Broinowski, Alison, *About Face: Asian accounts of Australia*, Carlton North: Scribe, 2003.

Brooke, Micool, 'India courts Vietnam with arms and nuclear technology', *Asia-Pacific Defence Reporter*, Vol.25, August/September 2000, pp.20–21.

Brown, Jeffrey G. Vijay Mukherji and Kang Wu, 'The energy race between China and India: motivations and potential opportunities for cooperation', in *China, India and the United States: competition for energy resources*, Abu Dhabi: The Emirates Centre for Strategic Studies and Research, 2008, pp.223–54.

Bruce, Robert H., *Australia and the Indian Ocean: strategic dimensions of increasing naval involvement*, Perth: Centre of Indian Ocean Studies, 1988.

—— (ed.), *The Modern Indian Navy in the Indian Ocean: developments and implications*, Perth: Centre for Indian Ocean Regional Studies, 1989.

Budianto, Lilian, 'Indonesia told to initiate new Asia Pacific forum', *The Jakarta Post*, 6 May 2009.

Bull, Hedley, 'The new balance of power in Asia and the Pacific', *Foreign Affairs*, Vol.49, 1971, pp.669–81.

—— *The Anarchical Society: a study of order in world politics*, London: Macmillan, 1977.

Burns, William J., speech to Council on Foreign Relations, Washington DC, 1 June 2010.

Buszynski, Leszek, 'Emerging naval rivalry in East Asia and the Indian Ocean: implications for Australia', *Security Challenges*, Vol.5 No.3, 2009, pp.73–93.

Buzan, Barry and Gowher Rizvi, *South Asian Insecurity and the Great Powers*, New York: St Martin's Press, 1986.

Buzan, Barry, Ole Waever and Jaap de Wilde, *Security: a new framework for analysis*, Boulder, CO: Lynne Rienner Publishers, 1998.

Camilleri, Joseph A., *Regionalism in the New Asia-Pacific Order*, Cheltenham: Edward Elgar, 2003.

Centre for Strategic and International Studies, 'The United States, Japan and India: toward new trilateral cooperation', 16 August 2007. http://csis.org/files/media/csis/pubs/070816_us_j_ireport.pdf (accessed 28 February 2011).

—— 'Bridging strategic Asia: the rise of India in East Asia and implications for the US-Japan alliance', Winter 2008. http://csis.org/programs/international-security-program/asia-division/bridging-strategic-asia-rise-india-east-asia-a (accessed 28 February 2011).

—— 'US-Japan-India strategic dialogue October 17–19 in Delhi, India – key recommendations', 6 November 2008. http://csis.org/files/media/csis/pubs/081105_india-japan-us_trilateral_delhi_statement.pdf (accessed 28 February 2011).

Cha, Victor D., 'The ideational dimension of America's alliances in Asia', in Amitav Acharya and Evelyn Goh (eds), *Reassessing Security Cooperation in the Asia Pacific: competition, congruence and transformation*, Cambridge, MA: The MIT Press, 2007, pp.41–70.

Chakraborty, Debashis, 'China factor in India-ASEAN relations', IPCS China Seminar Report No.273, 15 December 2008.

Chambers, Michael R. (ed.), *South Asia in 2020: future strategic balances and alliances*, Carlisle, PA: Strategic Studies Institute, 2002.

Chanda, Nayan, *Brother Enemy: the war after the war*, New York, Harcourt Brace Jovanovich, 1986.

——'After the bomb', *Far Eastern Economic Review*, 13 April 2000, p.20.

Chandrasekaran, Rajiv, 'India offers bases to U.S. for retaliatory attacks', *Washington Post*, 17 September 2001.

Cheeseman, Graeme, *Selling Mirages: the politics of arms trading*, Canberra: Strategic and Defence Studies Centre, 1992.

Chellaney, Brahma (ed.), *Securing India's Future in the New Millennium*, New Delhi: Centre for Policy Research, 1999.

——*Asian Juggernaut: the rise of China, India and Japan*, New Delhi: HarperCollins, 2006.

——'Dragon's foothold in Gwadar', *Asian Age*, 7 April 2007.

——'Assessing India's reactions to China's "Peaceful Development" doctrine', *NBR Analysis*, Vol.18, No.5 April 2008, pp.23–36.

——'Towards Asian power equilibrium', *The Hindu*, 1 November 2008.

Chellaney, Brahma and Horimoto Takenori, 'Indo kara mita Nihon, Ajia' [Japan–India links critical for Asia–Pacific Security], *Gaiko Forum*, Vol.7, No.2, Fall 2007.

Cheng, Sun, 'A comparative analysis of Abe's and Fukada's Asia diplomacy', *China International Studies*, Spring 2008, pp.58–72.

Chie, Nakane, 'Logic and the smile: when Japanese meet Indians', *Japan Quarterly*, Vol.11, No.4, October/December 1964, pp.434–38.

'China-ASEAN FTA to accelerate RMB regionalization', *Peoples Online Daily*, 23 October 2009.

'China attracts $52 bln investment from ASEAN', *Xinhua*, 21 October 2008.

'China mulling naval base in Gulf of Aden: admiral', *Agence-France Presse*, 29 December 2009.

CIA World Factbook. www.cia.gov/library/publications/the-world-factbook/geos/in. html (accessed 28 February 2011).

Coates, Austin, *China, India and the Ruins of Washington*, New York: The John Day Company, 1972.

Cohen, Saul Bernard, *Geography and Politics in a World Divided* (2nd edn), New York: Oxford University Press, 1973.

Cohen, Stephen P., *India: emerging power*, Washington: Brookings Institute, 2001.

Cohen, Stephen P. and Sunil Dasgupta, *Arming without Aiming: India's military modernisation*, Washington D.C.: Brookings Institution Press, 2010.

Crocker, Walter, *Australian Ambassador*, Melbourne: Melbourne University Press, 1971.

Crocombe, R.G., *Asia in the Pacific Islands: replacing the West*, Suva: IPS Publications, 2007.

Daly, John, 'Can the Dragon swim? The naval balance in the Taiwan Strait', *China Brief*, Vol.4, No.2, 20 January 2004. www.jamestown.org/programs/chinabrief/single/?tx_ttnews[tt_news]=3621&tx_ttnews[backPid]=194&no_cache=1 (accessed 15 July 2011).

Daniels, Paul R., 'Beyond "better than ever": Japanese independence and the future of US-Japan relations', Institute for International Policy Studies, IIPS Policy Paper 308E, July 2004.
Das, Durga, *India: from Curzon to Nehru and after*, London: Collins, 1969.
——'Japan's role in Asia', *Indian and Foreign Review*, Vol.7, No.18, 1 July 1970, pp.11–17.
Das, Gurcharan, *India Unbound: the social and economic revolution from independence to the Global Information Age*, New Delhi: Viking, 2000.
Datta-Ray, Sunanda K., 'Invasion of Vietnam brings an end to the thaw between India and China', *Canberra Times*, 21 March 1979.
——*Looking East to Look West: Lee Kuan Yew's mission India*, Singapore: ISEAS Publishing, 2009.
Denmark, Abraham M., Dr James Mulvenon, Frank G. Hoffman, Lt Col Kelly M. Martin, Oliver Fritz, Eric Sterner, Dr Greg Rattray, Chris Evans, Jason Healey and Robert Kaplan, *Contested Commons: the future of American Power in a multipolar world*, Washington DC: Center for a New American Security, 2010.
Devare, Sudhir, *India and Southeast Asia: towards security convergence*, Singapore: Institute of Southeast Asian Studies, 2006.
Dhar, A.K., 'Indian Air Force carries out exercise from Andaman Islands Base', *Press Trust of India*, 15 April 2005.
Dikshit, Sandeep, 'Japanese energy security is dependent on the Indian Navy', *The Hindu*, 1 October 2007.
——'No strings attached to sale of ships', *The Hindu*, 29 March 2008.
Dixit, J.N., *Makers of India's Foreign Policy: Raja Ram Mohun Roy to Yashwant Sinha*, New Delhi: HarperCollins, 2004.
Downer, Alexander, 'Australian response to India's nuclear tests', media release, 14 May 1998.
Dutt, V.P., *India's Foreign Policy*, New Delhi: Vikas, 1984.
Easley, Leif-Eric, Tetsuo Kotani and Aki Mori, 'Electing a new Japanese security policy? Examining foreign policy visions within the Democratic Party of Japan', *Asia Policy*, No.9, January 2010, pp.x–xx.
Eayres, James, *Commonwealth and Suez: a documentary survey*, London: Oxford University Press, 1964.
Elegant, Simon and Michael Elliot, 'Lee Kuan Yew reflects', *Time Asia*, 5 December 2005.
Ellings, Richard J. and Aaron L. Friedberg (eds), *Strategic Asia 2001–02: power and purpose*, Seattle: National Bureau of Asian Research, 2002.
Elsbree, Willard H., *Japan's Role in Southeast Asian Nationalist Movements 1940 to 1945*, New York: Russell & Russell, 1970.
Emirates Centre for Strategic Studies and Research, *China, India and the United States: competition for energy resources*, Abu Dhabi, 2008.
Emmers, Ralf, 'Regional hegemonies and the exercise of power in Southeast Asia: a study of Indonesia and Vietnam', *Asian Survey*, Vol.45, No.4, July–August 2005, pp.645–65.
Emmerson, Donald K., 'Indonesia's eleventh hour in Aceh', *PacNet Newsletter*, No.49, 17 December 1998.
Enoki, Yasukuni, 'The Japan–India new partnership', speech to the United Services Institute, New Delhi, 28 May 2004.
Fair, Christine, 'India and Iran: New Delhi's balancing act', *The Washington Quarterly*, Vol.30, No.3, Summer 2007, pp.145–59.

Flournoy, Michele, 'Investing in the future of U.S.–India defense relations', speech to the Asia Society, Washington DC, 1 July 2010.

Frankel, Francine R. and Harry Harding (eds) *The India–China Relationship: what the United States needs to know*, New York: Columbia University Press, 2004.

Frazier, Mark W., 'Quiet competition and the future of Sino-Indian relations', in Francine R. Frankel and Harry Harding, *The India–China Relationship: what the United States needs to know*, New York: Columbia University Press, 2004, pp.294–318.

Ganguly, Sumit, *India as an Emerging Power*, London: Frank Cass, 2003.

Ganguly, Sumit, Brian Shoup and Andrew Scobell (eds), *US–Indian Strategic Cooperation into the 21st Century: more than words*, London: Routledge, 2006.

Garamone, Jim, 'Officials praise growth of U.S.–India military partnership', *American Armed Services Press*, 23 July 2010.

Garver, John W., 'Chinese–Indian rivalry in Indochina', *Asian Survey*, Vol.27, No.11, November 1987, pp.1205–19.

——*Protracted Contest: Sino-Indian rivalry in the twentieth century*, Seattle: University of Washington Press, 2001.

——'Asymmetrical Indian and Chinese threat perceptions', in Sumit Ganguly, *India as an Emerging Power*, London: Frank Cass, 2003, pp.109–134.

George Mulgan, Aurelia, 'Breaking the mould: Japan's subtle shift from exclusive bilateralism to modest minilateralism', *Contemporary Southeast Asia*, Vol.30, No.1, 2008, pp.52–72.

Gerace, Michael P., *Military Power, Conflict and Trade*, London: Frank Cass, 2004.

Ghazali Bin Shafie, Muhammed, 'Defence pattern for South East Asia', in K.K. Sinha (ed.), *Problems of Defence of South and East Asia*, New Delhi: Rawat Publications, 1978, pp.241–46.

Ghose, Sankar, *Jawaharlal Nehru, a Biography*, New Delhi: Allied Publishers, 1993.

Gill, Amandeep and Rory Medcalf, *Unconventional Partners: Australia–India cooperation in reducing nuclear dangers*, Lowy Institute Policy Brief, October 2009.

Goh Chok Tong, 'Constructing East Asia', speech to Asia Society, 15th Asian Corporate Conference, Bangkok, 9 June 2005.

Gopal, D. (ed.), *Australia in the Emerging Global Order: evolving Australia–India relations*, New Delhi: Shipra, 2002.

Gopal, Krishan and Sarbjit Sharma, *India and Israel: towards strategic partnership*, New Delhi: Authorspress, 2007.

Gopalan, Sita, *India and Non-Alignment*, New Delhi: Spick & Span, 1984.

Gordon, Sandy, *Widening Horizons: Australia's new relationship with India*, Canberra: Australian Strategic Policy Institute, 2007.

——'India "Looks East" as history', *East Asia Forum*, 17 July 2010. www.eastasiaforum.org/2010/07/17/india-looks-east-as-history/ (accessed 28 February 2011).

Gordon, Sandy and Stephen Henningham (eds), *India Looks East: an emerging power and its Asia Pacific neighbours*, Canberra: Strategic and Defence Studies Centre, 1995.

Gosh, Nirmal, 'India govt "should try to change its mindset"', *Straits Times*, 20 January 2000.

Gowa, Joanne, *Allies, Adversaries and International Trade*, Princeton, NJ: Princeton University Press, 1994.

Grare, Frederick, 'In search of a role: India and the ASEAN Regional Forum', in Frederick Grare and Amitabh Mattoo (eds), *India and ASEAN: the politics of India's Look East policy*, New Delhi: Centre de Sciences Humaines, 2001, pp.119–45.

Grare, Frederick and Amitabh Mattoo (eds), *India and ASEAN: the politics of India's Look East policy*, New Delhi: Centre de Sciences Humaines, 2001.

Grezebrook, A.W., 'The Indian naval buildup: has Defence Central got it wrong?', *Pacific Defence Reporter*, February 1990, pp.14–15.

Gupta, Amit, 'US-India-China: assessing tripolarity', *China Report* (New Delhi), Vol.42, No.1, March 2006, pp.69–83.

Gupta, Sourabh, 'Japan–India joint declaration on security cooperation: groping towards an Asia-wide security architecture', *Nautilus Institute Policy Forum Online* 08-085A, 4 November 2008. www.nautilus.org/fora/security/08085Gupta.html (accessed 28 February 2011).

——"Japan–India economic ties and the promise of the Delhi–Mumbai industrial corridor," *East Asia Forum*, 4 November 2010. www.eastasiaforum.org/2010/11/04/japan-india-economic-ties-and-the-promise-of-the-delhi-mumbai-industrial-corridor (accessed 28 February 2011).

Gurry, Meg, *India: Australia's neglected neighbour? 1947–1996*, Griffith: Centre for the Study of Australia–Asia Relations, 1996.

Haacke, Jürgen, 'Seeking influence: China's diplomacy towards ASEAN after the Asian crisis', *Asian Perspective*, Vol.26, No.4, 2002, pp.13–52.

Hanoist, The, 'Vietnam hedges China risk', 30 July 2010, *Asia Times Online*, www.atimes.com/atimes/Southeast_Asia/LG30Ae01.html (accessed 28 February 2011).

Harrison, Selig, 'A nuclear bargain with India', paper presented at the conference India at the Crossroads, Southern Methodist University, Dallas, Texas, 27 March 1998.

Hauner, Milan, *India in Axis Strategy: Germany, Japan, and Indian nationalists in the Second World War*, Stuttgart: Klett-Cotta, 1981.

Hawksworth, John 'The world in 2050: how big will the major emerging market economies get and how can the OECD compete?', PricewaterhouseCoopers, March 2006. www.pwc.com/en_GX/gx/world-2050/pdf/world2050emergingeconomies.pdf (accessed 28 February 2011).

Hewitt, Vernon Marston, *The International Politics of South Asia*, Manchester: Manchester University Press, 1992.

Hirose, Takako, 'Japan's role in South Asia in the post-Cold War period', in K.V. Kesavan and Lalima Varma (eds), *Japan–South Asia: security and economic perspectives*, New Delhi: Lancer's Books, 2000, ch.6.

Hitachi Research Institute, 'Manmohan Singh's visit to Japan: recent trends, historical perspectives', 7 February 2007.

Ho Weizan, *Examining Singapore-India Security Relations after the Cold War: motivating factors, trends and implications for Singapore*, unpublished thesis, National University of Singapore, 2008.

Hoffman, Steven A., 'Perception and China policy in India', in Francine R. Frankel and Harry Harding (eds) *The India–China Relationship: what the United States needs to know*, New York: Columbia University Press, 2004, pp.33–74.

Holmes, James R., 'India and the proliferation security initiative: a US perspective', *Strategic Analysis*, Vol.31, No.2, 2007, pp.315–37.

Holmes, James R. and Toshi Yoshihara, 'India's "Monroe Doctrine" and Asia's maritime future', *Strategic Analysis*, Vol.32, No.6, November 2008, pp.997–1011.

Holmes, James R., Andrew C. Winner and Toshi Yoshihara, *Indian Naval Strategy in the Twenty-First Century*, London: Routledge, 2009.

Hongyi Lai (ed.), *Asian Energy Security: the maritime dimension*, London: Palgrave Macmillan 2009.

Horimoto, Takenori, 'The world as India sees it' *Gaiko Forum*, Vol.6, No.3, Fall 2006, pp.4–5.
Humphrey, Hubert H., *The Education of a Public Man: my life and politics*, New York: Doubleday, 1976.
Huxley, Timothy, *Defending the Lion City: the armed forces of Singapore*, St Leonards: Allen & Unwin, 2000.
IDSA News Review on Southeast Asia and Australia, June 1990.
Ikenberry, G. John, *Liberal Order and Imperial Ambition: essays on American power and world politics*, Malden, MA: Polity, 2006.
India Brand Equity Foundation, 'India and Japan', n.d. www.ibef.org/india/indiajapan.aspx (accessed 28 February 2011).
India, Department of Commerce and Industry. http://commerce.nic.in/eidb (accessed 28 February 2011).
India Integrated Headquarters, Ministry of Defence Navy, *Indian Maritime Doctrine*, 2004.
India, Ministry of Defence, *Annual Report 2000–2001*, n.d. http://mod.nic.in/reports/welcome.html (accessed 20 October 2011).
India Defence Consultants, 'What's hot? – analysis of recent happenings – Indian Navy update', *IDC Analysis*, 20 November 2005. www.indiadefence.com/navyupdate.htm (accessed 28 February 2011).
'India not competing with China: Navy Chief', *NDTV India*, 26 December 2007.
'India, Japan ink action plan on security cooperation', *NetIndian News Network*, 29 December 2009. http://netindian.in/news/2009/12/29/0004571/india-japan-ink-action-plan-security-cooperation (accessed 28 February 2011).
'India, Japan will have close defence ties, says Fernandes', *Times of India*, 16 January 2000.
'India must not ignore S.E. Asia: Fernandes', *The Hindu*, 28 March 2000.
'Indian Navy awaits regional nod for patrolling Malacca Straits', *India Defence*, 7 June 2006.
Indian Navy, 'Freedom to use the seas: India's maritime military strategy', May 2007.
'India's nuclear forces, 2007', *Bulletin of Atomic Scientists*, Vol.63, No.4, July/August 2007, pp.74–78.
Indo-Asian News Service, 'Want dialogue? Then contain terror, PM tells Gilani', *Thaindian News*, 16 July 2009.
'Indonesia and Malaysia keen on buying Brahmos', *Frontier India Strategic and Defence*, 13 April 2007. http://frontierindia.net/indianesia-and-malasia-keen-on-buying-brahmos (accessed 28 February 2011).
'Indonesia asks India to help maintain Malacca Strait security', *Xinhua*, 5 March 2009.
'Indonesia for security cooperation with India', *The Hindu*, 30 July 1999.
Inoguchi, Takashi (ed.), *Japan's Asian Policy: revival and response*, New York: Palgrave, 2002.
Jaffrelot, Christophe, 'India's Look East policy: an Asianist strategy in perspective', *India Review*, Vol.2, No.2, April 2003, pp.35–68.
Jain, Purnendra, 'India's calculus of Japan's foreign policy in Pacific Asia', in Takashi Inoguchi (ed.), *Japan's Asian Policy: revival and response*, New York: Palgrave, 2002, pp.211–36.
——'From condemnation to strategic partnership: Japan's changing view of India 1998–2007', Institute of South Asian Studies Working Paper No.41, 10 March 2008.
——'Westward ho! Japan eyes India strategically', *Japanese Studies*, Vol.28, Issue 1, May 2008, pp.15–30.

Jaishankar, S., 'India–Japan relations after Pokharan II', *Seminar* New Delhi, No.487, March 2000.
Jane's Information Group, *Jane's Sentinel Southeast Asia*, No.22, 2008.
Jencks, Harlan W., 'China's "Punitive" War on Vietnam: a military assessment', *Asian Survey*, Vol.19, No.8, 1979, pp.801–15.
Jenkins, H., 'Dwindling support throws *Status Quo* into Sea of Change', *Insight*, 14 January 1991, p.29.
Jha, Pankaj K., 'India-Indonesia: emerging strategic confluence in the Indian Ocean', *Strategic Analysis*, Vol.32, No.3, May 2008, pp.439–58.
Ji, You, 'Dealing with the Malacca dilemma: China's effort to protect its energy supply', *Strategic Analysis*, Vol.31, No.3, May 2007, pp.467–89.
'Joint statement of Prime Minister Singh and Prime Minister Abe', 16 December 2006.
'Joint statement on the advancement of the strategic and global partnership between Japan and India', 22 October 2008.
Joseph, Josy, 'Navy hails successful South China Sea visit', *Rediff on the Net*, 17 October 2000. www.rediff.com/news/2000/oct/17spec.htm (accessed 28 February 2011).
Kanwal, Colonel Gurmeet, 'Countering China's strategic encirclement of India', *Indian Defence Review*, Vol.15, No.3, July–September 2000, p.13.
Kapila, Dr Subhash, 'India–Vietnam strategic partnership: the convergence of interests', *South Asia Analysis Group*, Paper No.177, 2 January 2001.
——'Japan–India "Strategic Dialogue" March 2007. A misnomer', *South Asia Analysis Group*, Paper No.2187, 29 March 2007.
Kaplan, Robert D., 'Center stage for the twenty-first century', *Foreign Affairs*, Vol.88, 2009, pp.16–32.
——*Monsoon: the Indian Ocean and the future of American power*, New York: Random House, 2010.
——'Power plays in the Indian Ocean: the Maritime Commons in the 21st Century', in Abraham M. Denmark, Dr James Mulvenon, Frank G. Hoffman, Lt Col Kelly M. Martin, Oliver Fritz, Eric Sterner, Dr Greg Rattray, Chris Evans, Jason Healey and Robert Kaplan, *Contested Commons: the future of American power in a multipolar world*, Washington DC: Center for a New American Security, 2010, pp.177–94.
Kapur, Ashok, *India, from Regional to World Power*, New York: Routledge, 2006.
Karnad, Bharat, 'China uses Pak, Vietnam opens to India', *Express India*, 3 October 2005.
——'India's future plans and defence requirements', in N. Sisodia and C. Udaya Bhaskar (eds), *Emerging India: security and foreign policy perspectives*, New Delhi: Institute for Defence Studies and Analysis, 2005, pp.61–76.
——*Nuclear Weapons and Indian Security: the realist foundations of strategy*, Delhi: Macmillan India, 2005.
Kassim, Annuar, 'New Delhi want use of Hanoi naval facilities', *Asian Defense Journal*, Vol.9, 1990, p.108.
Kassim, Yang Razali, 'India angered by claim over Soviet subs', *Straits Times*, 13 October 1986.
Katzenstein, Peter J., *Rethinking Japanese Security: internal and external dimensions*, London: Routledge, 2008.
Kaul, Man Mohini, 'Australia–India relations: a critical survey', in D. Gopal (ed.), *Australia in the Emerging Global Order: evolving Australia–India relations*, New Delhi: Shipra, 2002, pp.220–34.

Kaul, T.N., *India, China and Indochina*, New Delhi: Lancer Press, 1987.
Keenleyside, T.A., 'Nationalist Indian attitudes toward Asia: a troublesome legacy for post-Independence Indian foreign policy', *Pacific Affairs*, Vol.55, No.2, Summer 1982, pp.210–30.
Kellerhals Jr, Merle David, 'India an indispensable partner, U.S. officials say', 1 June 2010. www.america.gov/st/peacesec-english/2010/June/20100601090431dmslahrellek0.7037622.html (accessed 28 February 2011).
Kennedy, Paul, *The Rise and Fall of the Great Powers: economic change and military conflict from 1500 to 2000*, New York: Random House, 1987.
Kenny, Henry J., *Shadow of the Dragon: Vietnam's continuing struggle with China and its implications for U.S. foreign policy*, Washington D.C.: Brassey's, 2002.
Kesavan, K.V. and Lalima Varma (eds), *Japan–South Asia: security and economic perspectives*, New Delhi: Lancer's Books, 2000.
——'The Indo-Japanese partnership: the security factor', Observer Research Foundation, ORF Issue Brief No.19, May 2009.
Kesavapany, K, *India's Tryst with Asia*, New Delhi: Asian Institute of Transport Development, 2006.
Khalik, Abdul, 'Indonesia – India security pact comes into effect', *Jakarta Post*, 3 April 2007.
Khalilzad, Zalmay, David T. Orletsky, Jonathan D. Pollack, Kevin L. Pollpeter, Angel Rabasa, David Shlapak, Abram Shulsky and Ashley J. Tellis, *The United States and Asia: towards a new US strategy and force posture*, Santa Monica, CA: Rand Corporation, 2001.
Khurana, Gurpreet S., 'Safeguarding the Malacca Straits', *IDSA Comment*, 5 January 2005.
——'Security of sea lines: prospects for India–Japan cooperation', *Strategic Analysis*, Vol.31, No.1 2007, pp.139–53.
——'Indian Ocean Naval Symposium IONS: where from. ... whither-bound?', *IDSA Comment*, 22 February 2008.
——'China–India maritime rivalry', *Indian Defence Review*, Vol.23, No.4, 2009. www.bannedthought.net/China/Capitalism-Imperialism/China-IndiaMaritimeRivalry-090409.pdf (accessed 23 June 2011).
Kim Il-young and Lakhvinder Singh, 'The North Korean nuclear program and external connections', *The Korean Journal of Defense Analysis*, Vol.16, No.1, Spring 2004, pp.73–98.
Kirsch, Marian P., 'Soviet security objectives in Asia', *International Organization*, Vol.24, No.3, Summer 1970, pp.451–78.
Kissinger, Henry, *Diplomacy*, New York: Touchstone, 1994.
Klintworth, Gary, 'Chinese perspectives on India as a great power', in Ross Babbage and Sandy Gordon (eds), *India's Strategic Future: regional state or global power?* London: Macmillan, 1992, pp.94–106.
Klux, Dennis, *India and the United States: estranged democracies, 1941–1991*, Washington DC: National Defense University Press, 1992.
Komai, Hiroshi, *Foreign Migrants in Contemporary Japan*, Melbourne: Trans Pacific Press, 1999.
Kroef, Justus M. van der, 'The Gorton Manner: Australia, Southeast Asia and the U.S.', *Pacific Affairs*, Vol.42, No.3, Fall 1969, pp.311–33.
Kumar, A. Vinod, 'Indo-US missile defence cooperation: hype or happening?', *ISDA Strategic Comments*, 30 January 2009.

Kumar, Madhurendra, *Super Power India and the Indian Ocean*, Allahabad: Chugh, 1995.

Kumar, Nagesh, 'Regionalism with an "Asian Face": an agenda for the East Asia Summit', *RSIS Policy Briefs* No.28, October 2006.

Kumar, Pranav, 'Singapore as a gateway for Indian companies', Institute of Peace and Conflict Studies, Paper No.2593, 10 June 2008.

Kumaraswamy, P.R. (ed.), *Security Beyond Survival: essays for K. Subrahmanyam*, New Delhi: Sage Publications, 2004.

Kuruppu, N.R.H., *An Indian Perspective of the Relationship between India and Australia, 1947 to 1975: personalities and policies, peaks and troughs*, unpublished doctoral thesis, Victoria University of Technology, 2000.

Kwa, Chong Guan (ed.), *S. Rajaratnam on Singapore: from ideas to reality*, Hackensack, NJ: World Scientific, 2006.

Lacey, Terry, 'Indonesia looks to play on the world stage', *Asia Sentinel*, 1 February 2010.

'Lack of consensus holding back Anti-piracy policy', *Thaindian News*, 20 November 2008.

Lai, Hongyi (ed.), *Asian Energy Security: the maritime dimension*, London: Palgrave Macmillan 2009.

Latif, Asad-ul Iqbal, *Between Rising Powers: China, Singapore and India*, Singapore: ISEAS Publishing, 2007.

Lebra, Joyce C. (ed.), *Japan's Greater East Asia Co-Prosperity Sphere in World War II: selected readings and documents*, London: Oxford University Press, 1975.

Lee Kuan Yew, *From Third World to First: the Singapore story: 1965–2000*, New York: HarperCollins, 2000.

——'India's peaceful rise', *Forbes*, 24 December 2007.

'Lee to urge guardian role for India', *Straits Times*, 3 September 1966.

Leifer, Michael, *Singapore's Foreign Policy: coping with vulnerability*, London: Routledge, 2000.

Li Hongmei, 'India's "Look East policy" means "look to encircle China"?', *People's Daily Online*, 27 October 2010. http://english.peopledaily.com.cn/90002/96417/7179404.html (accessed 28 February 2011).

Limaye, Satu P., 'Tokyo's dynamic diplomacy: Japan and the subcontinent's nuclear tests', *Contemporary Southeast Asia*, Vol.22, No.2, August 2000, pp.322–39.

Lintner, Bertil, 'Enter the Dragon', *Far Eastern Economic Review*, 22 December 1994, pp.22–24.

Loudon, Bruce and Mark Dodd, 'Confusion over uranium sales grows as Stephen Smith reaches India', *The Australian*, 10 September 2008.

Luce, Edward, *In Spite of the Gods: the strange rise of modern India*, New York: Doubleday, 2007.

McDonald, Hamish, 'Nuclear posturing – out on a street-cred limb', *Sydney Morning Herald*, 8 February 1999.

Macdonald, Juli A., 'Indo–U.S. military relationship: expectations and perceptions', Booz Allen Hamilton, report for the Director, net assessment, office of the Secretary of Defense, October 2002.

Mahalingam, Sudha, 'India-China energy cooperation: commonalities, synergies and complementarities', in Ligia Noronha and Anant Sudarshan (eds), *India's Energy Security*, London: Routledge, 2009, pp.97–107.

Mahizhnan, Arun, 'Developing Singapore's external economy', *Southeast Asian Affairs*, Vol.21, 1994, pp.285–301.

Maitra, Ramtanu, 'India bids to rule the waves', *Asia Times*, 19 October 2005.
Makekar, D.R., *The Guilty Men of 1962*, Bombay: Tulsi Shah Enterprises, 1968.
'Malaysia warns India against Thailand', *Newsinsight*, 3 January 2005.
Malik, Mohan, 'Sino-Indian relations and India's Eastern Strategy', in Sandy Gordon and Stephen Henningham (eds), *India Looks East: an emerging power and its Asia Pacific neighbours*, Canberra: Strategic and Defence Studies Centre, 1995, pp.119–63.
——'The Proliferation Axis: Beijing-Islamabad-Pyongyang', *Korean Journal of Defense Analysis*, Vol.15, No.1, Spring 2003, pp.57–100.
——'Eyeing the Dragon: India's China debate', Asia-Pacific Center for Security Studies, Special Assessment, December 2003. www.apcss.org/Publications/SAS/ChinaDebate/ChinaDebate_Malik.pdf (accessed 28 February 2011).
——'India and China: bound to collide', in P.R. Kumaraswamy (ed.), *Security Beyond Survival: essays for K. Subrahmanyam*, New Delhi: Sage Publications, 2004, pp.127–65.
——'China and the East Asian Summit: more discord than accord', Asia-Pacific Center for Security Studies, February 2006. www.apcss.org/Publications/APSSS/ChinaandEastAsiaSummit.pdf (accessed 28 February 2011).
——'China's strategy of containing India' Power and Interest News Report, 6 February 2006. www.pinr.com/report.php?ac=view_report&report_id=434 (accessed 28 February 2011).
Malik, V.P., 'Indo-US defense and military relations: from "estrangement" to "strategic partnership"', in Sumit Ganguly, Brian Shoup and Andrew Scobell (eds), *US–Indian Strategic Cooperation into the 21st Century*, London: Routledge, 2006, pp.82–112.
Malnotra, 'Japanese not interested in Indian pact', *The Australian*, 26 June 1969.
'Manmohan Singh leaves Japan, heads to Malaysia', *The Times of India*, 26 October 2010.
Mansfield, Edward D., *Power, Trade & War*, Princeton, NJ: Princeton University Press, 1994.
Maswood, S. Javed, *Japan and East Asian Regionalism*, London: Routledge, 2001.
Mearsheimer, John, *The Tragedy of Great Power Politics*, New York: W.W. Norton & Co, 2001.
Medcalf, Rory, 'Australia–India relations: hesitating on the brink of partnership', *Asia Pacific Bulletin*, No.13, 3 April 2008. www.eastwestcenter.org/fileadmin/stored/pdfs/apb013.pdf (accessed 23 June 2011).
——'Squaring the triangle: an Australian perspective on Asian security minilateralism', in William Tow, Michael Auslin, Rory Medcalf, Akihiko Tanaka, Zhu Feng and Sheldon Simon, *Assessing the Trilateral Strategic Dialogue*, NBR Special Report, December 2008, pp.23–31.
Medeiros, Evan S., Keith Crane, Eric Heginbotham, Norman D. Levin, Julia F. Lowell, Angel Rabasa and Sovil Soong, *Pacific Currents: the responses of U.S. allies and security partners in East Asia to China's rise*, Santa Monica: Rand Corporation, 2008.
Mehta, V.R. and Thomas Pantham (ed.), *Political Ideas in Modern India: thematic explorations*, New Delhi: Sage, 2006.
Menon, Shiv Shankar, 'Maritime imperatives of Indian foreign policy', speech to the National Maritime Foundation, New Delhi, 11 September, 2009.
Miller, J.D.B. (ed.), *India, Japan, Australia, Partners in Asia?*, Canberra: Australian National University Press, 1968.
Mohan, C. Raja, 'The Asian balance of power', *Seminar*, No.487, 2000.
——*Crossing the Rubicon: the shaping of India's new foreign policy*, New York: Palgrave Macmillan, 2003.

——'India, China and Asian security', *The Hindu*, 27 January 2003.
——'Superpower in the South Pacific', *The Hindu*, 30 July 2003.
——'Look East policy: phase two', *The Hindu*, 9 October 2003.
——'India in East Asia', Australia–India Strategic Lecture, Melbourne, 21 February 2007.
——'Balancing interests and values: India's struggle with democracy promotion', *The Washington Quarterly*, Vol.30, No.3, Summer 2007, pp.99–115.
——'The importance of being Vietnam', *indiaexpress.com*, 9 July 2007. www.indianexpress.com/story_print.php?storyid=204292 (accessed 28 February 2011).
——'Japan and India: the making of a new alliance?', *RSIS Commentaries*, 27 August 2007.
——'India's changing strategic profile in East and Southeast Asia', paper presented at the Regional Outlook Forum, Singapore, 8 January 2008. www.iseas.edu.sg/rof08/s1_raja.pdf (accessed 28 February 2011).
——'India's geopolitics and Southeast Asian security', in Daljit Singh and Tin Maung Maung (eds), *Southeast Asian Affairs 2008*, Singapore: Institute of Southeast Asian Studies, 2008, pp.43–60.
——'Is India an East Asian power? Explaining New Delhi's security politics in the Western Pacific', ISAS Working Paper No.81, 11 August 2009.
——'The evolution of Sino-Indian relations: implications for the United States', in Alyssa Ayres and C. Raja Mohan, *Power Realignments in Asia: China, India and the United States*, New Delhi: Sage Publications, 2009, pp.270–90 at p.288.
——'India in the emerging Asian architecture', in William T.Tow and Chin Kin Wah, *Asean India Australia: towards closer engagement in a New Asia,* Singapore: Institute of Southeast Asian Studies, 2009, pp.40–57.
——'India and the changing geopolitics of the Indian Ocean', speech at the National Maritime Foundation, New Delhi, 19 July 2010.
——'Rising India: partner in shaping the global commons?', *The Washington Quarterly*, July 2010, pp.133–48.
Monsonis, Guillem, 'India's strategic autonomy and rapprochement with the US', *Strategic Analysis*, Vol.34, No.4, July 2010, pp.611–24.
Muhibat, Shafiah Fifi, 'Competing to secure the Straits of Malacca and Singapore', *The Indonesian Quarterly*, Vol.35, No.3, 2007, pp.242–53.
Mukherjee, Pranab, address to the 7th Asian Security Conference, 29 January 2005.
——Address to the 5th IISS Asian Security Summit, 3 June 2006.
——Speech for the Admiral A.K. Chatterjee Memorial Lecture, Kolkata, 30 June 2007.
Mullen, Mike, speech in New Delhi, 23 July 2010.
Muni, S.D., *India's Foreign Policy: the democracy dimension*, Foundation Books: New Delhi, 2010.
Muni, S.D. and C. Raja Mohan, 'Emerging Asia: India's options', *International Studies*, Vol.41, No.3, 2004, pp.313–33.
Munro, Ross H., 'The loser: India in the nineties', *National Interest*, No.33, Summer 1993, pp.62–63.
Murthy, P.A. Narasimha, *India and Japan: dimensions of their relations: historical political*, New Delhi: ABC Publishing House, 1986.
Naidu, G.V.C., 'The Indian Navy and Southeast Asia', *Contemporary Southeast Asia*, Vol.13, No.1, June 1991, p.81.
——'Indo-Japan relations: emerging contours of strategic partnership', paper presented at the 10th IDSA-JIIA Bilateral Seminar, New Delhi, 15–16 December 2008.

Nalapat, M.D., 'Will the USS Kitty Hawk cement U.S.–India military ties?', *UPI Asia.com*, 28 November 2007. www.upiasia.com/Security/2007/11/28/commentary_will_the_uss_kitty_hawk_cement_usindia_military_ties/7273/ (accessed 28 February 2011).

Nanda, Prakash (ed.), *Rising India: friends and foes*, New Delhi: Lancer, 2007.

National Institute of Defense Studies, *East Asian Strategic Review 1998–99*, Tokyo: National Institute of Defense Studies, 1999.

——*East Asian Strategic Review 2005*, Tokyo: National Institute of Defense Studies, 2005.

——*East Asian Strategic Review 2008*, Tokyo: National Institute of Defense Studies, 2008.

Natsukawa, Kazuya, 'Opening address, Indo-Japan dialogue on ocean security', Tokyo, 12 October 2006.

Nayar, Baldev Raj, 'Political structure and India's economic reforms of the 1990s', *Pacific Affairs*, Vol.71, No.3, Autumn 1998, pp.335–58.

——*India and the Major Powers after Pokhran II*, New Delhi: Har-Anand Publications, 2001.

Nayar, Baldev Raj and T.V. Paul, *India in the World Order: searching for major power status*, Cambridge: Cambridge University Press, 2003.

Nayar, K.P., 'Vajpayee describes India and US as natural allies', *The Telegraph*, 29 September 1998.

Noronha, Ligia and Anant Sudarshan (eds), *India's Energy Security*, London: Routledge, 2009.

Noronha, Paul, 'China woos Mauritius and eyes the Indian Ocean', *The Hindu*, 1 July 2009.

'Northrop Grumman sees India sealing $11 billion deal in "11"', Reuters, 7 February 2011. http://in.reuters.com/article/2011/02/07/idINIndia-54710520110207 (accessed 28 February 2011).

Novotny, Daniel, *Torn between America and China: elite perceptions and Indonesian foreign policy*, Singapore: ISEAS Publishing, 2010.

'Nuclear anxiety; Indian's letter to Clinton on the nuclear testing', *The New York Times*, 13 May 1998.

Nye, Joseph S., *Soft Power: the means to success in world politics*, New York: Public Affairs, 2004.

OECD Nuclear Energy Agency and International Atomic Energy Agency, *Uranium 2007: production, resources and demand*, Paris: OECD, 2008.

Olson, Lawrence, *Japan in Postwar Asia*, London: Council on Foreign Relations, 1970.

Ong, Yong, 'Advancing the ASEAN-India partnership in the new millenium', address in New Delhi, 18 October 2004.

Pai, Nitin and Aruna Urs 'Look before you hop: a discussion on strategic affairs with Stephen Cohen', *Pragati: The Indian National Interest Review*, No.15, June 2008, p.9.

Pandit, Rajat, 'US eyes naval ties with India', *Times of India*, 19 April 2007.

Panikkar, K.M., *The Future of Southeast Asia: an Indian view*, New York: The Macmillan Company, 1943.

——*India and the Indian Ocean: an essay on the influence of sea power on Indian history*, London: George Allen and Unwin, 1945.

Pant, Harsh V., 'India in the Indian Ocean: growing mismatch between ambitions and capabilities', *Pacific Affairs*, Vol.82, No.2, Summer 2009, pp.279–97.

Pardesi, M., *Deducing India's Grand Strategy of Regional Hegemony from Historical and Conceptual Perspectives*, Singapore: Institute of Defence and Strategic Studies, 2005.
Parthasarathy, G., 'New US thinking on India: coming Obama visit offers an opportunity', *The Tribune*, 22 July 2010.
Percival, Bronson, *The Dragon Looks South: China and Southeast Asia in the new century*, Westport, CT: Praeger Security International, 2007.
——'Growing Chinese and Indian naval power: U.S. recalibration and coalition building', in Sam Bateman and Joshua Ho (eds), *Southeast Asia and the Rise of Chinese and Indian Naval Power: between rising naval powers*, London: Routledge, 2010, pp.36–47.
——'Regional security environment in the Indian Ocean: threats on the margins; partnership with India', in C. Uday Bhaskar and Kamlesh K. Agnihotri (eds), *Security Challenges along the Indian Ocean Littoral: Indian and US perspectives*, Delhi: National Maritime Foundation, 2010, pp.21–32.
Perkovich, George, 'Is India a major power?', *The Washington Quarterly*, Vol.27, No.1, Winter 2003-4, pp.129–44.
Perlez, Jane, 'Faster ASEAN integration urged', *International Herald Tribune*, 29 November 2004.
Pham, Cao Phong, 'Vietnam's new security perception: the role of economic security', paper prepared for the 43rd annual ISA convention, New Orleans, 24–27 March 2002.
Poddar, Tushar and Eva Yi, 'India's rising growth potential', Goldman Sachs Global Economics Paper No.152, January 2007. www.usindiafriendship.net/viewpoints1/Indias_Rising_Growth_Potential.pdf (accessed 28 February 2011).
Prakash, Arun, 'A vision of India's maritime power in the 21st century', *USI Journal*, July–September 2006, pp.454–63.
——'China and the Indian Ocean region', *Indian Defence Review*, Vol.21, No.4, October–December 2006, pp.7–12.
——'India's maritime strategy', *Indian Defence Review*, Vol.137, No.568 (April–June 2007), pp.157–76.
Press Trust of India, 'Reaction to Indo-Soviet Treaty – Japan's isolation heightened', *The Patriot*, 19 August 1971.
——'Vietnam for greater economic engagement with India', *Times of India*, 20 June 2007.
Pubby, Manu, 'China proposed division of Pacific, Indian Ocean regions, we declined: US Admiral', *Indian Express*, 15 May 2009.
Pyle, Kenneth B., 'Abe Shinzo and Japan's change of course', *NBR Analysis*, Vol.17, No.4, October 2006, pp.5–9.
——*Japan Rising: the resurgence of Japanese power and purpose*, New York: Public Affairs, 2007.
Rajagopalan, Rajesh and Varun Sahni, 'India and the great powers: strategic imperatives, normative necessities', *South Asian Survey*, Vol.15, No.5, 2008, pp.5–32.
Rajan, D.S., 'China: media fears over India becoming part of western alliance', Chennai Centre for China Studies Paper No.46, 29 August 2007.
——'Is China wary of India's "Look East policy"?', Chennai Centre for China Studies, C3S Paper No.97, 13 January 2008.
——'Beijing: suspicions on Japan–India Security Declaration targeting China', Chennai Centre for China Studies Paper No.221, 2 November 2008.

Rajan, Mannaraswamighala Sreeranga, *Studies on Nonalignment and the Nonaligned Movement: theory and practice*, New Delhi: ABC Publishing House, 1986.

Rajghatta, Chidanand, 'Singhing Bush's praise', *Times of India*, 13 April 2001.

Ramachandran, Sudha, 'China moves into India's back yard', *Asia Times*, 13 March 2007.

——'What are friends for ... ?', *AsiaTimes Online*, 25 August 2007. www.atimes.com/atimes/Japan/IH25Dh03.html (accessed 28 February 2011).

Raman, B., 'India & Japan: democracy as a strategic weapon', South Asia Analysis Group, Paper No.206, 17 December 2006.

——'China & India: reality behind statistics', South Asia Analysis Group, Paper No.2567, 28 January 2008.

——'Obama ducks Dalai Lama issue', South Asia Analysis Group, Paper No.3418, 16 September 2009.

Ranjan, Amitav, 'India says not yet to Indonesian plea', *Indian Express*, 21 April 2004.

ReCAAP Information Sharing Centre, *Annual Report 2009*, Singapore, 2009.

Rehman, Iskander, 'Keeping the Dragon at bay: India's counter-containment of China in Asia', *Asian Security*, Vol.5, No.2, May 2009, pp.114–43.

Rice, Condoleezza, speech at Sophia University, Tokyo, 19 March 2005.

——'US–India civil nuclear cooperation agreement: opening remarks before House International Relations Committee', 5 April 2006.

Richardson, Michael, 'East Asia and western Pacific brace for Indian ascendency', *The International Herald Tribune*, 4 October 1989.

Rodham Clinton, Hillary, 'America's engagement in the Asia-Pacific', address at Honululu, 28 October 2010.

Rogin, Josh, 'U.S. and India take their relationship beyond South Asia', *The Cable*, 15 November 2010. http://thecable.foreignpolicy.com/posts/2010/11/15/the_us_and_india_take_their_relationship_beyond_south_asia (accessed 28 February 2011).

Roy, Mihir K., *War in the Indian Ocean*, New Delhi: Lancer, 1995.

Roy-Chaudhury, Rahul, *Sea Power and India's Security*, London: Brassey's, 1995.

Rudd, Kevin, 'From fitful engagement to strategic partnership', address to the Indian Council of World Affairs in New Delhi, 12 November 2009.

Saaler, Sven and J. Victor Koschmann (eds), *Pan Asianism in Modern Japanese History: colonialism, regionalism and borders*, New York: Routledge, 2007.

Sagar, Rahul, 'State of mind: what kind of power will India become', *International Affairs*, Vol.85, No.4, 2009, pp.801–16.

Sahni, Varun, 'India and the Asian security architecture', *Current History*, Vol.105, No.680, April 2006, pp.163–67.

Samuels, Richard J., *Securing Japan: Tokyo's Grand Strategy and the future of East Asia*, Ithaca, NY: Cornell University Press, 2007.

Saran, Shyam, 'India and its neighbours', address in New Delhi, 14 February 2005.

SarDesai, D.R., *Indian Foreign Policy in Cambodia, Laos and Vietnam 1947–1964*, Berkeley: University of California Press, 1968.

Sato, Heigo, 'Arc of freedom and prosperity', in Centre for Strategic and International Studies, *Bridging Strategic Asia: the rise of India in East Asia and implications for the US-Japan alliance*, Winter 2008. http://csis.org/programs/international-security-program/asia-division/bridging-strategic-asia-rise-india-east-asia-a (accessed 28 February 2011).

Sawhney, Rajeev, 'Redefining the limits of the Straits: a composite Malacca Straits security system', *RSIS Commentaries* No.37, 18 May 2006.

Schaffer, Teresita C., *India and the United States in the 21st Century: reinventing partnership*, Washington DC: The CSIS Press, 2009.
Schaller, Michael, *Altered States: the United States and Japan since the Occupation*, New York: Oxford University Press, 1997.
Scobell, Andrew, '"Cult of Defense" and "Big Power Dreams": the influence of strategic culture on China's relationship with India', in Malcolm R.Chambers (ed.), *South Asia in 2020: future strategic balances and alliances*, Carlisle: US Army War College, Strategic Studies Institute, 2002, pp.329–59.
Scott, David, 'India's "Grand Strategy" for the Indian Ocean: Mahanian visions', *Asia-Pacific Review*, Vol.13, No.2, 2006, pp.97–129.
——'India's drive for a "Blue Water" navy', *Journal of Military and Strategic Studies*, Vol.10, Issue 2, Winter 2007, pp.1–42.
Selth, Andrew, 'Chinese military bases in Burma: the explosion of a myth', Griffith University Regional Outlook Paper No.10, 2007.
Shanahan, Denis, 'Pacific allies enlist India', *The Australian*, 15 March 2007.
Sheridan, Greg, 'Region notices bias for Beijing', *The Australian*, 3 May 2008.
Shirk, Susan L., 'One-sided rivalry: China's perceptions and policies toward India', in Francine R. Frankel and Harry Harding (eds) *The India–China Relationship: what the United States needs to know*, New York: Columbia University Press, 2004, pp.75–100.
Sikdar, Bimal Kumar and Amitabh Sikdar, *India & China: strategic energy management and security*, New Delhi: Manas Publications, 2009.
Sikri, Rajiv, *Challenge and Strategy: rethinking India's foreign policy*, New Delhi: Sage, 2009.
Singh, Bilveer, *The Vulnerability of Small States Revisited: a study of Singapore's post-Cold War foreign policy*, Yogyakarta: Gadjah Mada University Press, 1999.
Singh, Daljit and Tin Maung Maung (eds), *Southeast Asian Affairs 2008*, Singapore: Institute of Southeast Asian Studies, 2008.
Singh, Jaswant, 'Statement by Deputy Chairman Planning Commission of India Jaswant Singh on the occasion of the ASEAN 31st Post Ministerial Conference (ASEAN+9) Plenary Session', 28 July 1998.
Singh, Manmohan, 'PM's address at the combined commander's conference', 24 October 2004.
——'PM's speech at India Today conclave', New Delhi, 25 February 2005. www.pmindia.nic.in/speech/content.asp?id=510 (accessed 28 February 2011).
Singh, Sinderpal and Syeda Sana Rahman, 'The next stage of Singapore–India relations: possibilities and prospects', ISAS Working Paper No.91, 24 September 2009.
Sinha, K.K. (ed.), *Problems of Defence of South and East Asia*, New Delhi: Rawat Publications, 1978.
Sinha, Rakesh, 'Jakarta says no to Indian patrol in Malacca Straits', *Indian Express*, 13 July 2005.
Sinha, Yashwant, 'Geopolitics: what it takes to be a world power', speech in New Delhi, 12 March 2004.
Sisodia, N. and C. Udaya Bhaskar (eds), *Emerging India: security and foreign policy perspectives*, New Delhi: Institute for Defence Studies and Analysis, 2005.
Sisodia, N.S. and Sreeradha Datta (eds), *Changing Security Dynamics in Southeast Asia*, New Delhi: Magnum Books, 2008.
Smith, Vincent, 'Australia urged to seek own defence', *The Australian*, 1 October 1968.

Sreenivasan, T.P., 'Obama has gone further than Bush on India', *Rediff.com*, 9 June 2010. http://news.rediff.com/column/2010/jun/09/tps-sreenivasan-on-the-obama-platter-for-india.htm (accessed 28 February 2011).
Sridharan, Kripa, *The ASEAN Region in India's Foreign Policy*, Aldershot: Dartmouth Publishing, 1996.
——'Regional perceptions of India', in Frederick Grare and Amitabh Mattoo (eds), *India and ASEAN: the politics of India's Look East policy*, New Delhi: Centre de Sciences Humaines, 2001, pp.67–89.
——'Transcending the region: Singapore's India policy', in N.N. Vohra (ed.), *Emerging Asia: challenges for India and Singapore*, New Delhi: Manohar, 2003, pp.15–32.
Stobdan, P., 'Central Asia and India's security', *Strategic Analysis*, Vol.28, No.1, 2004, pp.54–83.
Stockholm International Peace Research Institute. http://milexdata.sipri.org/result.php4 (accessed 28 February 2011).
Storey, Ian, 'Indonesia's China policy in the new order and beyond: problems and prospects', *Contemporary Southeast Asia*, Vol.22, No.1, April 2000, pp.145–74.
——'Securing Southeast Asia's sea lanes: a work in progress', *Asia Policy*, No.6, July 2008, pp.95–127.
Storey, Ian and Carlyle A. Thayer, 'Cam Ranh Bay: past imperfect, future conditional', *Contemporary Southeast Asia*, Vol.23, No.3, December 2001, pp.452–73.
Subrahmanyam, K., *Indian Security Perspectives*, New Delhi: ABC Publishing House, 1982.
——'Strategic developments in the Indian and South Pacific Ocean regions', in Robert H. Bruce, *Australia and the Indian Ocean: strategic dimensions of increasing naval involvement*, Perth: Centre of Indian Ocean Studies, 1988, pp.79–95.
Suryanarayan, Dr V., 'India–Singapore relations: an overview', Chennai Centre for China Studies, C3S Paper No.140, 2 April 2008.
——'Malaysian Indian society in ferment', *South Asia Analysis Group*, Paper No.2880, 14 October 2008.
Suryanarayana, P.S., 'A vision for Asia', *Frontline*, Vol.22, Issue 1, 1–14 January, 2005. www.flonnet.com/fl2201/stories/20050114000406000.htm (accessed 23 June 2011).
——'India, Singapore hold "maritime exercise"', *The Hindu*, 6 March 2005.
——'Indonesia for defence tie-up with India', *The Hindu*, 5 June 2007.
——'India, Malaysia to step up defence ties', *The Hindu*, 8 January 2008.
——'Indonesia to "learn" from India's defence sector', *The Hindu*, 18 June 2010.
Talbott, Strobe, *Engaging India: diplomacy, democracy and the bomb*, Washington DC: Brookings Institution, 2004.
Tanham, George, *Indian Strategic Thought: an interpretative essay*, Santa Monica, CA: Rand, 1992.
Tanham, George K., Kanti P. Bajpai and Amitabh Mattoo (eds), *Securing India: strategic thought and practice in an emerging power*, New Delhi: Manhora, 1996.
Tavan, Gwenda, *The Long Slow Death of White Australia*, Melbourne: Scribe, 2005.
Tellis, Ashley J., 'The changing political-military environment: South Asia', in Zalmay Khalilzad, David T. Orletsky, Johnathan D. Pollack, Kevin L. Pollpeter, Angel Rabasa, David Shlapak, Abram Shulsky and Ashley J. Tellis (eds), *The United States and Asia: towards a new US strategy and force posture*, Santa Monica, CA: Rand Corporation, 2001, pp.203–40.

——'South Asia', in Richard J. Ellings and Aaron L. Friedberg (eds), *Strategic Asia 2001– 02 Power and Purpose*, Seattle: National Bureau of Asian Research, 2002, pp.223–26.
——'Assessing America's War on Terror: confronting insurgency, cementing primacy', *NBR Analysis*, Vol.15, No.4, 2004.
——'China and India in Asia', in Francine R. Frankel and Harry Harding (eds) *The India–China Relationship: what the United States needs to know*, New York: Columbia University Press, 2004, pp.134–77.
——*India as a New Global Power: an action agenda for the United States*, Washington DC: Carnegie Endowment for World Peace, 2005.
——'India in Asian geopolitics', in Prakash Nanda (ed.), *Rising India: friends and foes*, New Delhi: Lancer, 2007, pp.118–30.
Terada, Takashi, 'The origins of Japan's APEC policy: Foreign Minister Takeo Miki's Asia-Pacific policy and current implications', *The Pacific Review*, Vol.11, No.3, 1988, pp.337–63.
'Thai to join RI patrolling Malacca Strait', *The Jakarta Post*, 16 March 2009.
Thakur, Ramesh, 'India and overseas Indians: the case of Fiji', *Asian Survey*, Vol.25, No.3, 1985, pp.356–70.
Thakur, Ramesh and Carlyle A. Thayer, *Soviet Relations with India and Vietnam*, New York: St Martin's Press, 1992.
Thayer, Carlyle A., 'Vietnam's defence policy and its impact on foreign relations', paper delivered to EuroViet 6, Asien-Afrika Institüt, Universität Hamburg, Hamburg, Germany, 6–8 June 2008.
Thomas, Raju G.C., 'The sources of Indian naval expansion', in Robert H. Bruce (ed.), *The Modern Indian Navy in the Indian Ocean: developments and implications*, Perth: Centre for Indian Ocean Regional Studies, 1989, pp.95–107.
Tow, William T., 'Strategic dimensions of energy competition in Asia', in Michael Wesley (ed.), *Energy Security in Asia*, London: Routledge, 2008, pp.161–73.
Tow, William T. and Chin Kin Wah, *Asean India Australia: towards closer engagement in a New Asia*, Singapore: Institute of Southeast Asian Studies, 2009.
Tow, William, Michael Auslin, Rory Medcalf, Akihiko Tanaka, Zhu Feng and Sheldon Simon, *Assessing the Trilateral Strategic Dialogue*, NBR Special Report, December 2008.
Trager, Frank N., *Why Vietnam?*, London: Pall Mall Press, 1966.
Tsai, Ting-I, 'For Taiwan, India's in the slightly-less-hard basket', *AsiaTimes Online*, 15 February 2006. www.atimes.com/atimes/China_Business/HB15Cb02.html (accessed 28 February 2011).
Twining, Daniel, 'America's grand design in Asia', *The Washington Quarterly*, Vol.30, No.3, 2007, pp.79–94.
United States Department of Defense, *Quadrennial Defence Review Report, February 2010*.
——*Annual Report to Congress: military and security developments involving the People's Republic of China 2010*. www.defense.gov/pubs/pdfs/2010_CMPR_Final.pdf (accessed 28 February 2011).
United States Department of State, Memorandum of Harriman-Shiga Conversation, 14 November 1962.
——Memorandum of Conversation, Washington, 3 December 1962, 5.30pm, FRUS 1961–63, Vol.XXII Doc # 362.
——Office of Spokesman, 'Background briefing by administration officials on U.S.-South Asia relations', Washington DC, 25 March 2005.
——'Global maritime partnerships', Unclassified Telegram, 13 May 2008.

Unnithan, Sandeep, 'The hijack dilemma', *India Today*, 17 October 2008.
US Navy, US Marine Corps and US Coast Guard, *Cooperative Strategy for 21st Century Seapower*, October 2007.
'US offers F-35 for Indian Navy', *Indian Military*, 13 January 2010.
Vajpayee, Atal, 'India's perspective on ASEAN and the Asia-Pacific region', speech to Institute of Southeast Asian Studies, Singapore, 9 April 2002.
Varadarajan, Siddharth, 'Bush, India and two degrees of separation', *The Hindu*, 3 March 2006.
——'India, Japan say new security ties not directed against China', *The Hindu*, 23 October 2008.
Venugopal, K., 'Japan's guarded, positive response on nuclear issue', *The Hindu*, 16 December 2006.
'Vietnam's risky game in the South China Sea', *Stratfor*, 20 May 2004. www.stratfor.com/vietnams_risky_game_south_china_sea (accessed 28 February 2011).
Vohra, N.N. (ed.), *Emerging Asia: challenges for India and Singapore*, New Delhi: Manohar, 2003.
Vuving, Alexander L., 'Strategy and evolution of Vietnam's China policy: a changing mixture of pathways', *Asian Survey*, Vol.XLVI, No.6, November/December 2006, pp.805–24.
Walt, Stephen M., *The Origins of Alliances*, Ithaca, NY: Cornell University Press, 1987.
Waltz, Kenneth, *Theory of International Politics*, New York: McGraw Hill, 1979.
Wanandi, Jusuf, *Global, Regional and National: strategic issues and linkages*, Jakarta: Centre for Strategic and International Studies, 2006.
——'The ASEAN Charter and remodelling regional architecture', *The Jakarta Post*, 3 November 2008.
Wang, Vincent Wei-cheng, 'The logic of China–ASEAN free trade agreement: economic statecraft of "Peaceful Rise"', paper presented at Institute of China Studies University of Malaya Conference, 5–6 August 2007.
Welfield, John, *An Empire in Eclipse: Japan in the postwar American alliance system: a study of the interaction of domestic politics and foreign policy*, London: The Athlone Press, 1988.
Wesley, Michael (ed.), *Energy Security in Asia*, London: Routledge, 2008.
White, Hugh, *Power Shift: Australia's future between Washington and Beijing*, Collingwood: Black Inc., 2010.
Wilson, Dominic and Anna Stupnytska, 'The N11: more than an acronym', Goldman Sachs Global Economics Paper No.153, 28 March 2007. www.chicagobooth.edu/alumni/clubs/pakistan/docs/next11dream-march%20'07-goldmansachs.pdf (accessed 28 February 2011).
Womack, Brantly, *China And Vietnam: the politics of asymmetry*, Cambridge: Cambridge University Press, 2006.
Yahya, Faizal, 'Challenges of globalisation: Malaysia and India engagement', *Contemporary Southeast Asia*, Vol.27, No.3, 2005, pp.472–98.
Ye Hailin, 'Securing SLOCs by cooperation – Chinese perspectives of maritime security in the Indian Ocean', paper presented at Karichi, Pakistan, 2009.
Yeo, George, speech to India Economic Summit 2002, New Delhi.
——Speech in New Delhi, 18 February 2004.
——Address to the Global Leadership Forum in Kuala Lumpur, 6 September 2005.
Yoshihara, Toshi and James R. Holmes, *Red Star over the Pacific: China's rise and the challenge to U.S. maritime strategy*, Annapolis, MD: Naval Institute Press, 2010.

Zhang Guihong, 'US–India strategic cooperation: implications for China', paper submitted to The Asia Fellow China Alumni Conference, Beijing University, China, 13–14 November 2005.

Zhang Ming, 'The Malacca dilemma and the Chinese Navy's strategic choices', *Modern Ships*, No.274, October 2006, p.23.

Zhao Hong, 'India's changing relations with ASEAN in China's perspective', East Asia Institute Background Paper No.313, 7 December 2006.

Index

Abe, Shinzo 65, 71, 72, 77, 78, 80, 127
Acheson, Dean 31
Aden 28, 30, 154
ADMM + 8 15
Afghanistan 9, 10, 28, 30, 49, 50, 52, 59; and Australia 123; and Japan 81
Albuquerque, Alfonso de 135
Andaman and Nicobar Islands 57, 106, 111, 117, 135–6, 139, 153; Great Nicobar Island 104–5
Andaman Sea 30; China 40, 118; Indian Navy 112, 116, 117, 135, 136; Soviet Navy 104
Angola 37
Antony, A.K. 97
APEC *see* Asia-Pacific Economic Cooperation
ARF *see* ASEAN Regional Forum
ASEAN + 3 16, 43, 46, 107, 152
ASEAN Regional Forum (ARF) 15, 46, 48, 69; Indonesia 105, 115; Malaysia 112, Singapore 105, 107; Vietnam 96
Asian economic community 16
Asia-Pacific Economic Cooperation (APEC) 3, 13, 16, 69, 127, 152
Aso, Taro 71, 73, 77, 82
Australia: Beazley, Kim 120; cooperation with India in Asia Pacific 131–2; cooperation with India in Indian Ocean 129–30; Downer, Alexander 121; economic relationship 124–5; Evans, David 120; Howard, John 121, 125; Joint Security Declaration 122–3; Malacca Strait 114, 115, 117, 118, 137; Menzies, Robert 119, 120; Nuclear Suppliers Group 125; race 127–9; relationship with India generally 119–33; Rudd, Kevin 122, 125; security relationship 121–5; uranium sales 125
Australia Group 52

Badawi, Abdullah 139
Bajpai, Kanti 20, 24
balance of power 22–4, 146–50; and Australia 149; balance of threats 146; and China 147; Indonesia 115, 148; intra-regional balance in Southeast Asia 48, 149–50; and Japan 76, 79, 81, 147; naval 140; Singapore 148; Vietnam 101, 149
Bangladesh 9, 26; and China 32, 39
Bay of Bengal 12, 26, 30, 120, 135; naval exercises in 54, 60, 71, 111
Bay of Bengal Initiative (BIMSTEC) 15
Beazley, Kim 120
Bhagat, B.R. 103
Bhutan 9, 35
BIMSTEC *see* Bay of Bengal Initiative
Bose, Subhas 78, 177
BrahMos cruise missiles 95–6, 116
Brazil 1
Britain 31, 58, 123, 153; and Australia 127, 128; British India 67; and Singapore 106
Bull, Hedley 4, 5, 68
Burma 15, 26, 30, 63, 96, 134; and Japan 65, 66, 68; relationship with China 26, 32, 37–40, 101, 113, 118, 149, 157
Burns, William J. 52, 61
Bush administration 50–2, 54, 77, 114, 149
Buzan, Barry 42, 43

Cambodia 48, 92–3, 96, 104
Cam Ranh Bay 95, 97–9, 141–2, 155, 184

Index

Central Intelligence Agency (US) 23, 50
Chellaney, Brahma 24; Japan 82, 83
Cheney, Richard 77
Chiang, Antonio 75
Chie, Nakane 65
Chile 13
China: and Australia 122, 124, 127, 130, 131, 132; balancing against China 18, 22–4, 33, 145, 146–50; counter-encirclement of 32; democratic values 25–6; economic relationship with ASEAN 45–6; economic relationship with India 16, 36–7, 146; energy security 37–8; great power 5, 8, 14, 16, 27, 30; India–China–Russia trilateral 19; India's Monroe Doctrine/sphere of influence 9, 32, 152–5; and Indonesia 114–18; and Japan 44, 64–88; Malacca Strait 31, 137–40; and Malaysia 112–13; nuclear target 6; perceptions of India 42; relationship with India generally 15, 16, 17, 26, 34–48; relationship with Pakistan 32, 34, 35, 38, 39, 42, 43, 74, 91, 101, 149, 157, 159; rivalry with India in Asia Pacific 13, 41–8, 158–60; rivalry with India in Indian Ocean 11, 12, 13, 38–41, 136, 157, 158; rivalry with India in Southeast Asia 44–8, 102–3; Singapore 105, 107–10; Sino-Indian war, 1962 18, 35; in South Asia 28, 32; South China Sea 136, 140–3; strategic competition with India 30, 33; String of Pearls 32, 38–40, 57, 117–18, 130, 136, 154; and Taiwan 63, 74–6, 81; and Tibet 35, 43; and United States 50–63; and Vietnam 29, 90–101
Clinton administration 50, 51
Clinton, Hillary Rodham 62, 76, 98
Coco Islands (Burma) 39
Cohen, Saul Bernard 32
Cohen, Stephen 1, 3, 20, 51, 152
Combined Task Force 151 (CTF 151) 39, 59, 176
Comprehensive Test Ban Treaty (CTBT) 85
concert of powers 115, 131, 152, 158, 163
Cooperative Strategy for 21st Century Seapower 58
Crocker, Walter 128
Curzon, Lord 28, 30, 106

Das, Durgas 65
Defence Research and Development Organisation 56
'Democratic Peace' 25
democratic values 24–6
Deng Xiaoping 7, 153
Devare, Sudhir 47
Diego Garcia 31, 130
Djibouti 39
Downer, Alexander 121
DPRK *see* North Korea

East Asian Economic Community 16
East Asia Summit 16, 152; Australia 131; China 43; Indonesia 116, 186; Japan 79; Malaysia 112; Singapore 107; United States 62; Vietnam 96
Enoki, Yasukuni 65, 80
Evans, David 120
'Eye in the Sky' 139

Fernandes, George 27, 71, 75; and Vietnam 94, 95, 97, 141
Fiji 126
Fissile Material Cut-off Treaty (FMCT) 85
Forward Policy 28–30
Framework for Maritime Security Cooperation 56
France 80, 91, 123
Frazier, Mark 41

Gandhi, Indira 19, 68, 91, 103, 104, 106, 126
Gandhi, Rajiv 7
Garver, John 42
Goh Chok Tong 104, 109, 145
Greater East Asia Co-Prosperity Sphere 66
Green, Michael 77
Gujral, I.K. 9
Gwadar (Pakistan) 39, 172

Hambantota (Sri Lanka) 39, 172
Harriman, Averill 67
Harrison, Selig 3
Hauner, Milan 66
Hindutva beliefs 2
Ho Chi Minh 90
Holmes, James R. 12, 38, 39
Howard, John 121, 125
Huang Hua 92
Hu Jintao 38, 41, 72
Humphrey, Hubert 91

Ikeda, Hayato 67
India, major power status 1–17, 151–2
Indian National Congress 67, 177
Indian Navy 6, 11, 12, 26, 30, 38, 120, 134; Australia 123; Britain 123; Cam Ranh Bay 155; Fiji 126; France 123; Gulf of Aden 59, 60; Indian Ocean Naval Symposium 129, 136; Indonesia 112; Japan 80, 84; Malacca Strait 137; Malaysia 112; Maritime Doctrine 40, 135; MILAN naval gathering 105, 136; Pacific Ocean 62, 75, 162; Russia 123; Singapore 106, 111; South China Sea 141, 142; Southeast Asia 135; Thailand 112; tsunami, 2004 60, 136; US Navy 55, 56, 59, 123; Vietnam 95; Western Pacific Naval Symposium 62
Indian Ocean, strategic convergence with Pacific 157
Indian Ocean Naval Symposium 12, 129, 136
Indian Ocean Rim-Association for Regional Cooperation 129
Indonesia: Aceh 117; concerns about India in Andaman Sea 104–5; Defence Cooperation Agreement 116; economic relationship 116, 145; IndIndocorpat Agreement 117; Malacca Strait 139–40; relationship with India generally 113–8
IONS *see* Indian Ocean Naval Symposium
IOR-ARC *see* Indian Ocean Rim-Association for Regional Cooperation

Japan: Cold War 67–9; Delhi–Mumbai Industrial Corridor 87–8, 146; economic relationship with India 85–8, 145–6; Indian National Army 66, 78; Joint Security Declaration with India 72–3, 82; Pacific War 66–7; Pokhran II nuclear tests 69–71; Pal, Radhabinod 78; Nuclear Suppliers Group 85; nuclear technology 85; Official Development Aid 87; relationship with India generally 65–89; Sino-Indian war 67
Jiang, Yili 75
Johnson, Lyndon 92

Kampuchea *see* Cambodia
Kaplan, Robert 23, 40, 57, 137, 157
Kargil crisis 50

Karnad, Bharat 101
Kashmir 50, 51, 70, 84, 96, 114, 117
Katzenstein, Peter 76
Kaul, T.N. 91
Keating, Timothy J. 57.
Kennedy, Paul 3,4
Kesavan, K.V. 84
Kesavapany, K. 154
Khurana, Gurpreet 40
Kissinger, Henry 1
Kumar, Sushil 26, 27
Kyaukpyu (Burma) 39

Laos 96
Lee Kuan Yew 25, 106, 154; Indonesia 115; nuclear weapons 103; Monroe Doctrine 153
Leifer, Michael 148
Li Peng 92
Look East policy 14–16, 44, 107, 123, 144
Look West policy 10

Ma Ying-jeou 75
McMahon Line 35
Madagascar 12
Mahan, Alfred Thayer 28
Malabar naval exercises 54–5, 60: Exercise *Malabar 2007* 54, 60, 71, 111; Exercise *Malabar 2009* 62; Exercise *Malabar 2010* 55, 124
Malacca Strait 13, 30, 31, 32, 38, 41, 50, 57, 59, 80, 135–40, 160; Australia 114, 115, 117, 118, 137; Indonesia 139–40; Malaysia 112, 139–40; Singapore 110, 111, 139
Malaysia: Bay of Bengal Initiative 15; concerns about India in Andaman Sea 104; economic relationship 113, 145; Malacca Strait 112, 139–40; relationship with India generally 112–3
Maldives 9, 12, 29, 104
Malik, Mohan 41, 74
MALSINDO co-ordinated naval patrols 138
Manh, Nong Duc 94, 95
Mauritius 12, 27, 109, 157
Mehta, Suresh 39
Mekong Ganga Cooperation (MGC) 15, 96
Menon, Shiv Shankar 82, 87, 157, 158
Menon, V.K. Krishna 90, 127

Menzies, Robert 119, 120
Miki, Takeo 69
MILAN naval gathering 105, 136, 188
Ministerial Conference for Economic Development of Southeast Asia (MEDSEA) 69
Missile Technology Control Regime 52
Mohan, C. Raja 19, 30, 31, 36, 41, 47, 61, 165; and balance of power 22, 23; Forward Policy 29; Indonesia 118; Japan 83, Singapore 141; South Pacific 126; strategic autonomy 21; Vietnam 101;
Mongolia 32, 125
Monroe Doctrine, India's 9, 28, 29, 103, 153
Moraes, Frank 128
Mori, Yoshiro 71
Mozambique 12
Mozambique Channel 135
Mukherjee, Pranab 22, 27, 30, 108
Mullen, Michael 53, 57
multipolar regional order 150–1
Myanmar *see* Burma

Nagashima, Akihisa 81
Najib, Razak 113
Natsukawa, Kazuya 80
Nehru, Jawaharlal 1, 2, 34, 169; and Australia 120, 127; and China 34, 35, 44; and Japan 67, 78; and Southeast Asia 103; and Vietnam 90, 91, 182
Nehruvian strategic doctrine 18–20
Nepal 9, 32, 35
New Zealand 125–6
Nguyen, Tan Dun 97
Nigeria 37
Nixon, Richard 26
North Korea 63, 70, 74, 84
Novotny, Daniel 115
NSG *see* Nuclear Suppliers Group
Nuclear Suppliers Group 52, 85, 125, 127
nuclear tests, 1998 *see* Pokhran II nuclear tests
nuclear weapons, India 2, 3, 5, 6, 9, 19, 36, 50, 51, 69, 70, 85, 96, 101, 103, 129, 156, 184

Obama, Barack 51–3
Obama administration 51–3, 55, 114
Ohira, Masayoshi 67
Oman 12

Pace, Michael 137
Pakistan: and Australia 121, 123, 124; and Indonesia, 114, 117, 187; and Iran 10; and Japan 70, 71, 148; and Malaysia 112; maritime threat to India 38; relationship with China 32, 34, 35, 38, 39, 42, 43, 74, 91, 101, 149, 157, 159; relationship with India 6, 7, 9, 10, 15, 16, 25, 26, 30, 47, 52, 75, 134, 184; and Singapore 107; and United States, relationship generally 49, 50, 53, 54; United States – naval cooperation 57, 59; and Vietnam 96
Panchsheel 35, 90
Panikkar, K.M. 27, 102, 106, 141
Papua New Guinea 37
Percival, Bronson 51, 62
Peru 13
Pokhran II nuclear tests 19, 36, 50, 69–71, 115, 121
Prakash, Arun 12, 32, 39, 139
Prithvi missiles 95–6
Proliferation Security Initiative (PSI) 58, 60
Pyle, Kenneth 79

Qatar 12
Quadrennial Defence Review 2010 (US) 53
Quadrilateral proposal 23, 71–2, 77, 124

Rahman, Tunku Abdul 106
Rajagopolachari, C. 120
Rajaratnam, S. 148
Rao, P.V. Nasimha 7, 14, 105
ReCAAP 138
Rice, Condoleezza 50, 77
Rithauddeen, Ahmad 104
Roy, Mihir 126
Rudd, Kevin 122, 125
Rusk, Dean 67
Russia 13, 15, 59, 125, 162; as defence technology supplier 55, 56; as great power x, 5, 8, 14, 16, 150, 156, 159; India–Russia–China trilateral 19; India–Russia–Japan trilateral 82; and Indonesia 116; and Malaysia 113; relationship with India 17, 22; Russian Navy 123; and Vietnam 94–9, 149

Sagar, Rahul 20
Saran, Shyam 26

Sato, Eisaku 68, 146
Schaffer, Teresita 52, 62
Seychelles 12, 157
Sharma, Anand 88
Shastri, Lal Bahadur 92, 106
Shiga, Kenjiro 67
Sikkim 35
Sikri, Rajiv 27
Singapore: concerns about India in Andaman Sea 104; economic relationship with India 108–9, 145; Malacca Strait 110, 111, 139; relationship with India generally 102–12; security relationship with India 109–12
Singh, Manmohan 25, 27, 44; Japan 75, 81, 83, 87; Malaysia 139
Singh, Natwar 96
Sinha, Yashwant 2
Sino-Indian war, 1962 35, 67
Smith, Stephen 124
Sonadia (Bangladesh) 39
South China Sea 97–9, 101, 111, 140–3
South Korea 14, 15, 16, 51, 54, 122, 139, 152, 159; economic relationship with India 74, 86, 87, 99; nuclear technology 74; relationship with India generally 19, 25, 32, 161; security relationship with India 74, 84, 141, 155
Soviet Union 44, 48, 66, 68, 69, 93; and Australia 120; as defence technology supplier 110; as great power 27, 134; and Japan 177; relationship with India generally 7, 18, 19, 35, 49, 104, 105, 107; and Singapore 110; Soviet Navy 104, 110, and Vietnam 93, 98, 101, 104
sphere of influence 27, 29–32, 91, 152–5
Sri Lanka 9, 27, 29, 104, 185; relationship with China 39, 157, 172
Strait of Hormuz 39, 50, 135
Strait of Malacca *see* Malacca Strait
strategic autonomy 21–2, 82
String of Pearls theory 32, 38–40, 57, 117–18, 130, 136, 154; and Australia 130; and Indonesia 118; and United States 57
Subrahmanyam, K. 29
Sudan 37
Sudarsono, Juwono 139
swing state, India as 23, 50, 146, 150

Taiwan 63, 74–6, 81
Taiwan Strait 38, 62, 63, 75
Tajikistan 32
Tanham, George 28, 30
Tellis, Ashley 20, 23, 42, 44, 45
Thailand 96, 155; and BIMSTEC 15; and China 37, 45, 46; and India–ASEAN Summit 185; joint naval patrols with India 112, 136; Malacca Strait 138, 139; and Malaysia 139, 150; and Mekong Ganga Cooperation 15, 183; and Singapore 186; and Vietnam 104
Tibet 28, 32, 35, 43, 75, 98
Treaty of Amity and Cooperation 46, 93
Trilateral Security Dialogue, US–Japan–Australia 71, 124

United Nations Security Council 3, 52, 70, 73, 96
United States: Acheson, Dean 31; and Australia 119–21, 123–33; balance of power 23, 24, 33, 146–50; and Burma 63; Burns, William J. 52, 61; Bush administration 50–2, 54, 77, 114, 149; Central Intelligence Agency (US) 23, 50; Cheney, Richard 77; Clinton, Hillary Rodham 62, 76, 98; Clinton administration 50, 51; Cold War 19; Combined Task Force 151 (CTF 151) 39, 59, 176; as defence technology supplier 55–6; democratic values 24–5; Diego Garcia 31, 130; economic relationship with India 49; Exercise *Malabar 2007* 54, 60, 71, 111; Exercise *Malabar 2009* 62; Exercise *Malabar 2010* 55, 124; Global Maritime Partnership 58; as a great power 5, 8, 12, 26, 30, 156, 159; Harriman, Averill 67; Humphrey, Hubert 91; and India in Asia Pacific 13–17, 41, 44, 48, 61–3; Indian Ocean region 10–13, 31; Indonesia 114–16; and Iran 10, 63; and Japan 67–88; Kargil crisis 50; Keating, Timothy J 57; Kissinger, Henry 1; Malacca Strait 137–40; MILAN naval gathering 136; military cooperation with India 53–61; naval cooperation with India in the Indian Ocean region 56–61; naval cooperation with India in the Pacific Ocean 141, 142, 153; Nehruvian strategic doctrine 18–20; Nixon, Richard 26; North Korea 63;

nuclear cooperation with India 51; Nuclear Suppliers Group (NSG) 52; Obama, Barack 51–3; Obama administration 51–3, 55, 114; Operation *Enduring Freedom* 59; Pace, Michael 137; Pokhran II nuclear tests 19, 50; Proliferation Security Initiative (PSI) 58, 60; Quadrenniel Defense Review 2010 (QDR 2010) 53; Quadrilateral proposal 23, 71–2, 77, 124; relationship with India generally 2, 49–63, 160–3; Rusk, Dean 67; and Saudi Arabia 63; and Singapore 106, 108, 111; and Southeast Asia 104, 153; and Taiwan 63; US Africa Command (USAFRICOM) 54; US Central Command (USCENTCOM) 54, 59; US Pacific Command (USPACOM) 53–4, 59, 62; and Vietnam 91–5, 98, 101

US Africa Command (USAFRICOM) 54

US Pacific Command (USPACOM) 53–4, 59, 62

US Central Command (USCENTCOM) 54, 59

USS Enterprise 26, 54, 120

Vajpayee, Atal 16, 41, 50, 53, 92, 94
Venezuela 37
Vietnam: Cam Ranh Bay 95, 97–9, 141–2, 155, 184; economic relationship with India 99–100, 145; nuclear technology 100; relationship with India generally 90–101; and South China Sea 97–9, 101

Waltz, Kenneth 4
Wassenaar Agreement 52
Wen Jiabao 43
Western Pacific Naval Symposium (WPNS) 12, 62, 136
Winner, Andrew C. 12
Winter, Donald 56

Xinjiang 75

Yang, Jiechi 124
Yemen 27
Yeo, George 145, 157
Yoshida Doctrine 79
Yoshihara, Toshi 12, 38, 39
Yudhoyono, Susilo Bambang 47, 114, 116
Yusgiantoro, Purnomo 139

Zhou Enlai 92

Routledge Paperbacks Direct

Bringing you the cream of our hardback publishing at paperback prices

This exciting new initiative makes the best of our hardback publishing available in paperback format for authors and individual customers.

Routledge Paperbacks Direct is an ever-evolving programme with new titles being added regularly.

To take a look at the titles available, visit our website.

www.routledgepaperbacksdirect.com

ROUTLEDGE Revivals

Are there some elusive titles you've been searching for but thought you'd never be able to find?

Well this may be the end of your quest. We now offer a fantastic opportunity to discover past brilliance and purchase previously out of print and unavailable titles by some of the greatest academic scholars of the last 120 years.

Routledge Revivals is an exciting new programme whereby key titles from the distinguished and extensive backlists of the many acclaimed imprints associated with Routledge are re-issued.

The programme draws upon the backlists of Kegan Paul, Trench & Trubner, Routledge & Kegan Paul, Methuen, Allen & Unwin and Routledge itself.

Routledge Revivals spans the whole of the Humanities and Social Sciences, and includes works by scholars such as Emile Durkheim, Max Weber, Simone Weil and Martin Buber.

FOR MORE INFORMATION

Please email us at **reference@routledge.com** or visit: **www.routledge.com/books/series/Routledge_Revivals**

www.routledge.com